Longman
Spanish
Pocket
Traveller

L. G. Alexander
Carolina Haro
Peter Vickers

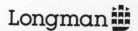

Longman Group UK Limited
Longman House, Burnt Mill
Harlow, Essex CM20 2JE, England
and Associated Companies throughout the world.

© Longman Group Limited 1983

First published 1983
Eighth impression 1989

Phototypeset in 7/8 Linotron 202 Helvetica Light

Produced by Longman Group (FE) Ltd.
Printed in Hong Kong

ISBN 0 582 79962 7

Drawings by Ed McLachlan

Contents

Indice

Preface

The Longman Spanish Pocket Traveller contains

a bilingual dictionary which gives you all the words you're likely to need to cope with social situations whether you're travelling for pleasure or on business

a section to 'help you get around' with lists of basic words, key sentence patterns and some short conversations to enable you to make the best use of the dictionary

For example, suppose you want to ask for a ticket or a coffee. All you have to do is to look up 'ticket' or 'coffee' in the dictionary and slot the Spanish words into the appropriate key sentence pattern:

Quiero /un billete/ , por favor   I'd like /a ticket/ please
Quiero /un café/ , por favor   I'd like /a coffee/ please

a reference section to help you find all the essential information you need to cope abroad, everything from choosing a meal to understanding Spanish currency

Prólogo

Este libro contiene

un diccionario bilingüe que le da todas las palabras que podría
necesitar para enfrentarse con situaciones de tipo social y de viaje,
ya sea de placer o de negocios

una sección para ayudarle a desenvolverse, con listas de palabras
básicas, estructuras clave, y algunas conversaciones cortas que le
permitan hacer el mejor uso del diccionario

Por ejemplo, supongamos que quiere un billete o un café. Busque
la palabra que quiere (por ej. 'billete' o 'café') e inmediatamente
podrá decir:

I'd like /a ticket/ please   Quiero /un billete/ , por favor
I'd like /a coffee/ please   Quiero /un café/ , por favor

una sección de referencia para encontrar toda la información
esencial que pueda necesitar para entenderse con moneda
extranjera, en viajes en coche, al comer fuera etc.

English – Spanish

Inglés – Español

To help you get around

Basics

If you learn these by heart, you'll find it easier to get around

Please	Por favor [*por fa**vor***]
Thank you	Gracias [***gra**theeas*]
Yes	Sí [*see*]
No	No [*no*]
Yes please	Sí, por favor [*see por fa**vor***]
No thank you	No, gracias [*no **gra**theeas*]
Sorry?	¿Cómo? [***ko**mo*]
Excuse me!	¡Perdone! [*per**don**eh*]
I'm sorry	¡Lo siento! [*lo **see-en**to*]
That's all right	Está bien [*esta **bee-en***]
Good!	¡Bien! [***bee-en***]
I don't understand	No entiendo [*no en**tee-en**do*]
Hello	Hola [***ola***]
My name's _____	Me llamo _____ [*meh **ya**mo _____*]
Goodbye	Adiós [*ad**ee**os*]
Good morning	Buenos dias [***bwe**nos **dee**as*]
Good afternoon	Buenas tardes [***bwe**nas **tar**dehs*]
Good evening	Buenas tardes [***bwe**naş **tar**dehs*]
Good night	Buenas noches [***bwe**nas **no**chehs*]
How are you?	¿Cómo está? [*komo esta*]
Fine thanks	Bien, gracias [*bee-en **gra**theeas*]
Cheers!	¡Salud! [*sa**lood***]
It was nice to meet you	Me alegro de haberle conocido [*me alegro deh a**ber**leh kono**thee**do*]
Could you repeat that please?	¿Podría repetirlo, por favor? [*podr**ee**a repe**teer**lo por favor*]
Slower please	Más despacio, por favor [*mas des**path**eeo por favor*]

| How much is it? | ¿Cuánto es? [*kwanto es?*] |
| How much are they? | ¿Cuánto valen? [*kwanto **ba**len?*] |

Key sentence patterns

Once you've learnt these key sentence patterns by heart, you'll be able to make up your own sentences using the words from the dictionary.

Where's /the (nearest) bank/ please?	¿Dónde está /el banco (más cercano)/ , por favor? [*dondeh esta el **ban**ko (mas ther**ka**no) por favor*]
Is there /a car park/ near here?	¿Hay /un aparcamiento/ por aquí? [*I oon aparka**mee-en**to por akee*]
Are there any /restaurants/ near here?	¿Hay /restaurantes/ por aquí? [*I restaoo**ran**tehs por akee*]
I'd like to /go swimming/	Me gustaría /ir a bañarme/ [*meh goostareea **eer** a ban**yar**meh*]
Would you like to /go shopping/?	¿Le gustaría /ir de compras/? [*leh goostareea **eer** de com**pras**]
Have you got /a streetmap/ please?	¿Tiene /un plano de la ciudad/ , por favor? [*tee-eneh oon **pla**no deh la theeoo**dad** por favor*]
Have you got any /envelopes/ please?	¿Tiene /sobres/ , por favor? [*tee-eneh **so**brehs por favor*]
I haven't got any /change/	No tengo /cambio/ [*no tengo **kam**beeo*]
I need /a doctor/	Necesito /un medico/ [*nethes**ee**to oon **me**deeko*]
I need some /traveller's cheques/	Necesito /cheques de viajero/ [*nethes**ee**to **che**kehs de beea**he**ro*]

I'd like /a room/ please

Quiero /una habitación/ , por favor [*kee-ero oona abeeta***theeon** *por favor*]

I'd like some /stamps/ please

Quiero /sellos/, por favor [*kee-ero* **se***yos por favor*]

Would you like /a coffee/?

¿Quiere /un café/? [*kee-ereh oon ka***feh**]

Would you like some /chocolates/?

¿Quiere /bombones/? [*kee-ereh bom***bo***nehs*]

Could you /call/ /a taxi/ for me please

Podría /llamarme/ /un taxi/ por favor [*podreea ya***mar***meh oon* **ta***ksee por favor*]

When does /the (next) train/ to /Valencia/ leave?

¿Cuándo sale /el (próximo) tren/ para /Valencia/? [*kwando saleh el (***prok***seemo) tren para ba***len***theea*]

When do /the banks/ open (close)?

¿Cuándo abren (cierran) /los bancos/? [*kwando abren (thee-erran) los* **ban***kos*]

Do you like /this colour/?

¿Le gusta /este color/? (singular) [*leh goosta* **es***teh ko***lor**]

Do you like /these shoes/?

¿Le gustan /estos zapatos/? (plural) [*leh goostan* **es***tos tha***pa***tos*]

I like /this style/

Me gusta /este estilo/ [*meh goosta* **es***teh es***tee***lo*]

I don't like /this shape/

No me gusta /esta forma/ [*no meh goosta* **es***ta* **for***ma*]

Conversations

Now that you've learnt the basics and the key sentence patterns, here are a few examples of conversations you can take part in.

Introductions

Buenos días, Señor García. Le presento a Marian Harwood	Good morning Señor García. This is Marian Harwood
¡Encantado! (male)	How do you do
¡Encantada! (female)	How do you do

Meeting someone you know

Buenas tardes	Good evening
Buenas tardes, Señor Gómez	Good evening Señor Gomez
¿Cómo está?	How are you?
Bien, gracias. ¿Y usted?	Fine thanks. And you?
Bien, gracias	Fine thanks

Finding your way

¡Perdone!	Excuse me
¿Sí?	Yes?
¿Dónde está el Hotel Bristol, por favor?	Where's the Hotel Bristol please?
Todo recto, y a la derecha	Straight on, then right
Gracias	Thank you
De nada	Not at all

At the station

Un billete de ida para Valencia, por favor	A single to Valencia please
500 ptas (quinientas pesetas)	500 pesetas
¿Cuándo sale el próximo tren?	When does the next train leave?
A las dieciocho quince	At 6.15 (p.m.)
¿Cuándo llega el tren a Valencia?	When does the train arrive in Valencia?
A las diecinueve treinta y seis	At 7.36
Gracias	Thank you

At a hotel – you want a room

Buenas tardes. ¿Desea alguna cosa?	Good afternoon. Can I help you?
Buenas tardes. Quiero una habitación doble, por favor	Good afternoon. I'd like a double room please
¿Para cuántas noches?	For how many nights?
Para dos noches, por favor	For two nights please
¿Quiere una habitación con baño o sin baño?	Would you like a room with or without bath?
Con baño	With bath
Sí, está bien	Yes, that's fine
¿Cuánto es, por favor?	How much is it please?
Tres mil pesetas la noche	3000 pesetas a night
Sí. De acuerdo, gracias	Yes. OK, thanks

Buying something

Buenos días. ¿Desea alguna cosa?	Good morning. Can I help you?
Buenos días ¿Tiene café?	Good morning. Have you got any coffee?
Sí. ¿Cuánto quiere?	Yes. How much would you like?
Quiero quinientos gramos, por favor	I'd like 500 grams please
Bien. ¿Algo más?	Good. Anything else?
Sí. Quiero manzanas, por favor	Yes. I'd like some apples please
¿Cuántas?	How many?
Cuatro, por favor	4 please
De acuerdo. Doscientas cincuenta pesetas, por favor	OK. 250 pesetas please
Gracias	Thank you

Choosing something

Buenos días. ¿Desea alguna cosa?	Good afternoon. Can I help you?
Quiero una camiseta, por favor	I'd like a T-shirt please
¿Qué talla quiere?	What size would you like?
Cuarenta	40
¿Le gusta ésta?	Do you like this one?
No. No me gusta este color. ¿La tiene en rojo?	No. I don't like that colour. Have you got a red one?
Sí, por supuesto	Yes, of course
¿Cuánto es, por favor?	How much is it please?
Quinientas cincuenta pesetas	550 pesetas
Me la llevo. Gracias	I'll take it. Thank you

A few tips

1 You – 'usted/ustedes' or 'tú/vosotros'?

There are two ways of addressing people in Spanish.
'Usted' (you, singular) and 'ustedes' (you, plural) are used with
people you don't know well or with older people. To be on the safe
side, start by using 'usted' or 'ustedes'. Wait for people to use 'tú' to
you first.
'Tú' (you, singular) and 'vosotros' (you, plural) are used with people
you know well and with children. Young people usually use these
forms when talking to each other.

However, the equivalent of 'I/you' etc in Spanish is only used for
emphasis or when it isn't clear whom you are talking about. It is
usually the verb ending which tells you who is the subject of the verb.

eg *Quiero vino*	I'd like some wine
¿Quiere (usted) vino?	Would you like some wine?

2 Masculine or feminine?

In Spanish names of things are either masculine or feminine, and the
Spanish for 'the/a/to the' changes accordingly. Here is a table to
help you.

masculine		feminine	
el tren	the train	*la cama*	the bed
un billete	a ticket (train)	*una entrada*	a ticket (theatr
al autobús	to the bus	*a la habitación*	to the room
los trenes	the trains	*las camas*	the beds
a los autobuses	to the buses	*a las habitaciones*	to the rooms

3 Plurals

The plural of words ending in a vowel is formed by adding '*s*'.
The plural of words ending in a consonant or in '*y*' is formed by adding '*es*'.

> eg   *perro perros* (dog)
>   *cuidad ciudades* (town)
>   *ley leyes* (law)

all irregular plurals are given

> eg   *lápiz lápices* (pencil)

4 Adjectives

Adjectives are given in the masculine singular form.
Change '*–o*' to '*–a*' for the feminine form.

> eg   *un coche rojo* (a red car)
>   *una camisa roja* (a red shirt)

Adjectives ending in '*–e*' or a consonant do not change.

> eg   *un coche grande* (a big car)
>   *una camisa grande* (a big shirt)

All adjectives add '*s*' in the plural.

5 Comparisons

In Spanish '*más*' (more) can be used with all adjectives to form the comparative.

> eg   *Quiero algo más grande*   I'd like something bigger
>   *Quiero algo más barato*   I'd like something cheaper

'*Menos*' (less) is used in a similar way.

> eg   *Quiero algo menos caro*   I'd like something less expensive

Irregular Comparisons
Although the following adjectives can form their comparatives with '*más*' you may also hear these irregular forms:

bueno – mejor	good – better
malo – peor	bad – worse
grande – mayor	big – bigger
pequeño – menor	small – smaller

6 A note on quantity

'Some' and 'any' usually need no translation in Spanish.

   eg *¿Tiene (usted) cerveza?*   Have you got any beer?
       Tengo sellos   I've got some stamps

However, when talking about 'some' meaning 'a few' eg 'some cigars', use '*unos*':

   eg *Quiero unos puros*   I'd like some cigars

'*Unos*' changes to '*unas*' when the noun is feminine:

   eg *Quiero unas naranjas*   I'd like some oranges

However, the dictionary will also enable you to indicate very precise amounts. For example, if you look up 'match' (*cerilla*) you will also find 'a box of matches' (*una caja de cerillas*).

Quantity can also be indicated precisely in terms of volume or weight eg '20 litres of petrol', 'a kilo of tomatoes', etc. See Equivalents p144.

If you remember these six 'quantity words' you will be able to ask for almost anything:

una botella de /cerveza/	a bottle of /beer/
una caja de /cerillas/	a box of /matches/
una lata de /tomates/	a·tin of /tomatoes/
una cortada de /jamón/	a slice of /ham/
un paquete de /cigarrillos/	a packet of /cigarettes/
un vaso de /leche/	a glass of /milk/

NB In Spanish you may come across several different words for
     'slice'. '*Cortada*' is the general term but you may also hear:

un trozo de /queso/	a slice of /cheese/
una rebanada de /pan/	a slice of /bread/
una rodaja de /limón/	a slice of /lemon/
una loncha de /fiambre/	a slice of /cold meat/

7 Verbs

In the dictionary verbs are usually given in the infinitive form only eg
'*escribir*' (write)

Certain verbs always need the Spanish equivalent of 'myself',
'yourself' etc. These are the verbs ending in '*se*' in this dictionary eg
'*lavarse*' (have a wash), '*entrenarse*' (to practise). This is the form of
the verb you will be likely to need:
    ¿Quiere (usted) lavarse?   Would you like to have a wash?
If you are talking about yourself remember to change the '*–se*'
(yourself) to '*–me*' (myself).
    Quiero lavarme   I'd like to have a wash

8 To be – '*ser*' or '*estar*'

There are two words for 'to be' in Spanish. '*ser*' and '*estar*'.

'*Estar*' is used to describe the position of things or people and to
describe temporary things and situations.
    eg   *Está en la nevera*   It's in the fridge
        ¿Cómo está?   How are you?
'*Ser*' is used to describe permanent and inherent characteristics
    eg   *Soy arquitecto*   I'm an architect

9 Very common expressions

'*Hay*' means 'there is' or 'there are'
    eg   *Hay sopa*   There is some some soup
        Hay asientos   There are some seats
By raising the tone of your voice at the end of the sentence you can
make '*hay*' mean 'is there/are there?'
    eg   *¿Hay sopa?*   Is there any soup?
        ¿Hay asientos?   Are there any seats?

Be careful with '*por favor*' (please). The Spanish don't use '*por favor*' as
often as the English use 'please'. You can still sound polite without it.

Pronunciation guide

Spanish consonants

Most Spanish consonants are pronounced in the same way as English but you should be careful with the following:

'c' is pronounced like 'k' (in key) before 'a' 'o' or 'u', eg coche (car) but like 'th' (in think) before 'i' or 'e', eg centro (centre) gracias (thank you).

'g' is pronounced like 'g' (in game) before 'a' 'o' or 'u', eg galleta (biscuit) but like ch (in loch) before 'e' or 'i', eg gente (people).

NB 'gu' is pronounced like 'g' (in game) before 'e' or 'i', eg guia (guide) but like 'gw' (in Gwent) before 'a', eg agua (water).

'h' is never pronounced, eg huevo (egg).

'j' is pronounced like ch (in loch), eg jamón (ham).

'll' is pronounced like 'y' (in yes), eg llave (key).

'ñ' is pronounced like 'ni' (onion), eg mañana (morning).

'r' is pronounced with a trill, eg pero (but) but 'rr' and 'r' at the beginning of a word are pronounced with a stronger trill (tip of tongue against the gums and close to the upper teeth), eg perro (dog) reloj (watch).

'v' is pronounced like 'b' (in bath), eg vino (wine).

'z' is pronounced like 'th' (in think), eg jerez (sherry).

NB In South America substitute 's' for 'th' in the table above.

Spanish vowel sounds never change:

'a' is pronounced as 'a' (in cat), eg cama (bed).

'e' is pronounced as 'e' (in bed), eg tren (train).

'i' is pronounced as 'ee' (in meet), eg vino (wine).

'o' is pronounced as 'o' (in knot), eg todo (everything).

'u' is pronounced as 'oo' (in zoo), eg uno (one).

NB In Spanish accents usually indicate the stressed part of the word – they do not affect the sound of the vowel. Usually the next to last syllable of a word is stressed.

Abbreviations

Abreviaturas

(adj)	adjective	adjetivo
(adv)	adverb	adverbio
(n)	noun	nombre (sustantivo)
(prep)	preposition	preposición
(pron)	pronoun	pronombre
(vb)	verb	verbo
(m)	masculine	masculino
(f)	feminine	femenino
(s)	singular	singular
(pl)	plural	plural
(infml)	informal	familiar
(tdmk)	trademark	marca de fábrica
(eg)	for example	por ejemplo
(etc)	et cetera	etcétera

Dictionary
A – Z
Diccionario

A

a (an) *un (m) una (f) (artículo)*
about (=approximately) *alrededor de (aproximadamente)*
about (=concerning) *acerca de*
  about /your problem/ *acerca de /su problema/*
above (adv) *encima*
  above /my head/ *encima de /mi cabeza/*
abroad *al extranjero*
  he's abroad *él está en el extranjero*
accept *aceptar*
accident *accidente (m)*
accommodation *alojamiento*
accountant *contable (m)*
ache *dolor (m)*
  I've got backache *tengo dolor de espalda*
  I've got earache *tengo dolor de oído*
  I've got stomachache *tengo dolor de estómago*
actor *actor (m)*
actress -es *actriz (f) actrices (pl)*
adaptor plug *adaptador(m)*
add *añadir*
address -es *dirección (f) (domicilio)*
  temporary address *dirección eventual*
adjust *ajustar*
admission (=cost) *precio de entrada*
adult *adulto*
  adults only *sólo adultos*
advance (advance of money) *adelanto*
  advance booking *reserva por adelantado*
  in advance *por adelantado*
advantage *ventaja*
advertise *anunciar*
advertisement *anuncio*
advice *consejo*
  I'd like some advice *quiero consejo*
advise a rest *aconsejar un descanso*
aerial *antena*
aeroplane *avión (m)*
  by air *por avión*

aerosol *aerosol (m)*
afraid
  be afraid (of / /) *tener miedo (de / /) (algo)*
  I'm afraid of / / *tengo miedo de / / (alguien)*
after *después (de) (prep)*
afternoon *tarde (f) (n)(hasta las 6)*
  good afternoon *buenas tardes*
  this afternoon *esta tarde*
  tomorrow afternoon *mañana por la tarde*
  yesterday afternoon *ayer por la tarde*
aftershave lotion *loción (f) para después del afeitado*
afterwards *después (adv)*
again *otra vez*
against *contra*
age *edad (f)*
agency -ies *agencia*
agenda *orden (m) del día*
agent (of company) *agente (m)*
ago *hace*
  /three years/ ago *hace /tres años/*
agree *estar de acuerdo*
  agree to / / *consentir en / /*
  I agree *estoy de acuerdo*
agreement *acuerdo (convenio)*
ahead *delante*
air *aire (m)*
  air pressure *presión (f) de aire*
  by air *por avión*
  some fresh air *aire fresco*
air conditioning *aire (m) acondicionado*
air letter *carta aérea*
air terminal *terminal (f) aérea*
  air terminal bus *autobús servicio terminal*
airline *línea aérea*
airmail *correo aéreo*
  by airmail *por avión*
airport *aeropuerto*
  airport bus -es *autobús (m) servicio aeropuerto*
alarm clock *despertador (m)*
alcohol *alcohol (m)*

alcoholic (adj) *alcohólico*
alive *vivo (con vida)*
  he's alive *está vivo*
all *todo*
  all /the children/ *todos /los niños/*
  all /the time/ *todo /el tiempo/*
allergic *alérgico*
  I'm allergic /to penicillin/ *soy alérgico /a la penicilina/*
allow *permitir*
  allow /smoking/ *permitir /fumar/*
allowed *permitido*
almost *casi*
alone *solo (=no acompañado)*
alphabet *alfabeto*
already *ya*
also *también*
alter (change) *cambiar*
alter (=clothes) *reformar (ropa)*
alternative (n) *alternativa*
always *siempre*
a.m. *de la mañana*
  /four/ a.m. */las cuatro/ de la mañana*
ambassador *embajador (m) embajadora (f)*
ambulance *ambulancia*
amenities (pl) *comodidades (fpl)*
among *entre (varios)*
  among /my friends/ *entre /mis amigos/*
amusement arcade *sala de juegos recreativos*
amusing *divertido*
anaemic *anémico*
  I'm anaemic *estoy anémico*
anaesthetic (n) *anestésico*
anchor *ancla*
and *y*
angry *enfadado*
  I'm angry with/ him/ *estoy enfadado con /él/*
animal *animal (m)*
ankle *tobillo*
  ankle socks *calcetines (mpl) cortos*
anniversary -ies *aniversario*
  wedding anniversary *aniversario de boda*

announcement *comunicación (f)*
  make an announcement *hacer una comunicación*
annoying *molesto (ser)*
annual *anual*
anorak *anorak (m)*
another *otro*
  another /glass of wine/ *otro /vaso de vino/*
answer (n) *contestación (f)*
answer (vb) *contestar*
ant *hormiga*
antibiotic *antibiótico*
antifreeze *anticongelante (m)*
  a can of antifreeze *un bidón de anticongelante*
antique (n) *antigüedad (f)*
antique shop *tienda de antigüedades*
antiseptic *antiséptico*
  antiseptic cream *pomada antiséptica*
  a tube of antiseptic (cream) *un tubo de pomada antiséptica*
any
  have you got /any stamps/? *¿tiene /sellos/?*
  I haven't got /any money/ *no tengo /dinero/*
anything *¿algo?*
  anything else? *¿algo más?*
aperitif *aperitivo*
apologise *disculparse*
  I apologise *me disculpo*
apology -ies *disculpa*
appendicitis *apendicitis (f)*
apple *manzana*
  apple juice *zumo de manzana*
application form *impreso de solicitud*
apply *solicitar*
apply to / / for /a visa/ *solicitar /un visado/ a / /*
  apply for /a job/ *solicitar /un trabajo/*
appointment *cita*
  I've got an appointment *tengo una cita*
  make an appointment *hacer una cita*
apricot *albaricoque (m)*

April abril (m)

aqualung botella de oxígeno para bucear

architect arquitecto

area (of town) zona

area (of country) región (f)

argue discutir

argument discusión (f)

arm brazo

army ejército

around alrededor
  around /the table/ alrededor /de la mesa/

arrange concertar
  arrange /a meeting/ concertar /una reunión/

arrangement acuerdo (disposición)

arrival llegada
  time of arrival hora de llegada

arrive llegar
  arrive at /four-thirty/ p.m. llegar a /las cuatro y media/
  arrive in /July/ llegar en /julio/
  arrive on /Monday/ llegar el /lunes/
  arrive in /Madrid/ llegar a /Madrid/

arrow flecha

art gallery -ies galería de arte

artichoke alcachofa

artificial artificial
  artificial respiration respiración (f) artificial

artist artista (m&f)

ashamed
  be ashamed (of / /) estar avergonzado (de / /)
  I'm ashamed of /him/ estoy avergonzado de /él/

ashtray cenicero

ask preguntar
  please ask how much it is por favor pregunte cuánto es

ask (a favour) pedir (un favor)

asleep dormido (adj)
  he's asleep duerme

asparagus espárrago
  asparagus tips puntas (fpl) de espárrago

aspirin aspirina
  a bottle of aspirins una botella de aspirinas
  a packet of aspirins una caja de aspirinas

assistant dependiente (m)
  shop assistant dependiente de una tienda

asthma asma (m)

at
  at /seven-thirty/ a /las siete y media/
  at /the hotel/ en /el hotel/
  at /the university/ en /la universidad/

atlas -es atlas (m)

attack (n) ataque (m)
  an attack of / / un ataque de / /

attend asistir
  attend a /Catholic/ service asistir a una ceremonia /católica/

attendant empleado (n)

attractive atractivo

au pair au pair (f)

aubergine berenjena

auction (n) subasta

auction (vb) subastar

audience público (teatro, etc)

August agosto

aunt tía

author autor (m)

authorities (pl) autoridades (fpl)

automatic automático

autumn otoño
  in autumn en otoño

available disponible

avalanche alud (m)

average (n) medio (=normal)

avocado aguacate (m)

avoid evitar

awake despierto
  he's awake está despierto

away fuera (de la ciudad)

away (absent) ausente

awful (of people) desagradable

awful (of things) horrible

B

baby **-ies** *bebé (m)*
baby-sit *cuidar niños*
baby-sitter *persona que cuida niños*
back *espalda*
  backache *dolor de espalda*
back door *puerta trasera*
backwards *hacia atrás*
bacon *bacón (m)*
bad *mal (adj)*
badly *mal (adv)*
  badly hurt *malherido*
badminton *badminton (m)*
  a game of badminton *un partido de badminton*
  play badminton *jugar a badminton*
bag *bolsa*
  carrier bag *bolsa de compra*
  string bag *bolsa de cuerda*
bake *cocer (al horno)*
baker's *panadería*
balcony **-ies** *balcón (m)*
bald *calvo*
  he's bald *es calvo*
ball *pelota*
  a ball of /string/ *un ovillo de /cordón/*
  beach ball *pelota de playa*
  football *pelota de fútbol*
  golf ball *pelota de golf*
  squash ball *pelota de squash*
  table tennis ball *pelota de ping-pong*
  tennis ball *pelota de tenis*
ball (=dance) *baile (m)*
ballet *ballet (m)*
  ballet dancer *bailarín (m) bailarina (f)*
balloon *globo*
ballpoint pen *bolígrafo*
ballroom *salón (m) de baile*
banana *plátano*
band (=orchestra) *orquesta*
bandage (n) *venda*
bandage (vb) *vendar*
bank *banco*
  bank account *cuenta bancaria*
  current account *cuenta corriente*

bar (=for drinks) *bar (m)*
barbecue *barbacoa*
bare *desnudo*
bargain (n) *ganga*
  it's a bargain *es una ganga*
bargain (vb) *regatear*
  bargain with / / *regatear con / /*
barrel *barril (m)*
  a barrel of / / *un barril de / /*
barrier *barrera*
basement *sótano*
basket *cesta*
  a basket of / / *una cesta de / /*
  shopping basket *cesta de compra*
  waste paper basket *papelera*
basket (small)
basketball (=game) *baloncesto*
  a game of basketball *un partido de baloncesto*
  play basketball *jugar al baloncesto*
bat (cricket) *palo (cricket)*
bath *baño (en bañera)*
  have a bath *tomar un baño*
  Turkish bath *baño turco*
bath mat *alfombrilla de baño*
bath salts (pl) *sales (fpl) de baño*
bath salts (pl) *sales (fpl) de baño*
bathe (eyes etc) *bañar*
bathe (in the sea etc) *bañarse*
bathing costume (one piece) *traje (m) de baño*
bathing trunks (pl) *bañador (m)*
bathroom *cuarto de baño*
battery **-ies** (radio) *pila (radio)*
battery **-ies** (car) *batería*
  I've got a flat battery *tengo la batería descargada*
bay (=part of sea) *bahía*
be (see ''A few tips'') *ser/estar*
be called (a name) *llamarse*
beach **-es** *playa*
  beach hut *caseta de playa*
  beach umbrella *sombrilla*
beads (pl) *cuentas (fpl) (=collar)*
  string of beads *collar (m)*
bean *judía*
  broad bean *haba*

French bean *judía verde*
beautiful *hermoso*
beauty salon *salón (m) de belleza*
because *porque*
  because of /the weather/ *a causa /del tiempo/*
bed *cama*
  bed and breakfast *habitación (f) y desayuno*
  double bed *cama doble*
  go to bed *irse a la cama*
  in bed *en la cama*
  make the bed *hacer la cama*
  single bed *cama sencilla*
bed clothes (pl) *ropa (s) de cama*
bedpan *bacina*
bedroom *dormitorio*
bee *abeja*
  bee sting *picadura de abeja*
beef *carne (f) de vaca*
  beef sandwich *sandwich (m) de carne de vaca*
beer *cerveza*
  a beer *una cerveza*
  a bottle of beer *una botella de cerveza*
  a can of beer *una lata de cerveza*
  a pint of beer *un tercio de cerveza*
beetroot/beetroot (pl) *remolacha*
before (prep) *antes (de)*
  before /breakfast/ *antes /del desayuno/*
  before /leaving/ *antes de /salir/*
begin *empezar*
  when does it begin? *¿cuándo empieza?*
behalf
  on behalf of / / *en nombre de / /*
behaviour *conducta*
behind (prep) *detrás (de)*
  behind /the house/ *detrás /de la casa/*
beige *beige*
believe *creer*
  believe /me/ *creer/me/*
  I don't believe it *no lo creo*
bell *timbre (m)*

belongings (pl) *posesiones(fpl)*
below (adv)/**(prep)** *abajo (posición)*
  below /the chair/ *debajo /de la silla /*
belt *cinturón (m)*
bend (vb) *doblar (una curva)*
bend (in a road) *curva*
bent (adj) *doblado*
beret *boina*
berth *litera*
  /four/-berth cabin *camarote (m) de/cuatro/literas*
  lower berth *litera de abajo*
  upper berth *litera de arriba*
beside (prep) *junto (a)*
  beside /her/ *junto a /ella/*
best *mejor (superlativo)*
  the best /hotel/ *el mejor /hotel/*
bet (n) *apuesta*
bet (vb) *apostar*
better *mejor (comparativo)*
  he's better (health) *está mejor*
  it's better (things) *es mejor*
betting shop *agencia de apuestas*
between /London /and /Madrid/ *entre / Londres/ y /Madrid/*
beyond (prep) *más allá (de)*
  beyond /the station/ *más allá /de la estación/*
bib *babero*
Bible *Biblia*
bicycle/bike (infml) *bicicleta/bici (infml)*
big *grande*
bikini *bikini (m)*
bill (for food, hotel, etc.) *cuenta (de hotel etc)*
billiards *billar (ms)*
  a game of billiards *una partida de billar*
  play billiards *jugar al billar*
binoculars (pl) *prismáticos (mpl)*
  a pair of binoculars *unos prismáticos*
bird *pájaro*
biro (tdmk) *bolígrafo*
birth *nacimiento*
  birth certificate *certificado de nacimiento*

date of birth *fecha de nacimiento*
place of birth *lugar (m) de nacimiento*
birthday *cumpleaños (m) cumpleaños (mpl)*
biscuit *galleta*
bite (=insect b.) *picadura (de insecto)*
bitter (adj) *amargo (ácido)*
black *negro*
  black coffee *café (m) solo*
blackberry -ies *mora*
blackcurrant *grosella*
blanket *manta*
bleach (n) *lejía*
bleach (vb) (laundry) *poner en lejía*
bleed *sangrar*
  my nose is bleeding *me sangra la nariz*
  stop the bleeding *detener la hemorragia*
blind (adj) *ciego*
blinds (=Venetian-type) *persianas (fpl)*
blister *ampolla*
block of flats *edificio de apartamentos*
blocked (eg drain) *embozado*
blonde *rubio*
blood *sangre (f)*
  blood group *grupo sanguíneo*
  blood pressure *tensión (f) sanguínea*
blotting paper *papel (m) secante*
blouse *blusa*
blue *azul*
blunt (eg knife) *desafilado*
board (vb) (eg a plane) *embarcar (avión)*
board (n) (=cost of meals) *pensión (f) alimenticia*
  full board *pensión completa*
  half board *media pensión*
boarding card *tarjeta de embarque*
boat *barco*
  by boat *en barco*
  boat train *tren (m) de enlace con puerto*
  lifeboat *bote (m) salvavidas*
  motor-boat *lancha motora*
body -ies *cuerpo*
boil (vb) *hervir*
bomb *bomba (explosivo)*

bone *hueso (del cuerpo)*
book *libro*
  guide book *guía (m)*
booking *reserva*
  advance booking *reserva anticipada*
booking office *taquilla*
bookmaker *corredor (m) de apuestas*
bookshop *librería*
boots (pl) *botas (fpl)*
  a pair of boots *un par de botas*
  rubber boots *botas de agua*
  ski-boots *botas de esquí*
border (=frontier) *frontera*
bored (to be bored) *estar aburrido*
  I'm bored *estoy aburrido*
boring *aburrido*
borrow *pedir prestado*
  borrow /a pen/ *pedir prestada /una pluma/*
  may I borrow /your pen/? *¿me puede prestar /su pluma/?*
boss (n) *jefe (m) jefa (f)*
both *ambos/los dos*
bother (vb) *molestar*
  don't bother *no se moleste*
  I'm sorry to bother you *siento molestarle*
bottle *botella*
  a bottle of / / *una botella de / /*
  bottle -opener *abrebotellas (m) abrebotellas (mpl)*
  feeding bottle *biberón (m)*
bottom (part of body) *trasero (infml)*
  bottom of / / *fondo de / /*
bow tie *pajarita*
bowl *plato hondo*
bowling (=ten pin bowling) *bolos (mpl)*
  bowling alley *bolera*
bows (pl) (of ship) *proa (s)*
box -es *caja*
  a box of / / *una caja de / /*
box office *taquilla*
boxer *boxeador (m)*
boxing *boxeo*
  boxing match *pelea de boxeo*
boy *chico*
boyfriend *amigo*

bra *sujetador (m)*
bracelet *pulsera*
  silver bracelet *pulsera de plata*
braces (pl) *tirantes (mpl)*
  a pair of braces *unos tirantes*
brake fluid *líquido de frenos (coche)*
brake linings/pads (pl) (car) *forros (mpl) de freno (coche)*
brakes/braking system *frenos (mpl)*
branch (of company) **-es** *sucursal (m)*
brand (=of make) *marca*
  brand name *nombre (m) de la marca*
brandy -ies *coñac (m)*
  a bottle of brandy *una botella de coñac*
  a brandy *un coñac*
bread *pan (m)*
  a loaf of bread *una barra de pan*
  a slice of bread *una rebanada de pan*
  bread and butter *pan con mantequilla*
  brown bread *pan integral*
  bread roll *bollo de pan*
  sliced bread *pan de molde*
  white bread *pan blanco*
break (vb) *romper*
breakdown (car) *avería*
breakfast *desayuno*
  bed and breakfast *habitación (f) y desayuno*
  breakfast for /two/ *desayuno para /dos/*
  breakfast in my room *desayuno en mi habitación*
  continental breakfast *desayuno*
  English breakfast *desayuno al estilo inglés*
  have breakfast *desayunar*
  serve breakfast *servir el desayuno*
breast *pecho*
breast-feed *dar el pecho*
breath *aliento*
  out of breath *sin aliento*
breathe *respirar*
bride *novia*
bridegroom *novio*
bridge (=card game) *bridge (m)*
  a game of bridge *una partida de*
  bridge

bridge *puente (m)*
  toll bridge *puente de peaje*
bridle *brida*
briefcase *portafolios (m) portafolios (mpl)*
bring *traer*
broadcast (n) *emisión (f)*
broadcast (vb) *emitir*
broccoli *brécoles (mpl)*
brochure *folleto*
broken *roto*
brooch -es *broche (m)*
  cameo brooch *camafeo*
  silver brooch *broche de plata*
brother *hermano*
brother-in-law /brothers-in-law (pl) *cuñado*
brown *marrón*
  brown hair *pelo castaño*
bruise (n) *moradura*
bruised *amoratado*
brush -es *cepillo*
  clothes brush *cepillo de ropa*
  hair-brush *cepillo de pelo*
  nail-brush *cepillo de uñas*
  paint-brush *brocha*
  shaving brush *brocha de afeitar*
  shoe-brush *cepillo de zapatos*
  tooth-brush *cepillo de dientes*
bucket *cubo*
  a bucket and spade *un cubo y pala*
buckle *hebilla*
Buddhist *Budista (m&f)*
buffet car *coche (m) restaurante*
builder *constructor (m)*
building *edificio*
  public building *edificio público*
bulb (=light bulb) *bombilla*
  40/60/100/200 watt *40/60/100/200 watios*
bun (bread) *bollo*
bun (hair) *moño*
  in a bun *en un moño*
bunch -es *ramo*
  a bunch of /flowers/ *un ramo de /flores/*

bungalow *bungalow (m)*
bunk bed *litera*
buoy *boya*
burglary -ies *robo*
burn (n) *quemadura*
burn (vb) *quemar*
burnt *quemado*
burst (adj) *reventado*
  a burst pipe *una tubería reventada*
bury *enterrar*
bus -es *autobús (m)*

  **the bus for / ** *el autobús para / /*
  bus driver *conductor (m)*
businessman /businessmen (pl)
  hombre (m) de negocios
busy *ocupado*
but *pero*
butane *butano*
butcher's *carnicería*
butter *mantequilla*
butterfly -ies *mariposa*
button *botón (m)*
buy *comprar*
  buy /an umbrella/ *comprar /un paraguas/*
  where can I buy /an umbrella/?
  ¿dónde puedo comprar /un paraguas/?
by
  by /bus/ *en /autobús/*
  by /the station/ *cerca de /la estación/*
  by (time) *para (tiempo)*
  by /three o'clock/ *para /las tres/*
bypass (n) **-es** *circunvalación (f)*

C

cabbage *col (f)*
cabin *camarote (m)*
  cabin cruiser *lancha con camarotes*
  /four/ berth cabin *camarote de /cuatro/ literas*
cable (n) *cable (m)*

cable car *teleférico*
café *café (m)*
caffeine *cafeína*
cake *pastel (m)*
  a piece of cake *un trozo de pastel*
cake shop *pastelería*
calculate *calcular*
  calculate /the cost/ *calcular /el coste/*
calculator *calculadora*
  pocket calculator *calculadora de bolsillo*
calendar *calendario*
call (n) (telephone call) *llamada*
  alarm call *llamada de alarma*
  call box -es *cabina telefónica*
  early morning call *servicio despertador*
  international call *llamada internacional*
  local call *llamada local*
  long distance call *conferencia*
  make a long distance call *poner una conferencia*
  make a call *hacer una llamada*
  personal call *llamada personal*
  transferred charge call *llamada de cobro revertido*
call (vb) (=telephone) *llamar (por teléfono)*
  call again later *llamar más tarde*
  call /the police/ *llamar /la policía/*
**call on / ** (=visit) *visitar a / /*
calm (of sea) *en calma*
calor gas *butano*
calories (pl) *calorías (fpl)*
cameo *camafeo*
camera *cámara fotográfica*
  cine camera *cámara de cine*
  35 mm camera *cámara de 35mm*
camera shop *tienda de artículos de fotografía*
camp (n) *campamento*
  holiday camp *campamento de vacaciones*
camp bed *cama plegable*
campfire *fuego de campamento*

camping *camping (m)*
  go camping *ir de camping*
campsite *camping (m)*
can (n) *lata*
  a can of /beer/ *una lata de /cerveza/*
can (vb) *poder (vb)*
  I can /do it/ *puedo /hacerlo/*
  I can't /do it/ *no puedo /hacerlo/*
canal *canal (m)*
cancel /my flight/ *cancelar /mi vuelo/*
cancellation *cancelación (f)*
cancelled *cancelado*
candle *vela*
canoe (n) *canoa*
canoeing *piragüismo*
  go canoeing *hacer piragüismo*
canteen (eating place) *bar (m) (para comidas)*
canvas (=material) *lona*
  canvas bag *bolsa de lona*
cap (=hat) *gorro*
  shower cap *gorro de ducha*
  swimming cap *gorro de baño*
cap (n) (for tooth) *funda*
cap (vb) (tooth) *enfundar*
cape (=cloak) *capa*
cape (eg Cape of Good Hope) *cabo*
captain *capitán (m)*
car *coche (m)*
  by car *en coche*
  buffet car *coche restaurante*
  car ferry -ies *ferry (m)*
  car hire *alquiler (m) de coches*
  car park *aparcamiento*
  car wash *autolavado*
  sleeping car *coche-cama*
carafe *jarra*
  a carafe of /wine/ *una jarra de /vino/*
carat *quilate (m)*
  /nine/ carat gold *oro de /nueve/ quilates*
caravan *caravana*
  caravan site *aparcamiento de caravana*
  /four/ berth caravan *caravana de /cuatro/ camas*

card (business card) *tarjeta*
  birthday card *tarjeta de cumpleaños*
  green card (car insurance) *carta verde*
cardigan *rebeca*
cards (pl) *cartas (fpl)*
  a game of cards *una partida de cartas*
  a pack of cards *una baraja*
careful *cuidadoso*
careless *descuidado*
caretaker *portero*
carnation *clavel (m)*
carnival *carnaval (m)*
carpet *alfombra*
  fitted carpet *moqueta*
carriage (in a train) *coche (m) (de un tren)*
carrier bag *bolsa de compra*
carrot *zanahoria*
carry *llevar (en la mano)*
carrycot *cuna portátil*
carton
  carton of /cigarettes/ (=200) *cartón (m) de /cigarrillos/*
cartridge (=film cartridge) *carrete (m) (fotos)*
cartridge (for gun) *cartucho*
case (=suitcase) *maleta*
  cigarette case *pitillera*
case *caso*
cash (n) *dinero en efectivo*
  cash payment *pago en efectivo*
  cash price *precio al contado*
  pay cash *pagar en efectivo*
cash (vb) *cobrar (reintegro)*
  cash /a traveller's cheque/ *cobrar /un cheque de viajero/*
cash desk *caja*
cashier *cajero*
cashmere *cachemir (m)*
  cashmere sweater *suéter (m) de cachemir*
casino *casino*
casserole (meal) *puchero*
casserole (container) *cazuela*
cassette *cassette (f)*

cassette player cassette (f) (aparato)
cassette recorder grabadora
  pre-recorded cassette cassette
  grabada
castle castillo
casualty department (hospital) servicio
  de urgencias
cat gato (animal)
catalogue catálogo
catch (illness) coger (una enfermedad)
  catch a cold constiparse
catch (transport) tomar
  catch /the train/ tomar /el tren/
cathedral catedral (f)
Catholic (adj) católico
cattle (pl) reses (fpl)
cauliflower coliflor (f)
cause (n) causa (origen)
cave cueva
ceiling techo (habitación)
celery apio
  a head of celery una cabeza de apio
cellar bodega
cement (n) cemento
cemetery cementerio
centimetre centímetro
centre centro
  in the centre en el centro
  shopping centre centro commercial
  town centre centro ciudad
century -ies siglo
ceramic cerámico
cereal (=breakfast cereal) cereal (m)
ceremony -ies ceremonia
certain (adj) (=cierto)
  I'm certain estoy seguro
certainly desde luego
certificate certificado (n)
chain cadena
chain store tienda de una cadena
  comercial
chair silla
  chair lift telesilla
  high chair sillita alta
  wheelchair silla de ruedas
chairman /chairmen/ (pl) presidente (m)
chalet chalet (m)

chambermaid camarera (hotel)
champagne champán (m)
  a bottle of champagne una botella
  de champán
change (n) (= alteration) cambio
  (reforma)
change (n) (=money) cambio (dinero)
  small change moneda fraccionaria
change (vb) (clothes) cambiarse (de
  ropa)
change (vb) cambiar
  change /the tyre/ cambiar /la rueda/
  I'd like to change /some traveller's
  cheques/ quiero cambiar /unos
  cheques de viajero/
change at / / (of train) hacer
  trasbordo en / /
  do I have to change? ¿tengo que
  hacer trasbordo?
changing room vestuario
charcoal carbón (m) de leña
charge (n) (=payment) coste (m)
  (honorario)
charge (vb) (=payment) cobrar (hacer
  pagar)
charming encantador
chart (=sea map) carta (mapa)
charter flight vuelo charter
chauffeur chófer (m)
cheap barato
cheat (vb) hacer trampa
check (vb) comprobar
  could you check /the oil and water/
  please? ¿podría comprobar /el aceite
  y el agua/ por favor?
check in (vb) (=of hotel/plane) facturar
check up (n) (=of health) chequeo
cheek (of face) mejilla
cheers! (toast) ¡salud!
cheese queso
  cheese /omelette/ /tortilla/ de queso
chemist's farmacia
cheque cheque (m)/talón (m)
  cheque book talonario
  traveller's cheque cheque de viajero
  cheque card tarjeta de crédito
  crossed cheque cheque cruzado

pay by cheque *pagar con cheque*
cherry -ies *cereza*
chess (s) *ajedrez (m)*
  a game of chess *una partida de ajedrez*
  play chess *jugar a ajedrez*
chest (part of body) *pecho*
chest of drawers *cómoda (n)*
chestnut *castaña*
chewing gum *chicle (m)*
chicken *pollo*
chicken pox *varicela*
chilblain *sabañon (m)*
child /children (pl) *niño (m) niña (f)*
chill (vb) *enfriar (muy frío)*
chimney -ies *chimenea*
chin *barbilla*
china *porcelana*
chips (pl) (potato) *patatas fritas (fpl)*
chiropodist *callista (m&f)*
chocolate *chocolate (m)*
  a bar of chocolate *una barra de chocolate*
  a box of chocolates *una caja de bombones*
choice *elección (f) (preferencia)*
  choice between / / and / / *elección entre / /y / /*
choir *coro*
choose *elegir*
  choose between / / and / / *elegir entre / /y / /*
chop (n) *chuleta (con hueso)*
  lamb chop *chuleta de cordero*
  pork chop *chuleta de cerdo*
chop (vb) *cortar*
chopsticks (pl) *palillos (mpl) (para comer)*
Christ *Cristo*
Christian *cristiano*
Christmas *Navidad (f)*
  Christmas card *christmas (m) christmas (mpl)*
  Christmas Day *día (m) de Navidad*
church -es *iglesia*
  a /Protestant/ church *una iglesia /protestante/*

cider *sidra*
  a bottle of cider *una botella de sidra*
  a cider *una sidra*
cigar *puro (n)*
  a box of cigars *una caja de puros*
  a Havana cigar *un habano*
cigarette *cigarrillo*
  a carton of cigarettes (=200) *un cartón de cigarrillos*
  cigarette (American type) *cigarrillo rubio*
  cigarette (French type) *cigarrillo*
  filter-tipped cigarettes *cigarrillos con filtro*
  smoke a cigarette *fumar un cigarrillo*
  a packet of cigarettes *un paquete de cigarrillos*
cigarette case *pitillera*
cigarette lighter *encendedor (m)*
  gas lighter *encendedor de gas*
cigarette paper *papel (m) de fumar*
cinema *cine (m)*
circus -es *circo*
citizen *ciudadano (n)*
city -ies *ciudad (f)*
  the new part of the city *la parte nueva de la ciudad*
  the old part of the city *la parte vieja de la ciudad*
civil servant *funcionario del Estado*
civilisation *civilización (f)*
claim (vb) *pedir (=reclamar)*
  claim /damages/ *pedir /indemnización/*
  claim on /the insurance/ *pedir indemnización a la compañía de seguros*
clarify *aclarar*
class -es *clase (f)*
  cabin class *clase de camarote*
  /first/ class */primera/ clase*
  tourist class *clase turista*
classical (eg music) *clásico*
  classical music *música clásica*
clean (adj) *limpio*
clean (vb) *limpiar (en general)*
cleaner's *tintorería*

cleansing cream *crema limpiadora*
clear (=obvious) *claro (obvio)*
clear (=transparent) *transparente*
clear goods through Customs *pasar mercancías por la aduana*
clever (of people) *listo (de una persona)*
client *cliente (m&f)*
cliff *acantilado*
climate *clima (m)*
climb (vb) (=c. mountains) *escalar*
climbing *montañismo*
  go climbing *hacer montañismo*
clinic *clínica*
  private clinic *clínica privada*
cloakroom *guardarropa (m)*
clock *reloj (m) (de pared, mesa)*
  alarm clock *reloj despertador*
clogs (pl) *zuecos (mpl)*
  a pair of clogs *un par de zuecos*
close (vb) *cerrar*
closed (adj) *cerrado*
cloth (dishcloth) *paño*
clothes (pl) *ropa (s)*
  clothes brush *cepillo de ropa*
  clothes line *cuerda de tender*
  clothes peg *pinza de ropa*
cloud *nube (f)*
cloudy *nublado*
club *club (m)*
  gambling club *casino, club de juego*
  golf club (institution) *club de golf*
  golf club (object) *palo de golf*
clutch (n) (car) *embrague (m)*
coach -es *autocar (m)*
  by coach *en autocar*
  coach (on a train) *coche (m) (vagón de tren)*
coal *carbón (m)*
coarse (of person) *áspero (de una . persona)*
coast (n) *costa*
coastguard *guardacostas (m) guardacostas (mpl)*
coastline *línea de la costa*
coat *abrigo*
  showerproof coat *chubasquero*
coat hanger *percha*

cockroach -es *cucaracha*
cocktail *cóctel (m)*
cocoa *cacao*
  a cup of cocoa *una taza de cacao*
coconut *coco*
cod *bacalao*
code *código*
  dialling code *prefijo*
  postal code *distrito postal*
codeine *codeína*
coffee *café (m)*
  a cup of coffee *una taza de café*
  a pot of coffee *una cafetera llena*
  black coffee *café sólo*
  decaffeinated coffee *café descafeinado*
  filter coffee *café hecho en cafetera*
  ground coffee *café molido*
  instant coffee *café instantáneo*
  white coffee *café con leche*
coffeepot *cafetera*
coffin *ataúd (m)*
coin *moneda (dinero)*
cold (adj) *frío*
  I'm cold *tengo frío*
  it's cold (of things) *está frío*
  it's cold (of weather) *hace frío*
cold (n) *constipado (n)*
  I've got a cold *estoy constipado*
collar *cuello (ropa)*
  collar bone *clavícula*
  dog collar *collar (m) de perro*
colleague *colega (m&f)*
collect (from) *recoger (de)*
  collect /my luggage/ *recoger /mi equipaje/*
collection (in a church) *colecta*
collection (of objects) *colección (f)*
  last collection (of post) *última recogida*
college *universidad (f)*
cologne *colonia*
colour *color (m)*
  what colour is it? *¿de qué color es?*
comb (n) *peine (m)*
come (from) *venir (de)*
come in *pasar (=entrar)*

come in! (command) ¡pase!
comfortable cómodo
comic (=funny paper) tebeo
commerce comercio
commission (=payment) comisión (f)
common (=usual) corriente
company (=firm) **-ies** empresa
compartment (in train) departamento (tren)
  non-smoking compartment departamento de no fumadores
  smoking compartment departamento de fumadores
compass -es brújula
compensation indemnización (f)
competition competición (f)
complain quejarse
  complain /to the manager/ quejarse /al director/
  complain /about the noise/ quejarse /del ruido/
complaint queja
complete (adj) completo (entero)
compulsory obligatorio
computer computador (m)
concert concierto
concert hall sala de conciertos
condition condición (f) (estado)
  in bad condition en malas condiciones (fpl)
  in good condition en buenas condiciones (fpl)
conditioner (for hair) acondicionador (m)
  a bottle of hair conditioner un frasco de acondicionador
conducted tour excursión (f) con guía
  go on a conducted tour ir en una excursión con guía
conference congreso
confirm /my flight/ confirmar /mi vuelo/
confused confuso
  I'm confused estoy confuso
congratulate /you/ on / / felicitar a /usted/ por / /
congratulations (pl) enhorabuena

connect conectar
connecting flight vuelo de conexión
constipated estreñido
consul cónsul (m)
consulate consulado
  the /British/ Consulate el consulado /británico/
contact lenses (pl) lentes (fpl) de contacto
contagious contagioso
contents (pl) (eg of a parcel) contenido (s)
continental continental
continual continuo
continue /a journey/ continuar /un viaje/
contraceptives (pl) anticonceptivos (mpl)
  the Pill la Píldora
  a packet of sheaths (=Durex) un paquete de preservativos
contract (n) contrato
convenient (of time and distance) coveniente
cook (vb) cocinar
cooked cocinado
cooker cocina
  electric cooker cocina eléctrica
  gas cooker cocina de gas
cooking cocina (española etc)
  do the cooking cocinar
cool (adj) templado (temperatura)
cool (vb) enfriar (=refrescar)
copper cobre (m)
copy (vb) copiar
copy (n) **-ies** copia
  make a copy copiar
coral coral (m)
cord cuerda (cordel)
corduroy pana
cork corcho
corkscrew sacacorchos (m) sacacorchos (mpl)
corn (eg on a toe) callo
  corn pads (pl) parches (mpl) de callos
corn maíz (m)

sweet corn *maíz dulce*

corner (inside) *rincón*

corner (outside) *esquina*

correct (adj) *correcto*

correct (vb) *corregir*

correction *corrección (f)*

corridor *pasillo*

corset *faja*

cost (n) *coste (m) (precio total)*

cost (vb) *costar*

cot *cuna*

cottage *casita de campo*

cotton *algodón (m)*
  a reel of cotton *un ovillo de algodón*

cotton wool *algodón (m) hidrófilo*

couchette *litera (tren)*

cough (n) *tos (f)*
  I've got a cough *tengo tos*

cough (vb) *toser*

cough mixture *jarabe (m) de la tos*
  a bottle of cough mixture *una botella de jarabe de la tos*

cough pastilles (pl) *pastillas (fpl) de la tos*

could
  could you /change/ /the tyre/ please? *¿podría /cambiar/ /la rueda/ por favor?*

count (vb) *contar (números)*

country (=countryside) *campo (el campo)*

country (=nation) **-ies** *país (m)*

countryside *paisaje (m) (campo)*

couple (married c.) *pareja*

coupon *cupón (m)*
  /petrol/ coupon *cupón de /gasolina/*

courrier *guía (m) (agente de turismo)*

course (of food) *plato (menú)*
  first course *primer plato*
  main course *plato principal*
  last course *último plato*

course
  of course! *¡por supuesto!*

court (law) *tribunal (m) de justicia*
  tennis court *pista de tenis*

cousin *primo (m) prima (f)*

cow *vaca*

crab *cangrejo*

crack (n) *grieta*

cracked *agrietado*
  it's cracked *está agrietado*

cramp (n) *calambre (m) (en la pierna etc)*

crash (into) *chocar (con)*

crash (car c.) **-es** *choque (m)*

crash helmet *casco*

crayon *lápiz (m) de color lápices (mpl) de color*

cream (from milk) *nata*

cream (=lotion) *crema*

crease (vb) *arrugar*
  does it crease? *¿se arruga?*

credit *crédito*
  on credit *a crédito*

credit terms *condiciones (fpl) de crédito*

credit card *tarjeta de crédito*

crew *tripulación (f)*
  air crew *tripulación aérea*
  ground crew *tripulación de tierra*
  ship's crew *tripulación de barco*

cricket *cricket (m)*
  a game of cricket *un partido de cricket*
  play cricket *jugar al cricket*

crime *crimen (m)*

criminal *criminal (m&f)*

crisps (=potato c.) *patatas (fritas en paquete)*

crocodile (leather) *de cocodrilo*

cross /the road/ *cruzar /la calle/*

crossroads /crossroads (pl) *cruce (m) (de calles)*

crossword puzzle *crucigrama (m)*

crowd *multitud (f)*

crowded *concurrido*

crown (vb) (tooth) *poner una corona*

cruise *crucero*
  go on a cruise *hacer un crucero*

cry (vb) *llorar*
  the baby's crying *el niño está llorando*

cube *cubo*

cucumber *pepino*
cuff links (pl) *gemelos (mpl) (camisa)*
  a pair of cuff links *un par de gemelos*
cup *taza*
  a cup of / / *una taza de / /*
  /plastic/ cup *taza de /plástico/*
cupboard *armario*
cure (vb) (health) *curar (salud)*
curl (vb) *rizar*
curlers (pl) *rulos (mpl)*
currant *pasa de corinto*
currency - ies *moneda (moneda corriente de un país)*
current (=electric c.) *corriente (f) (n)*
  A.C. *corriente alterna*
  D.C. *corriente directa*
  one hundred and twenty/ two hundred and forty volt *ciento veinte/doscientos cuarenta voltios*
current (of water) *corriente (f) (n) (de agua)*
  strong current *corriente fuerte*
current (adj) (eg account) *corriente (cuenta)*
  current account *cuenta corriente*
curry -ies *curry (m)*
  curry powder *polvos (mpl) de curry*
curtain *cortina*
cushion *cojín (m)*
custom *costumbre (f)*
Customs (pl) *aduana (s)*
  customs declaration form *impreso de declaración de aduana*
cut (n) *corte (m)*
  a cut and blow dry *un corte y secado a mano*
cut (vb) *cortar*
cut off (eg of telephone) *cortar(se) (teléfono)*
  I've been cut off *se ha cortado la comunicación*
cutlery *cubiertos (mpl)*
cutlet *chuleta (sin hueso)*
  lamb cutlet *chuleta de cordero*
  veal cutlet *chuleta de ternera*
cycling *ciclismo*
  go cycling *hacer ciclismo*

D

daily *diario*
damage (n) (s) *daño*
damaged *dañado*
damages (pl) (=compensation) *indemnización (fs)*
damn! *¡maldita sea!*
damp (adj) *húmedo (ropas)*
dance (n) *baile (m)*
dance (vb) *bailar*
dance hall *sala de baile*
dancer *bailarín (m) bailarina (f)*
dancing *bailar*
  go dancing *ir a bailar*
dandruff (s) *caspa (s)*
danger *peligro*
dangerous *peligroso*
dark (skin, hair) *moreno*
dark *oscuro*
  dark /green/ */verde/ oscuro*
  it's dark *está oscuro*
darn (vb) *zurcir*
dartboard *tablón (m) de dardos*
darts (pl) *dardos (mpl)*
  a game of darts *una partida de dardos*
  play darts *jugar a dardos*
date (calendar) *fecha*
  date of birth *fecha de nacimiento*
date (=fruit) *dátil (m)*
daughter *hija*
daughter-in-law/daughters-in-law (pl) *nuera*
dawn (n) *amanecer (m)*
day *día (m)*
  every day *cada día*
dead *muerto*
deaf *sordo*
decaffeinated *descafeinado*
December *diciembre (m)*
decide *decidir(se)*
  decide to /do something/ *decidir de /hacer algo/*
  decide on /a plan/ *decidirse por /un plan/*
deck *cubierta (n)*

lower deck *cubierta inferior*
upper deck *cubierta superior*
deckchair *hamaca*
declare /this watch/ *declarar /este reloj/*
deduct *descontar*
  deduct /five hundred pesetas/ from the bill *descontar /quinientas pesetas/ de la cuenta*
deep *profundo*
deep freeze (=machine) *congelador (m)*
definite *definitivo*
definitely *definitivamente*
degree (=university d.) *licenciatura*
degrees (pl) *grados (mpl) (temperatura)*
  Centigrade *centígrados*
  Fahrenheit *fahrenheit*
deicer *descongelante (m)*
delay (n) *retraso*
delayed *retrasado*
delicate (health) *delicado*
delicatessen (=food shop) *tienda de alimentos selectos*
deliver to *entregar a*
delivery (goods) *envío*
denim (=material) *paño estilo tejano*
  a pair of denim jeans *unos vaqueros*
dentist *dentista (m&f)*
  I must go to the dentist's *tengo que ir al dentista*
dentures (pl) *dentadura postiza*
depart *salir*
department *departamento (de tienda, sociedad)*
  children's department *departamento de niños*
  men's department *departamento de caballeros*
  women's department *departamento de señoras*
  accounts department *departamento de cuentas*
department store *grandes almacenes (mpl)*
departure lounge *sala de salidas*
departure time *hora de salida*

depend *depender*
  it depends *depende*
  it depends on /the weather/ *depende /del tiempo/*
deposit (n) *depósito (m)*
deposit (vb) *dejar (dinero)*
  deposit /some money/ *dejar en depósito /algo de dinero/*
  deposit /these valuables/ *dejar en depósito /estos artículos de valor/*
depth *profundidad (f)*
derv *aceite (m) diesel*
describe *describir*
description *descripción (f)*
design (n) *diseño*
design (vb) *diseñar*
desk *mesa de escritorio*
dessert *postre (m)*
destination *destino*
detail *detalle (m)*
detergent *detergente (m)*
detour *desviación (f) (rodeo)*
  make a detour *desviarse*
develop *revelar*
  develop and print (a film) *revelar y hacer copias*
diabetes *diabetes (f)*
diabetic *diabético*
dial *marcar (un número de teléfono)*
diamond *diamante (m)*
diarrhoea *diarrea*
diary -ies *diario (n) (personal)*
dice/dice (pl) *dados (mpl)*
dictionary -ies *diccionario*
  English/Spanish dictionary *diccionario de inglés/español*
  Spanish/English dictionary *diccionario de español/inglés*
  pocket dictionary *diccionario de bolsillo*
die (vb) *morir*
diesel oil *aceite (m) diesel*
diet (=slimming d.) *régimen (m)*
  be on a diet *estar a régimen*
different *diferente*
  different from / / *diferente de / /*
difficult *difícil*

difficulty **-ies** *dificultad (f)*
dig (vb) *cavar*
dinghy -ies *bote (m)*
  rubber dinghy *bote de goma*
  sailing dinghy *barco de vela*
dining room *comedor (m)*
dinner (=evening meal) *cena*
  dinner jacket *esmoquin (m)*
  have dinner *cenar*
diplomat *diplomático*
dipstick *varilla del nivel de aceite*
direct (adj) *directo*
  direct line *línea directa*
  direct route *ruta directa*
direction *dirección (f) (tráfico)*
director *director (m)*
directory -ies *listín (m)*
  telephone directory *guía (m) de
  teléfonos*
  Directory Enquiries *Información (f)
  (teléfono)*
dirty *sucio*
disagree with *no estar de acuerdo con*
  I disagree with /you/ *no estoy de
  acuerdo con /usted/*
  it disagrees with /me/ (food) */me/
  sienta mal*
disappointed *desilusionado*
disc *disco*
  a slipped disc *un esguince vertebral*
disco *discoteca*
disconnect *desconectar*
discount (n) *descuento*
disease *enfermedad (f)*
disembark *desembarcar*
disgusting *asqueroso*
dish (food) **-es** *plato (cocinado)*
dish (container for food) **-es** *plato (para
  servir)*
dishcloth *paño de secar*
dishonest *deshonesto*
dishwasher *lavaplatos (m) lavaplatos
  (mpl)*
disinfectant *desinfectante (m)*
  a bottle of disinfectant *una botella
  de desinfectante*
disposable *de usar y tirar*

disposable lighter *encendedor no
  recargable*
disposable nappies *pañales (mpl) de
  usar y tirar*
distance *distancia*
distributor (car) *distribuidor (m) de
  encendido*
dive into / / *zambullirse en / /*
  dive into /the water/ *zambullirse en
  /el agua/*
diversion *desviación (f) (obligatoria)*
divide (vb) *dividir*
diving *bucear*
  go diving *ir a bucear*
  skin-diving *bucear con equipo*
  scuba-diving *bucear con botellas de
  oxígeno*
divorced *divorciado*
dizzy *mareado (sentir vértigo)*
  I feel dizzy *estoy mareado*
do *hacer*
  do /some shopping/ *hacer /unas
  compras/*
  do /me/ a favour *hacer /me/ un favor*
  could you do /me/ a favour?
  ¿/podría hacer/me/ un favor?
docks (pl) *muelles (mpl)* (=puerto)
doctor *médico* (n)
  I must go to the doctor's *tengo que
  ir al médico*
documents (pl) *documentos (mpl)*
  car documents *documentos del
  coche*
  travel documents *documentos de
  viaje*
dog *perro*
  dog collar *collar (m) de perro*
doll *muñeca (juguete)*
dollar *dólar (m)*
domestic help *ayuda doméstica*
dominoes (pl) *dominó (s)*
  a game of dominoes *una partida de
  dominó*
  play dominoes *jugar al dominó*
donkey *burro*
door *puerta*
  back door *puerta trasera*

front door puerta delantera

doorbell timbre (m)

doorman /doormen (pl) portero (edificio)

dose of /medicine/ dosis (f) de /medicamento/ dosis (fpl) de /medicamento/

double doble

double room habitación doble

a double whisky un whisky doble

pay double pagar el doble

doubt (vb) dudar

I doubt it lo dudo

down abajo (=ascensor)

are you going down? ¿va Usted abajo? ¿baja Usted?

downstairs abajo (piso)

dozen docena

a dozen /eggs/ una docena de /huevos/

half a dozen media docena

drains (pl) (=sanitary system) desagüe (m)

the drain's blocked el desagüe está embozado

draught (of air) corriente (m) (n) (de aire)

draughts (pl)(game) damas (fpl)

a game of draughts una partida de damas

draw (a picture) dibujar

drawer cajón (m)

dreadful espantoso

dress (vb) (a wound) vendar

dress (n) -es vestido

dress (get dressed) vestir/se/

dress /the baby/ vestir /al niño/

dress shop tienda de vestidos

dressing (medical) venda

dressing (salad dressing) aliño

dressing gown batín (m)

dressmaker modista (m)

drink (n) bebida

alcoholic drink bebida alcohólica

soft drink bebida no alcohólica

drink (vb) beber

drip-dry no necesita plancha

a drip-dry shirt una camisa que no necesita plancha

drive (n) (=entrance) camino de acceso

drive (vb) conducir (coche)

go for a drive dar un paseo en coche

driver conductor (m) conductora (f)

driving licence carnet (m) de conducir

international driving licence carnet internacional de conducir

drop /of water/ gota /de agua/

drug droga

drunk (adj) (=not sober) borracho

dry (adj) seco

dry (vb) secar

dry cleaner's tintorería

dual carriageway carretera de dos carriles

duck/duckling pato

due (to arrive)

/the train/'s due /at two o'clock/ /el tren/ debe llegar /a las dos de la tarde/

dull (of people and entertainments) aburrido

dull (of the weather) gris (tiempo)

dummy (baby's d.) chupete (m)

during /the night/ durante /la noche/

dusk anochecer (m)

dust polvo (limpieza)

dustbin cubo de basura

dustman/dustmen (pl) basurero

duty (=tax) -ies impuesto (advana)

duty (=obligation) -ies deber (m)(n) (obligación)

duty-free goods (pl) artículos (mpl) libres de impuestos

duty-free shop tienda de artículos libres de impuestos

duvet sádana

duvet cover sádana-cubre (m)

dye (vb) teñir

dye /this sweater/ /black/ teñir /este suéter/ de /negro/

dysentry disentería

E

each *cada*
  each /of the children/ *cada uno /de los niños/*
  /50 pesetas/ each (on price-tag) */cincuenta pesetas/ por unidad*
ear *oreja (external) /oído (internal)*
  earache *dolor (m) de oído*
early *temprano*
  early train *tren (m) de primera hora*
  leave early *marcharse temprano*
earn *ganar (dinero)*
earplugs (pl) *tapones (mpl) (para los oídos)*
earrings (pl) *pendientes (mpl)*
  clip-on earrings *pendientes de clip*
  earrings for pierced ears *pendientes de agujero*
earth (=the earth) *tierra (nuestro planeta)*
easily *fácilmente*
east *este (m) (punto cardinal)*
Easter *Pascua*
easy *fácil*
eat *comer*
eau-de-Cologne *agua de colonia*
  a bottle of eau-de-Cologne *una botella de agua de colonia*
education *educación (f)*
educational *educativo*
EEC *CEE*
efficient *eficiente*
egg *huevo*
  boiled egg *huevo pasado por agua*
  fried egg *huevo frito*
  hardboiled egg *huevo duro*
  poached egg *huevo escalfado*
  scrambled eggs *huevos revueltos*
elaborate (adj) *detallado*
elastic (n) *elástico*
  elastic band *goma elástica*
Elastoplast (tdmk) *esparadrapo*
elbow *codo*
election (s) *elección (f) (política)*
electric *eléctrico*
  electric shock *calambre (m)*

electrical appliance shop *tienda de electrodomésticos*
electrical system (car) *sistema (m) eléctrico*
electrician *electricista (m)*
electricity *electricidad (f)*
elsewhere *en otra parte*
embark *embarcar (barco)*
embarkation *embarque (m)*
embassy -ies *embajada*
  the /British/ Embassy *la embajada /británica/*
embroidery *bordado*
emergency -ies *emergencia*
emergency exit *salida de emergencia*
emotional *emotivo*
  she's very emotional *es muy emotiva*
employed by / *empleado por / /*
empty (vb) *vaciar*
enclose *adjuntar*
  please find enclosed *le mandamos adjunto*
end (n) *final (m)(n)*
end (vb) *terminar*
endorse *endosar (documentos)*
  endorse my ticket to / *endosar mi billete para / /*
  endorse /my passport/ *endosar /mi pasaporte/*
engaged (to be married) *prometido*
engaged (telephone) *comunica*
engaged (toilet) *ocupado (servicios)*
engagement ring *sortija de compromiso*
engine (eg for a car) *motor (m) (coche)*
engineer *ingeniero*
engrave *grabar (arte)*
enjoy oneself *pasarlo bien*
  enjoy yourself! *¡que lo pase bien!*
enjoyable *divertido*
enlarge *ampliar*
enough *bastante*
  enough money *bastante dinero*
  fast enough *bastante rápido*
enroll *alistarse*

enter *entrar*
  enter **/a country/** *entrar en /un país/*
entertaining *entretenido*
entitled
  be entitled to **/petrol coupons/** *tener el derecho a /cupones de gasolina/*
entrance *entrada*
  entrance fee *precio de entrada*
  main entrance *entrada principal*
  side entrance *entrada lateral*
envelope *sobre (m)(n)*
  a packet of envelopes *un paquete de sobres*
  airmail envelope *sobre de correo aéreo*
epidemic (n) *epidemia*
epileptic (adj) *epiléptico*
equal *igual*
equip *equipar*
equipment *equipo (material)*
  office equipment *equipo de oficina*
  photographic equipment *equipo fotográfico*
eraser *borrador (m)*
escape from **/ /** *escapar de / /*
escort (n) *acompañante*
escort (vb) *acompañar*
espresso coffee *café (m) exprés*
estate agent *agente (m) de la propiedad*
estimate (n) *presupuesto*
even (surface) *liso*
evening *tarde (f) (n) (después de las 6)*
  good evening *buenas tardes*
  this evening *esta tarde*
  tomorrow evening *mañana por la tarde*
  yesterday evening *ayer por la tarde*
evening dress (for men) (s) *esmoquin (m)*
evening dress - evening dresses (for women) *traje (m) de noche*
every *cada (inv)*
every day *cada día*
everyone *todo el mundo*
everything *todo*

everywhere *por todas partes*
exact *exacto*
exactly *exactamente*
examination (=school etc.) *examen (m)*
  medical examination *chequeo médico*
examine (medically) *examinar*
example *ejemplo*
  for example *por ejemplo*
excellent *excelente*
except *excepto*
excess *exceso*
  excess baggage *exceso de equipaje*
  excess fare *suplemento*
exchange *cambiar*
  exchange **/this sweater/** *cambiar /este suéter/*
  exchange rate *tarifa (m) de cambio*
excited *ilusionado*
exciting *emocionante*
excursion *excursión (f)*
  go on an excursion *ir de excursión*
excuse (n) *excusa*
  make an excuse *dar una excusa*
excuse (vb) *perdonar*
  excuse me! *¡perdone!*
exhaust system (car) *sistema (m) de escape*
exhibition *exposición (f)*
exit *salida (puerta)*
  emergency exit *salida de emergencia*
expedition *expedición (f)*
expensive *caro*
experienced *con experiencia*
expert (adj) *experto (adj)*
expert (n) *experto (n)*
expire (= run out) *caducar*
  /my visa/ has expired *mi visado/ está caducado*
explain *explicar*
explanation *explicación (f)*
export (n) *exportación (f)*
export (vb) *exportar*
exposure meter *fotómetro*
express
  express letter *carta urgente*

express mail *correo urgente*
express service *servicio urgente*
express train *Talgo*
extension / seven/ (telephone) *extensión / siete/ (f)(de teléfono)*
extra *extra*
extras (pl) *extras (mpl)*
eye *ojo*
eye make-up *maquillaje (m) de ojos*
eyebrow *ceja*
eyelid *párpado*

F

face *cara*
facecloth *toallita de la cara*
facial (=face massage) *facial (m)(masaje)*
fact *hecho (n)*
factory -ies *fábrica*
factory worker *obrero*
faded (colour) *descolorido*
faint (vb) *desmayarse*
I feel faint *me siento desmayado*
fair (adj) (hair) *rubio*
fair (adj) (skin) *blanco (piel)*
fair (adj) (=just) *justo*
that's not fair *no es justo*
fair (=entertainment) *feria*
fall (n) *caída*
fall (vb) *caer*
I fell downstairs *me caí por las escaleras*
false *falso*
false teeth (pl) *dentadura postiza*
family -ies *familia*
famous *famoso*
fan (n) (electric) *ventilador (m)*
fan (n) (sports) *aficionado*
fancy dress (s) *disfraz (m) disfraces (mpl)*
far *lejos*
how far is it to /Segovia?/ *¿a qué distancia está /Segovia/?*
is it far? *¿está lejos?*
not far from / / *no lejos de / /*
fare *billete (m) (precio)*

air fare *billete de avión*
bus fare *billete de autobús*
full fare *billete entero*
half fare *medio billete*
return fare *billete de ida y vuelta*
single fare *billete de ida*
train fare *billete de tren*
farm *granja*
farmer *labrador (m)*
farmhouse *casa de labranza*
fashionable *de moda*
fast *rápido*
fast train *expreso*
fasten *abrochar*
fat (adj) *gordo (en general)*
father *padre (m)*
father-in-law/fathers-in-law (pl) *suegro*
fattening *que engorda*
fatty (of food) *grasoso (comida)*
fault *culpa*
it's my fault *es culpa mía*
faulty *defectuoso*
favour *favor (m)*
do me a favour *hacerme un favor*
could you do me a favour? *¿podría hacerme un favor?*
favourite (adj) *favorito*
feather *pluma (de animal)*
February *febrero*
fed up
be fed up *estar harto*
I'm fed up *estoy harto*
feeding bottle *biberón (m)*
feel *sentir*
I feel ill *me siento enfermo*
I feel sick *me siento mareado*
feel / / *ser / / al tacto*
it feels /rough/ *es /áspero/ al tacto*
felt (material) *fieltro*
felt-tip pen *rotulador (m)*
female (adj) *hembra*
feminine *femenino*
ferry -ies *ferry (m)*
by ferry *en ferry*
car ferry *transbordador (n)*
festival *festival (m)*
fetch *traer*

fever *fiebre (f)*
few *pocos (mpl)*
  a few *unos pocos*
  few /people/ *poca /gente/*
fewer *menos (más pocos)*
fiancé *novio*
fiancée *novia*
field (n) *campo (un campo)*
fig *higo*
fight (n) *lucha*
fight (vb) *luchar*
figure (body) *tipo*
file (n) (for papers) *fichero*
fill (tooth) *empastar*
fill (vessel) *llenar*
fill in (form) *rellenar*
  fill in /a form/ *rellenar /un impreso/*
fill up (petrol) *llenar*
  fill it up please! *¡llénelo, por favor!*
fillet (n) *filete (m)*
fillet (vb) *limpiar (pescado)*
filling (tooth) *empaste (m)*
filling station *gasolinera*
film (for camera) *película (para cámara)*
  ASA (tdmk) *ASA (marca)*
  black and white film *película en blanco y negro*
  cartridge film *carrete (m) de película*
  colour film *película de color*
  DIN (tdmk) *DIN (marca)*
  Polaroid film (tdmk) *carrete (m) polaroid*
  Super 8 *Super 8*
  16mm *16mm*
  35mm 20/36 exposures *35mm 20/36 fotos*
  120/127/620 *120/127/620*
film (=entertainment) *película (cine, TV)*
  horror film *película de terror*
  pornographic film *película pornográfica*
  thriller *película de miedo*
  Western *película del oeste*
filter-tipped cigarettes *cigarillos (mpl) con filtro*
find (vb) *encontrar*
  find /this address/ *encontrar /esta dirección/*
fine (adj) (of weather) *bueno (tiempo)*
  it's fine *hace buen tiempo*
fine (n) (=sum of money) *multa*
  pay a fine *pagar una multa*
fine (adj) (=OK) *bien (adj)*
  fine thanks! *¡bien gracias!*
finger *dedo*
finish (vb) *terminar*
  finish /my breakfast/ *terminar /mi desayuno/*
fire (n) *incendio*
  it's on fire *se ha incendiado*
fire alarm *alarma de incendios*
fire brigade *servicio de bomberos*
fire engine *coche (m) de bomberos*
fire escape *salida de incendios*
fire extinguisher *extintor (m) de incendios*
fireman /firemen (pl) *bombero*
fireworks (pl) *fuegos (mpl) artificiales*
  firework display *exhibición (f) de fuegos artificiales*
firm (n) (=company) *empresa*
first *primero*
  at first *al principio*
  first of all *en primer lugar*
first aid *primeros auxilios (mpl)*
  first aid kit *equipo de primeros auxilios*
first class (adj) *de primera clase*
first class (n) *primera clase*
first name *nombre (m)(de pila)*
fish *pescado*
fishing *pesca*
  go fishing *ir de pesca*
fishing line *línea (de pesca)*
fishing rod *caña de pescar*
fishmonger's *pescadería*
fit (adj) (health) *en forma*
  he's fit *está en forma*
fit (n) (=attack) *ataque (m)*
fit (vb) (eg exhaust) *colocar*
fit (vb) *venir bien (ajustar)*
  it doesn't fit me *no me viene bien*
  it's a good fit *viene bien*
fitting room (in shop) *probador (m)*

fix (vb) (=mend) *arreglar*
fizzy *efervescente*
flag *bandera*
flame (n) *llama*
flannel (=cloth) *franela*
flash -es *flash* (m) *flashes* (pl)
  flash bulb *lámpara de flash*
  flash cube *cubo flash*
flask (vacuum flask) *termo*
flat (adj) *plano*
flat (n) *piso (vivienda)*
  furnished flat *piso amueblado*
  unfurnished flat *piso sin amueblar*
flavour *sabor* (m)
  banana *a plátano*
  blackcurrant *a grosella negra*
  chocolate *a chocolate*
  strawberry *a fresa*
  vanilla *a vainilla*
flea *pulga*
flea market *rastro*
flea powder *polvos* (mpl) *para las pulgas*
fleabite *picadura de pulga*
flight *vuelo (avión)*
  charter flight *vuelo charter*
  connecting flight *vuelo de conexión*
  scheduled flight *vuelo programado*
  student flight *vuelo de estudiantes*
flippers (pl) *aletas* (fpl) *(natación)*
  a pair of flippers *un par de aletas*
float (vb) *flotar*
flood (n) *inundación* (f)
flooded *inundado*
floor (of room) *suelo (de habitación)*
floor (of building) *piso (suelo)*
  basement (B) *sótano (S)*
  ground floor (G) *planta baja (B)*
  /first/ floor */primer/ piso*
  top floor *último piso*
florist's *floristería*
flour *harina*
flower *flor* (f)
  a bunch of flowers *un ramo de flores*
flower pot *maceta*
flu *gripe* (f)
fly (=insect) *mosca*

fly spray *ahuyentador* (m) *de moscas*
fly to / / *volar a / /*
flying *vuelo (deporte)*
  go flying *hacer vuelo*
flywheel *volante* (m)
fog *niebla*
foggy *nebuloso*
  it's foggy *hay niebla*
fold (vb) *doblar* (=plegar)
folding *plegable*
  folding /bed/ */cama/ plegable*
  folding /chair/ */silla/ plegable*
folk (adj) *folklórico*
  folk art *arte* (m) *folklórico*
  folk dancing *baile* (m) *folklórico*
  folk music *música folklórica*
folklore *folklore* (m)
follow *seguir*
fond
  be fond of *tener cariño a*
  I'm fond of /him/ *tengo cariño a /él/*
food *comida (alimento)*
  where can I buy some food? *¿dónde puedo comer?*
  food poisoning *envenenamiento por ingestión de alimentos*
  health food *comida de régimen*
fool (n) *tonto* (n)
foolish *tonto* (adj)
foot /feet/ (pl) (=part of body) *pie* (m)
  on foot *a pie*
football (=game) *fútbol* (m)
  a game of football *un partido de fútbol*
  play football *jugar al fútbol*
football (=ball) *balón*
footpath (=through fields) *sendero*
for (prep) *para* (prep)
  for /me/ *para /mí/*
  what's it for? *¿para qué es?*
forehead *frente* (f) *(cara)*
foreign *extranjero* (adj)
foreigner *extranjero* (m) *extranjera* (f)
forest *bosque* (m) *(selva)*
forget *olvidar*
forgive *perdonar*
fork (cutlery) *tenedor* (m)

form (=document) *impreso*
fortunately *afortunadamente*
forward to *enviar a*
  please forward *se ruega hacer seguir*
fountain *fuente (f)*
fountain pen *pluma estilográfica*
foyer (in hotels and theatres) *vestíbulo*
fragile *frágil*
fragile with care (=on labels) *frágil*
frame (n) (=picture frame) *marco (marco de un cuadro)*
frame (vb) *enmarcar*
free (=unconstrained) *libre (=no obligado)*
free (=without payment) *gratis*
freeze *congelar*
  it's freezing *hace mucho frío*
frequent (adj) *frecuente*
fresh *fresco*
  fresh food (not stale, not tinned) *comida fresca*
  fresh water (ie not salt) *agua dulce*
Friday *viernes (m)*
  on Friday *el viernes*
  on Fridays *los viernes*
fridge *nevera*
friend *amigo (m) amiga (f) (en general)*
friendly *amistoso*
fringe (hair) *flequillo (pelo)*
from
  from /eight/ to /ten/ *de /ocho/ a /diez/*
  from /London/ to /Madrid/ *desde /Londres/ a /Madrid/*
  I come from / / *soy de / /*
front
  in front of / / *delante de / /*
frontier *frontera*
frost *escarcha*
frosty *escarchado*
frozen (=deep frozen) *congelado*
  frozen food *alimentos (mpl) congelados*
fruit *fruta*
  fresh fruit *fruta fresca*
  tinned fruit *fruta en lata*
fruit juice (see also under juice) *zumo de fruta*
  a bottle of fruit juice *una botella de zumo de fruta*
  a glass of fruit juice *un vaso de zumo de fruta*
fry *freír*
frying pan *sartén (f)*
full *completo (=lleno)*
  full board *pensión (f) completa*
fun *diversión (f)*
  have fun *divertirse*
funeral *entierro*
funicular *funicular (m)*
funny (=amusing) *gracioso*
fur *pieles (fpl)*
  fur coat *abrigo de pieles*
  lined with fur *forrado de pieles*
furnish *amueblar*
furnished *amueblado*
  furnished /flat/ */piso/ amueblado*
furniture *mobiliario*
furniture shop *tienda de muebles*
further *más lejos*
fuse (n) *fusible (m)*
  /three/ amp fuse *fusible de /tres/ amperios*
  fuse wire *.hilo de fusible*
fuse (vb) *fundirse (electricidad)*
  the lights have fused *se han fundido las luces*
future (adj) *futuro (adj)*
future (n) *futuro (n)*

G

gabardine coat *gaba. dina*
gadget *aparato*
gale *temporal (m) (n)*
gallery -ies *galería*
  art gallery *galería de arte*
gallon *galón*
gallop (vb) *galopar*
gamble (vb) *jugar por dinero*
gambling *juego de azar*
gambling club *club (m) de juego*
game (animals) *caza (animales)*
  grouse *ortega (m)*

hare liebre (f)
partridge perdiz (f)
pheasant faisán (m)
pigeon pichón (m)
quail codorniz (f) codornices (fpl)
wild boar jabalí (m)
game partido/partida
  a game of /tennis/ un partido de /tenis/
  play /tennis/ jugar al /tenis/
gaol cárcel (f)
  in gaol en la cárcel
garage garaje (m)
garden jardín (m)
garlic ajo
gas gas (m)
gate (=door) puerta
gate (=airport exit) salida (de aeropuerto)
gear equipo (para deporte)
  climbing gear equipo de escalar
  diving gear equipo de bucear
gears (pl) (car) marchas (fpl)
  first gear primera marcha
  second gear segunda marcha
  third gear tercera marcha
  fourth gear cuarta marcha
  fifth gear quinta marcha
  reverse marcha atrás
general (adj) general (adj)
generator generador (m)
generous generoso
Gents' (lavatory) servicios (mpl) caballeros
genuine auténtico
German measles rubeola
get (to) (= reach) llegar (a)
  how do I get there? ¿cómo se va allí?
  when does /the train/ get to /Toledo/? ¿cuándo llega /el tren/ a /Toledo/?
get /a taxi/ tomar /un taxi/
  where can I get /a taxi/? ¿dónde puedo tomar /un taxi/?
get off at / / bajar en / /
get on at / / subir en / /

gift regalo
gift shop tienda de regalos
gin ginebra
  a bottle of gin una botella de ginebra
  a gin una ginebra
  a gin and tonic un gin-tonic
ginger (flavour) jengibre (m)
girl chica
girlfriend amiga
give dar
  give it to /me/ please dé/me/lo por favor
glacier glaciar (m)
glad contento (feliz)
  he's glad está contento
glass (=substance) cristal (m)
glass -es vaso
  a glass of /water/ un vaso de /agua/
  a wine glass un vaso de vino
  a set of glasses un juego de vasos
glasses (pl) gafas (fpl) (óptica)
  a pair of glasses unas gafas
glassware shop cristalería
gliding vuelo sin motor
  go gliding hacer vuelo sin motor
gloves (pl) guantes (m)
  a pair of gloves un par de guantes
glue goma de pegar
go ir
  go /home/ ir /a casa/
  go on a picnic/ ir /de picnic/
  go out with / / salir con / /
  go /shopping/ ir /de compras/
  go to /a conference/ ir a /un congreso/
  let's go vamos
goal gol (m)
goalkeeper portero (=guardameta)
goat cabra
godfather padrino
God/god Dios/dios (m)
godmother madrina
goggles (pl) gafas (fpl) (para el deporte)
  underwater goggles gafas de bucear
go-kart coche (m) de karting
gold (adj) de oro
gold (n) oro

golf *golf (m)*
  a round of golf *una vuelta de golf*
  golf ball *pelota de golf*
  golf club (=institution) *club (m) de golf*
  golf club (=object) *palo de golf*
  golf course *campo de golf*
good *bueno (personas, cosas)*
goodbye *adiós*
good-looking *guapo*
  a good-looking man *un hombre guapo*
  a good-looking woman *una mujer guapa*
goods (=merchandise) (pl) *mercancías (fpl)*
  goods train *tren (m) de mercancías*
goose/geese (pl) *ganso*
  wild geese *gansos (mpl) salvajes*
government *gobierno*
grade (=level) *grado* (=nivel)
gradually *poco a poco*
graduate of / / *licenciado por / /*
grammar *gramática*
grams (pl) *gramos*
grandchild/grandchildren (pl) *nieto*
granddaughter *nieta*
grandfather *abuelo*
grandmother *abuela*
grandson *nieto*
grant (for studies) *beca*
grape *uva*
  a bunch of grapes *un racimo de uvas*
grapefruit (fresh) *pomelo*
  tinned grapefruit *pomelo en lata*
grass *hierba (campo)*
grateful *agradecido*
gravy *salsa para carne*
grease (vb) *engrasar*
greasy (of food) *graso*
greasy (of hair) *grasiento (pelo)*
great! *¡estupendo!*
green *verde (color)*
greengrocer's *verdulería*
grey *gris (color)*
grey (=grey-haired) *canoso (pelo)*
grill (vb) *asar a la parrilla*

groceries (pl) *comestibles (mpl)*
grocer's *ultramarinos (ms)*
ground (=the ground) *suelo (tierra)*
group *grupo*
  group ticket *billete (m) de grupo*
grow (of person) *crecer*
grow (=cultivate) *cultivar*
guarantee (n) *garantía*
guarantee (vb) *garantizar*
guardian *guardián (m)*
guess (vb) *adivinar*
guest *invitado (m) invitada (f)*
guide (=person) *guía (m) (persona)*
guide (vb) *guiar*
guide book *guía (m) (libro)*
guilty *culpable*
guitar *guitarra*
gum (of mouth) *encía*
  chewing gum *chicle (m)*
gun *arma de fuego*
gymnasium *gimnasio*

H

hair *pelo*
hair dryer *secador (m) de pelo*
hair oil *brillantina*
  a bottle of hair oil *un frasco de brillantina*
hairbrush *cepillo de pelo*
haircut *corte de pelo*
hairdresser *peluquero*
hairgrip *horquilla de pelo*
half -ves *medio (mitad)*
  half a /litre/ *medio /litro/*
  half a /slice/ *media /cortada/*
ham *jamón (m)*
  ham /sandwich/ */bocadillo/ de jamón*
  /six/ slices of ham */seis/ cortadas de jamón*
hammer *martillo*
hand *mano (f)*
hand luggage *bultos (mpl) de mano*
handbag *bolso de mano*
handcream *crema de manos*
handkerchief -ves *pañuelo (de nariz)*

handle (eg of a case) *asa*
handmade *hecho a mano*
hang *colgar*
happen *pasar* (=*suceder*)
happy *feliz* (s) *felices* (pl)
harbour *puerto (de mar)*
  harbour master *jefe* (m) *de tráfico portuario*
hard (=difficult) *difícil*
hard (=not soft) *duro (no blando)*
hare *liebre* (f)
harpoon gun *arpón* (m)
harvest *cosecha*
hat *sombrero*
hate (vb) *odiar*
have *tener*
  have fun *pasarlo bien*
  have got *tener*
  I've got /an appointment/ *tengo /una cita/*
hay fever *fiebre* (f) *de heno*
he *él*
head (part of body) *cabeza*
headache *dolor* (m) *de cabeza*
headlamp bulb *bombilla del faro*
headphones (pl) *auriculares* (mpl)
  a pair of headphones *un par de auriculares*
headwaiter *maître* (m)
health *salud* (f)
health certificate *certificado médico*
healthy *sano*
hear *oír*
hearing aid *aparato para sordos*
heart *corazón* (m)
  heart attack *ataque* (m) *de corazón*
  heart trouble *enfermedad* (f) *de corazón*
heat (n) *calor* (m)
  heat wave *ola de calor*
heater *calentador* (m)
heating *calefacción* (f)
  central heating *calefacción* (f) *central*
heavy *pesado*
heel (=part of body) *talón* (m) *(del pié)*
heel (=part of shoe) *tacón* (m)
  high heeled *tacón alto*

low heeled *tacón bajo*
height *altura*
helicopter *helicóptero*
hello *hola*
hello (on telephone) *¡díga!/¡dígame!*
help (n) *ayuda*
help (vb) *ayudar*
helpful *útil (que ayuda)*
henna *alheña*
her (adj) *su* (m&f) *sus* (pl)
  for her *para ella*
  her passport *su pasaporte* (m)
  her sister *su hermana* (f)
  her tickets *sus billetes* (mpl)
  her keys *sus llaves* (fpl)
herb *hierba (médica)*
here *aquí*
hero *héroe* (m)
heroine *heroína*
herring *arenque* (m)
hers
  it's hers *es suyo* (m) *es suya* (f)
he's away *está fuera*
hi! *¡hola!*
high *alto (cosas)*
  high chair *sillita alta*
  high water *marea alta*
hijack (n) *secuestro (de avión)*
hill *colina*
hilly *montañoso (colinas)*
him
  for him *para él*
hip *cadera*
hire (vb) *alquilar*
his *su* (m&f) *sus* (pl)
  his passport *su pasaporte* (m)
  his sister *su hermana* (f)
  his tickets *sus billetes* (mpl)
  his keys *sus llaves* (fpl)
  it's his *es suyo* (m) *es suya* (f)
history -ies *historia (universal etc)*
hit (vb) *golpear*
hitchhike *hacer autostop*
hobby -ies *afición* (f)
hockey *hockey* (m)
  a game of hockey *un partido de hockey*

play hockey jugar al hockey
hole agujero
holiday vacaciones (fpl)
  holiday camp campamento de
    vacaciones
  on holiday de vacaciones
  package holiday vacaciones en grupo
  public holiday fiesta oficial
    (= vacación)
hollow (adj) hueco
home casa (hogar)
  at home en casa (en el hogar)
  go home ir a casa
homemade hecho en casa
honest honrado
honey miel (f)
  a jar of honey un tarro de miel
honeymoon luna de miel
hood (of a garment) capucha
hook gancho
hoover (tdmk) aspiradora
hope (vb) esperar
  I hope not espero que no
  I hope so espero que sí
horrific horrendo
hors d'oeuvres entremeses (mpl)
horse caballo
  horse racing carreras (fpl) de caballos
hose (= tube) manga de riego
hose (car) tubo flexible
hospital hospital (m)
hospitality hospitalidad (f)
host anfitrión (m)
hostel (= youth hostel) albergue (m)
hostess -es anfitriona
hot caliente (alta temperatura)
  I'm hot tengo calor
  it's hot (of things/food) está caliente
  it's hot (of the weather) hace calor
hotel hotel (m)
  cheap hotel hotel económico
  first class hotel hotel de primera
    clase
  medium-priced hotel hotel de precio
    medio
hot-water bottle bolsa de agua caliente
hour hora

house casa (edificio)
housewife -ves ama de casa
hovercraft hovercraft (m)
  by hovercraft en hovercraft
how? ¿cómo?
  how are you? ¿cómo está?
  how do you do? encantado (m)
    encantada (f)
  how long? (time) ¿cuánto tiempo?
  how many? ¿cuántos? (mpl)
    ¿cuántas? (fpl)
  how much? ¿cuánto? (m) cuánta? (f)
humid húmedo (clima)
humour humor (m) (ironía)
  sense of humour sentido del humor
hundred cien (m) cientos (mpl)
  hundreds of / / cientos de / /
hungry
  be hungry tener hambre
  I'm hungry tengo hambre
hunting caza (deporte)
  go hunting ir de caza
hurry (n) prisa
  I'm in a hurry tengo prisa
hurry (vb) darse prisa
  please hurry ! ¡por favor dése prisa!
hurt (adj) herido (adj)
hurt (vb) (feel pain) doler
  my/arm/ hurts me duele /el brazo/
  my /foot/ hurts me duele /el pie/
hurt (vb) (inflict pain) hacer daño en
  I've hurt /my leg/ me he hecho daño
    en /la pierna/
husband marido
hut cabaña
hydrofoil hidrofoil (m)
  by hydrofoil en hidrofoil

I

I yo
ice hielo
ice cream helado
ice hockey hockey (m) sobre hielo
  a game of ice hockey un partido de
    hockey sobre hielo
  play ice-hockey jugar a hockey sobre
    hielo

ice skating *patinaje (m) sobre hielo*
  go ice-skating *hacer patinaje sobre hielo*
iced (drink/water) *con hielo*
icy *helado (adj)*
idea *idea*
ideal (adj) *ideal*
identification *identificación (f)*
identify *identificar*
identity card *carnet (m) de identidad*
if *si (condicional)*
  if you can *si puede*
  if possible *si es posible*
ignition system *sistema (m) de encendido*
ill (not well) *enfermo*
  he's ill *está enfermo*
illegal *ilegal*
illustration *ilustración (f)*
immediate *inmediato*
immediately *inmediatamente*
immigration *inmigración (f)*
  immigration control *control (m) de inmigración*
immune *inmune*
immunisation *vacunación (f)*
immunise *inmunizar*
immunity *inmunidad (f)*
  diplomatic immunity *inmunidad diplomática*
impatient *impaciente*
imperfect (goods) *con defecto*
import (n) *importación (f)*
import (vb) *importar (mercancías)*
important *importante*
impossible *imposible*
improve *mejorar*
in
  be in (adv) *estar en casa*
  in /July/ *en /julio/*
  in /summer/ *en /verano/*
  in the morning *por la mañana*
  in /the park/ *en /el parque/*
  in case of /fire/ *en caso de /incendio/*
  in front of / / *delante de / /*
inch -es *pulgada*

include *incluir*
  is /service/ included? *¿está incluido /el servicio/?*
including *incluyendo*
incredible *increíble*
independent *independiente*
indigestion *indigestión (f)*
  indigestion tablet *pastilla para la indigestión*
individual (adj) *individual*
indoors *en casa (dentro de casa)*
  indoor /swimming pool/ */piscina/ cubierta*
industry -ies *industria*
inefficient *ineficaz (s) ineficaces (pl)*
inexperienced *inexperto*
infected *infectado*
infectious *contagioso*
inflatable *hinchable*
inflate *hinchar*
inform *informar*
  inform /the police/ of / / *informar /a la policía/ de / /*
informal *informal*
information (s) *información (f)*
  I'd like some information about /hotels/ please *quiero información sobre /hoteles/ por favor*
  information desk *mostrador (m) de información*
  information office *oficina de información*
initials (pl) *iniciales (fpl)*
injection *inyección (f)*
  I'd like a /tetanus/ injection *quiero una inyección contra /el tétanos/*
injury -ies *herida (f)*
ink *tinta*
  a bottle of ink *un frasco de tinta*
inner tube (tyre) *cámara de aire*
innocent (=not guilty) *inocente*
inoculate *inocular*
inoculation *inoculación (f)*
inquiry -ies *pregunta*
  make an inquiry about / / *pedir información sobre / /*
insect *insecto*

insect bite *picadura de insecto*
insect repellent *ahuyentador (m) de insectos*
insecticide *insecticida*
  a bottle of insecticide *un frasco de insecticida*
inside (adv) *dentro*
inside (prep) *dentro de*
  inside /the house/ *dentro de /la casa/*
insomnia *insomnio*
instead (of) *en vez (de)*
  instead of /coffee/ *en vez de /café/*
instructions (pl) *instrucciones (fpl)*
  instructions for use *modo (s) de empleo*
instrument *instrumento*
  musical instrument *instrumento musical*
insulin *insulina*
insurance *seguro (n)*
  insurance certificate *certificado de seguros*
  insurance policy -ies *póliza de seguros*
insure *asegurar*
  are you insured? *¿está asegurado (m) asegurada (f)?*
  insure /my life/ *asegurar /mi vida/*
intelligent *inteligente*
intensive *intensivo*
intercontinental (flight) *intercontinental*
interested in / / *interesado en / /*
interesting *interesante*
internal *interno*
international *internacional*
interpret *interpretar*
interpreter *intérprete (m&f)*
interval (=break) *descanso (espectáculos)*
interval (in theatre) *intermedio*
interview (n) *entrevista*
  I've got an interview *tengo una entrevista*
interview (vb) *entrevistar*
into *dentro de*
introduce *presentar*

introduction *presentación (f)*
  letter of introduction *carta de presentación*
invalid (n) *inválido*
investment *inversión*
invitation *invitación (f)*
invite *invitar*
invoice (n) *factura*
iodine *yodo*
  a bottle of iodine *una botella de yodo*
iron (n) (object) *plancha*
  travelling iron *plancha de viaje*
iron (vb) (clothing) *planchar*
ironmonger's *ferretería*
irregular *irregular*
irritation (medical) *irritación (f)*
island *isla*
itch (n) *picazón (m)*

J

jack (car) *gato (coche)*
jacket *chaqueta*
  /tweed/ jacket *chaqueta de /tweed/*
jam *confitura*
January *enero*
jar *tarro*
  a jar of /jam/ *un tarro de /confitura/*
jaw *mandíbula*
jazz *jazz (m)*
jealous *celoso*
  he's jealous of /me/ *está celoso de /mí/*
jeans (pl) *vaqueros (mpl)*
  a pair of jeans *un par de vaqueros*
jelly *jalea*
jellyfish/jellyfish (pl) *medusa*
Jew *judío*
jeweller's *joyería*
jewellery *joyas (fpl)*
jigsaw puzzle *rompecabezas (m) rompecabezas (mpl)*
job *trabajo*
  what's your job? *¿cual es tu trabajo?*
jockey *jockey (m)*
joke *chiste (m)*
journey -ies *viaje (m)*

judo *judo*
  do judo *hacer judo*
jug *jarra*
  a jug of / / *una jarra de / /*
juice *zumo*
  grapefruit juice *zumo de pomelo*
  lemon juice *zumo de limón*
  orange juice *zumo de naranja*
  pineapple juice *zumo de piña*
  tomato juice *zumo de tomate*
juicy *jugoso*
July *julio*
jump (vb) *saltar*
junction *cruce (m) (carreteras)*
June *junio*
junk shop *tienda de trastos*

K

keep *guardar*
kettle *hervidora de agua*
key *llave (f)*
key ring *llavero*
khaki (colour) *caqui*
kick (n) *puntapié*
kick (vb) *dar un puntapié*
kidneys (pl) *riñones (mpl)*
kill (vb) *matar*
kilogramme/kilo *kilogramo/kilo*
kilometre *kilómetro*
kind (adj) (=friendly) *amable*
  it's very kind of you *es muy amable de su parte*
kind (n) (=type) *clase (f) (=tipo)*
  a kind of /beer/ *una clase de /cerveza/*
kindness -es *amabilidad (f)*
king *rey (m)*
kiss (vb) *besar*
kiss -es (n) *beso*
kit *equipo*
  first aid kit *botiquín (m)*
kitchen *cocina (lugar)*
kite *cometa*
Kleenex (tissues) (tdmk) *pañuelos de celulosa*
  a box of Kleenex *una caja de*

pañuelos de celulosa
knee *rodilla*
knife -ves *cuchillo*
  carving knife *cuchillo de cortar carne*
knit *hacer punto*
knitting *punto*
  do some knitting *hacer punto*
  knitting needles *agujas (fpl) de punto*
  knitting pattern *patrón (m)*
knitwear *prendas (fpl) de punto*
knob (door) *pomo*
knob (radio) *interruptor (m)*
know (a fact) *saber*
  I know *lo sé*
  I don't know *no sé*
know (a person) *conocer*
  I know him *le conozco*
Kosher *Kosher (comida judía)*

L

label (=luggage label) *etiqueta*
  stick-on label *etiqueta adhesiva*
lace (=material) *encaje (m)*
laces (pl) *cordones (mpl)*
ladder *escalera de mano*
Ladies' (=lavatory) *servicios (mpl) señoras*
lady -ies *señora*
lake *lago*
lamb *cordero*
  a leg of lamb *una pierna de cordero*
  lamb chop *chuleta de cordero*
lamp *lámpara*
  bicycle lamp *farol (m) de bicicleta*
lampshade *pantalla (de luz)*
land *tierra (en general)*
landed (of a plane) *aterrizado*
landlady -ies *propietaria (de piso en alquiler)*
landlord *propietario (de piso en alquiler)*
lane (=traffic lane) *carril (m)(tráfico)*
lane (=small road) *vereda*
language *idioma (m)*
large (size) *grande*
last (=final) *último*
  at last *por fin*

last (= previous) *pasado*
  last /Tuesday/ */el martes/ pasado*
late *tarde (adj)*
  he's late *llega tarde*
  I'm sorry I'm late *siento llegar tarde*
  it's late (= time of day) *es tarde*
later (= at a later time) *más tarde*
laugh (vb) *reír*
launder *lavar*
launderette *lavandería*
laundry (washing) *ropa sucia*
lavatory -ies *servicios (mpl) (wc)*
  Gents' *servicios caballeros*
  Ladies' *servicios señoras*
law *ley (f)*
lawyer *abogado*
laxative *laxante (m)*
  mild laxative *laxante suave*
  strong laxative *laxante fuerte*
  suppository *supositorio*
lay-by *zona de aparcamiento*
lazy *perezoso*
leaflet *folleto*
leak (n) *gotera*
leak (vb) *gotear*
  it's leaking *está goteando*
learn /Spanish/ *aprender /español/*
learner (driver) *alumno de auto-escuela*
leather *cuero*
  leather goods shop *tienda de artículos de cuero*
leave (= depart) *salir*
  leave /at four-thirty p.m./ *salir a /las cuatro y media/*
  leave in /July/ *salir en /julio/*
  leave on /Monday/ *salir el /lunes/*
leave *dejar*
  I've left /my suitcase/ behind *he dejado /mi maleta/*
  leave me alone *déjeme en paz*
  leave /my luggage/ *dejar /mi equipaje/*
left (= not right) *izquierda*
  left (direction) *a la izquierda*
left-handed *zurdo*
left-luggage office *consigna*
leg *pierna*

legal *legal*
lemon *limón (m)*
  a slice of lemon *una rodaja de limón*
  lemon juice *zumo de limón*
lemonade *limonada*
  a bottle of lemonade *una botella de limonada*
  a can of lemonade *una lata de limonada*
  a glass of lemonade *un vaso de limonada*
lend *prestar*
  could you lend me some /money/? *¿podría prestarme /dinero/?*
length *largo (n)*
  full length *largo hasta los pies*
  knee length *largo hasta la rodilla*
lengthen *alargar*
lens -es (of camera) *lente (f)*
  lens cap *tapa protectora de lente*
  wide-angle lens *lente amplio espectro*
  zoom lens *lente zoom*
less *menos (cantidad)*
lesson *lección*
  driving lesson *lección de conducir*
  /Spanish/ lesson *lección de /español/*
let (= allow) *dejar* (= permitir)
  let /me/ try *déje/me/ probar*
let's
  let's go! *¡vámonos!*
  let's /have a drink/ *vamos a /tomar una copa/*
  let's meet /at nine/ *quedemos /a las nueve/*
letter (= of the alphabet) *letra*
letter (correspondence) *carta (correspondencia)*
  air-letter *carta por correo aéreo*
  express letter *carta urgente*
  letter box -es *buzón (m)*
  registered letter *carta certificada*
lettuce *lechuga*
level (adj) *nivelado*
level (n) (= grade) *nivel (m)*
level crossing *paso a nivel*
library -ies *biblioteca*

licence permiso (documento)
lid (of eye) párpado
lid (of pot) tapadera
lie (n) (=untruth) mentira
lie (vb) (=tell an untruth) mentir
lie (vb) (=lie down) tumbarse
life jacket chaleco salvavidas
lifebelt salvavidas (m) / salvavidas (mpl)
lifeboat bote (m) salvavidas
lifeguard vigilante (m)
lift (vb) levantar
lift (n) (=elevator) ascensor (m)
lift (n) (=ride)
  could you give me a lift to / /? ¿podría llevarme a / /?
light (adj) (=not dark) claro (no oscuro)
light (adj) (=not heavy) ligero (=no pesado)
light (n) (electric light) luz (f) luces (fpl) (eléctrica)
  have you got a light? ¿puede darme fuego?
light /a fire/ encender /un fuego/
light bulb bombilla
  /forty/ watt /cuarenta/ watios
light switch -es interruptor (m) de luz
lighter (=cigarette lighter) encendedor (m)
  disposable lighter encendedor no recargable
lighter fuel gas (m) para encender
like (prep) como
  what's it like? ¿cómo es?
like (vb) gustar
  do you like /swimming/? ¿le gusta /la natación/?
  I like it me gusta
likely probable
lime lima
  lime juice zumo de lima
limit (n) límite (m)
  height limit límite de altura
  speed limit límite de velocidad
  weight limit límite de peso
line línea
  outside line línea exterior
  telephone line línea telefónica

linen (bed) ropa de cama
linen (table) mantelería
liner transatlántico
lingerie lencería
  lingerie department departamento de lencería
lining forro
  /fur/ lining forro de /pieles/
lip labio
  lower lip labio inferior
  upper lip labio superior
lipstick lápiz (m) de labios
liqueur licor (m)
liquid líquido
list lista
  shopping list lista de compras
  wine list carta de vinos
listen to /some music/ escuchar /música/
litre litro
litter basura
little (adj) pequeño
  a little boy un niño pequeño
  smaller más pequeño
  smallest el más pequeño
little (n) un poco
  a little money un poco de dinero
live vivir
  where do you live? ¿dónde vive?
liver hígado
load (vb) cargar
loaf -ves (of bread) barra
  a large loaf una barra grande
  a small loaf una barra pequeña
lobster langosta
local (adj) local
  local crafts artesanía local
lock (n) cerrojo
lock (vb) cerrar con llave
locker casillero
  left-luggage locker casillero de consigna
logbook (car) cartilla de propiedad
lonely solitario
long largo (adj)
look (vb) mirar
  look! ¡mire!

look out! ¡cuidado!
  I'm just looking sólo estoy mirando
look after cuidar
  look after /the baby/ cuidar /al niño/
look at mirar
  look at /this/ mirar /esto/
look for buscar
  look for /my passport/ buscar /mi pasaporte/
look /smart/ estar /elegante/
loose (of clothes) no apretado (ropa)
lorry -ies camión (m)
lorry driver camionero
lose perder
  I've lost /my wallet/ he perdido /mi cartera/
lost perdido
  I'm lost me he perdido
lost property office oficina de objetos perdidos
lot mucho
  a lot of /money/ mucho /dinero/
loud fuerte (ruido)
loudly ruidosamente
lounge (in hotel) salón (m)
  departure lounge sala de espera (aeropuerto)
  TV lounge sala de televisión
love (n) amor (m)
  give /Mary/ my love dale recuerdos a /Mary/
  make love hacer el amor
love (vb) amar
low bajo
  low water marea baja
lower (vb) rebajar
LP (=long playing record) LP (m)
luck suerte (f)
  good luck buena suerte
lucky afortunado
  be lucky ser afortunado
  he's lucky es afortunado
luggage equipaje (m)
  cabin luggage equipaje de cabina
  hand luggage equipaje de mano
luggage rack (in train) estante (m) de

equipaje
  luggage van (on train) vagón (m) de equipaje
lump (body) bulto (en el cuerpo)
  a lump of sugar un terrón de azúcar
lunch -es almuerzo
  have lunch almorzar
  packed lunch almuerzo para llevar
luxury -ies lujo

M

machine máquina
mad loco
made in /　/ fabricado en /　/
magazine revista
magnifying glass -es lupa
mahogany caoba
maid chica de servicio
mail correo
  by air-mail correo aéreo
  express mail correo urgente
  surface mail correo ordinario
main principal
  main road carretera principal
make (n) (eg of a car) marca
make (vb) hacer
  make /a complaint/ hacer /una queja/
  make /money/ hacer /dinero/
make-up (=face make-up) maquillaje (m)
  eye make-up maquillaje para de ojos
male (adj) varón
mallet mazo
man/men (pl) hombre (m)
  young man hombre joven
manager director (m)
manicure manicura
  manicure set juego de manicura
man-made sintético
  man-made fibre fibra sintética
many muchos
  not many no muchos
  too many demasiados
map mapa (m)
  large-scale map mapa a gran escala

map of /Spain/ *mapa de /España/*
road map *mapa de carreteras*
street map *plano de la ciudad*
marble (material) *mármol (m)*
March *marzo*
margarine *margarina*
mark (=spot/stain) *mancha*
market *mercado*
  fish market *mercado de pescado*
  fruit and vegetable market *mercado de frutas y verduras*
  market place *plaza del mercado*
  meat market *mercado de carnes*
marmalade *mermelada de naranja*
  a jar of marmalade *un tarro de mermelada de naranja*
maroon (colour) *castaño*
married *casado*
mascara *rímel (m)*
masculine *masculino*
mask *máscara*
  snorkel mask *máscara de bucear con tubo de respiración*
mass (=Catholic service) *misa*
massage (n) *masaje (m)*
mast *mástil (m)*
mat *alfombrilla*
  bath mat *alfombrilla de baño*
  door mat *alfombrilla de puerta*
match -es *cerilla*
  a box of matches *una caja de cerillas*
match -es (=competition) *partido*
  football match *partido de fútbol*
material (=cloth) *tela*
  checked material *tela de cuadros*
  heavy material *tela gruesa*
  lightweight material *tela ligera*
  plain material *tela lisa*
matter (vb)
  it doesn't matter *no importa*
  what's the matter? *¿qué le pasa?*
mattress -es *colchón (m)*
mauve *malva*
maximum (adj) *máximo*
May *mayo*
mayonnaise *mayonesa*
me *me (a mí)*

for me *para mí*
meal *comida (de cada día)*
  light meal *comida ligera*
mean (=not generous) *tacaño*
mean (vb) (of a word) *significar*
  what does it mean? *¿qué significa?*
measles *sarampión (m)*
measure (vb) *medir*
meat *carne (f)*
  cold meat *fiambre (m)*
  beef *carne de vaca*
  lamb *cordero*
  mutton *carnero*
  pork *cerdo*
mechanic *mecánico*
mechanism *mecanismo*
medical (adj) *médico*
medicine *medicamento*
  a bottle of medicine *un frasco de medicamento*
medium (size) *medio*
  medium-dry *semi-seco*
  medium-rare (eg of steak) *semi-hecho*
  medium-sweet *semi-dulce*
meet (=get to know) *encontrarse*
  meet /your family/ *encontrarse con /su familia/*
meet (at a given time) *quedar*
meeting (business) *reunión (f)*
melon *melón (m)*
  half a melon *medio melón*
  a slice of melon *una rodaja de melón*
member (of a group) *miembro*
memo *nota (para recordar algo)*
memory -ies *recuerdo*
  a good/bad memory *un buen/mal recuerdo*
  happy memories (pl) *recuerdos (mpl) felices*
mend *arreglar*
men's outfitter's *sastrería de caballero*
menu *menú (m)*
  à la carte menu *menú a la carta*
  set menu *menú del día*
mess -es *desorden (m)*
message *recado*
  can I leave a message please?

¿puedo dejar un recado por favor?
can I take a message? ¿quiere dejar algun recado?

metal metal (m)

meter contador (m)
  electricity meter contador de luz
  gas meter contador de gas

method método

methylated spirit alcohol (m) metilado
  a bottle of methylated spirits una botella de alcohol metilado

metre (=length) metro (medida)

microphone micrófono

midday mediodía

middle medio (=centro)
  in the middle of / / en el medio de / /

middle-aged de mediana edad

midnight medianoche

migraine jaqueca

mild suave

mild (of weather) templado (clima)

mile milla

milk leche (f)
  a bottle of milk una botella de leche
  a glass of milk un vaso de leche
  powdered milk leche en polvo
  tinned milk leche condensada

milk shake batido de leche

million millón (m)
  millions of / / millones de / /

mince (vb) picar
  minced meat carne (f) picada

mind (= look after/watch) cuidar
  could you mind /my bag/ please? ¿podría cuidarme /el bolso/ por favor?

mine (n) mina
  coal mine mina de carbón

mine (= belongs to me)
  it's mine es mío (m) es mía (f)

miner minero

mineral water agua mineral
  a bottle of mineral water una botella de agua mineral
  a glass of mineral water un vaso de agua mineral
  fizzy mineral water agua mineral con gas
  still mineral water agua mineral sin gas

minibus -es microbús (m)

minimum (adj) mínimo

mink visón (m)
  mink coat abrigo de visón

minus bajo (grados)

minute (time) minuto
  just a minute! ¡un momento!

mirror espejo
  hand-mirror espejo de mano

Miss / / señorita / /

miss /the train/ perder /el tren/

mist neblina

mistake (n) error (m)
  by mistake por equivocación

mix (vb) mezclar

mixer (of food) batidora

mixture mezcla

model (object) modelo (objeto)
  the latest model el último modelo
  model aeroplane aeromodelo

model (profession) modelo

modern moderno

moment momento

Monday lunes (m)
  on Monday el lunes
  on Mondays los lunes

money dinero
  make money hacer dinero

mono (adj) mono

month mes (m)
  last month el mes pasado
  next month el mes que viene
  this month este mes

monthly mensual

monument monumento

mood humor (m) (estado de ánimo)
  in a good/bad mood de buen/mal humor

moon luna

mop (n) fregona

moped moto (f) de pequeña velocidad

more más (cantidad)
  more /cake/ please más /pastel/, por favor

morning *mañana (tiempo)*
  good morning *buenos días*
  this morning *esta mañana*
  tomorrow morning *mañana por la mañana*
  yesterday morning *ayer por la mañana*
morning paper *periódico matutino*
mortgage (n) *hipoteca*
mosque *mezquita*
mosquito *mosquito*
  mosquito net *mosquitera*
most *la mayor parte*
  most /money/ *la mayor parte /del dinero/*
  most /people/ *la mayor parte /de la gente/*
motel *motel (m)*
mother *madre (f)*
mother-in-law/mothers-in-law (pl) *suegra*
motor *motor (m)*
  outboard motor *motor fuera bordo*
motor racing *carreras (fpl) de coches*
  go motor racing *hacer carreras de coches*
motorail (ie car on a train) *transporte (m) de coches por tren*
motorbike *motocicleta*
motorboat *lancha motora*
motorist *automovilista (m&f)*
motorway *autopista*
mouldy *enmohecido*
mountain *montaña*
mountaineer *montañero*
mountaineering *montañismo*
  go mountaineering *hacer montañismo*
mountainous *montañoso (montañas)*
mouse/mice (pl) *ratón (m)*
mousetrap *ratonera*
moustache *bigote (m)*
mouth *boca*
mouthwash -es *enjuague (m) bucal*
  a bottle of mouthwash *un frasco de enjuague bucal*
move (vb) *mover*

movement *movimiento*
Mr / / *señor / /*
Mrs / / *señora / /*
much *mucho*
mud *barro*
muddy *fangoso*
mug *jarrita*
mumps *paperas (fpl)*
murder (n) *asesinato*
murder (vb) *asesinar*
muscle *músculo*
museum *museo*
mushroom *champiñón (m)*
  mushroom /soup/ */crema/ de champiñón*
music *música*
  classical music *música clásica*
  folk music *música folklórica*
  light music *música ligera*
  pop music *música pop*
musical (=an entertainment) *musical (m)*
musician *músico*
Muslim *musulmán (m)*
mussel *mejillón (m)*
must *tener que*
  I must /go home/ now *tengo que /irme a casa/ ahora*
  must I /pay by cash/? *¿tengo que /pagar al contado/?*
  you mustn't /park/ /here/ *no se puede /aparcar/ /aquí/*
mustard *mostaza*
my *mi (m&f) mis (pl)*
  my passport *mi pasaporte (m)*
  my sister *mi hermana (f)*
  my tickets *mis billetes (mpl)*
  my keys *mis llaves (fpl)*

N

nail (metal) *clavo*
nail (finger/toe) *uña*
  nailbrush -es *cepillo de uñas*
  nail file *lima de uñas*
  nail scissors *tijeras (fpl) de uñas*
  nail varnish *esmalte (m) de uñas*

naked *desnudo*
name *nombre (m) (completo)*
  first name *nombre de pila*
  surname *apellido*
  my name's /Paul Smith/ *me llamo /Paul Smith/*
  what's your name please? *¿como se llama por favor?*
napkin *servilleta*
  napkin ring *servilletero*
  paper napkin *servilleta de papel*
nappy -ies *pañal (m)*
  disposable nappies *pañales (mpl) de usar y tirar*
narrow *estrecho*
nasty *desagradable*
nation *nación (f)*
national *nacional*
nationality -ies *nacionalidad (f)*
natural *natural*
nature *naturaleza*
naughty (usually of young children) *travieso*
nausea *náusea*
navigate *navegar*
navy -ies *marina*
near (adv) *cerca*
near (prep) **/the station/** *cerca /de la estación/*
neat (of a drink) *solo (bebidas)*
necessary *necesario*
necessity -ies *necesidad (f)*
neck *cuello (cuerpo)*
necklace *collar (m)*
née *apellido de soltera*
need (vb) *necesitar*
  I need /more money/ *necesito /más dinero/*
needle *aguja*
  knitting needles *agujas (fpl) de punto*
negative (=film negative) *negativo*
nephew *sobrino*
nervous (=apprehensive) *nervioso*
nervous breakdown *crisis nerviosa (f) crisis nerviosas (fpl)*
net (=fishing net) *red (f) (de pescar)*
  hair net *redecilla de pelo*

net weight *peso neto*
never *nunca*
new (of things) *nuevo*
news (s) *noticias (fpl)*
newsagent's *tienda de periódicos y revistas*
newspaper *periódico*
  /English/ newspaper *periódico /inglés/*
  evening paper *periódico de la tarde*
  local newspaper *periódico local*
  morning paper *periódico matutino*
newsstand *kiosco de periódicos*
next *siguiente*
next door *al lado*
  next door /to the station/ *al lado /de la estación/*
  the house next door *la casa de al lado*
next of kin *familiar (m) más cercano*
next to **/ /** *junto a / /*
nib *punta (de una pluma)*
nice *agradable*
niece *sobrina*
night *noche (f)*
  good night *buenas noches*
  last night *anoche*
  tomorrow night *mañana por la noche*
  tonight *esta noche*
night life *vida nocturna*
nightclub *club (m) nocturno*
nightdress -es *camisón (m)*
no (opposite of 'yes') *no (opuesto a 'sí')*
no /money/ *nada de /dinero/*
no one *nadie*
noisy *ruidoso*
nonsense *tontería*
nonstick *anti-adherente*
  nonstick /frying-pan/ */sartén/ (m) anti-adherente*
nonstop *sin parar*
normal *normal (=corriente)*
north *norte (m)*
  northeast *noreste (m)*
  northwest *noroeste (m)*
nose *nariz (f) narices (fpl)*
nosebleed *hemorragia nasal*

not no (con verbos etc)
  not at all (replying to 'thank you') de nada (respuesta a 'gracias')
  not yet todavia no
note (=money) billete (m) (dinero)
  /a hundred/ peseta note billete de /cien/ pesetas
note (written) nota (=apunte)
notebook cuaderno de notas
nothing nada
notice anuncio
  notice board tablón (m) de anuncios
November noviembre (m)
now ahora
nowhere en ninguna parte
nude desnudo
number número
  number /seven/ número /siete/
  telephone number número de teléfono
  wrong number número equivocado
nurse enfermera
nursery -ies (=day nursery for children) guardería infantil
nursery -ies (=school) jardín (m) de infancia
nut (metal) tuerca
  a nut and bolt una tuerca y un perno
nut nuez (f) nueces (fpl)
  almond almendra
  peanut cacahuete
nutcrackers (pl) cascanueces (m) cascanueces (mpl)
nylon nylon (m)
  a pair of nylons (stockings) un par de medias de nylon

O

oak roble (m)
oar (for rowing) remo
o'clock
  it's one o'clock es la una
  it's three o'clock son las tres
October octubre (m)
of de (posesión)
off (of light etc) apagado

offence infracción (f)
  parking offence infracción de tráfico
offer (n) oferta
  make an offer hacer una oferta
office despacho
office worker administrativo
official (adj) oficial
official (n) funcionario
often a menudo
oil (lubricating) aceite (m) (motor)
  a can of oil un bidón de aceite
  oil filter filtro de aceite
  oil pump bomba de aceite
oil (salad) aceite (m) (cocina)
  olive oil aceite de oliva
  vegetable oil aceite vegetal
oil painting óleo
oily aceitoso
ointment pomada
  a jar of ointment un tarro de pomada
  a tube of ointment un tubo de pomada
OK vale
old (of people and things) viejo
  he is /six/ years old tiene /seis/ años de edad
old-fashioned anticuado
olive aceituna
  black olive aceituna negra
  green olive aceituna verde
omelette tortilla
on
  on a coach en un autocar
  on /July 6th/ el /seis de julio/
  on Monday el lunes
  on the bed sobre la cama
  on /the table/ sobre /la mesa/
on (of light etc) encendido
once (=one time) una vez
one (adj) (number) un (m) una (f) (número)
one-way street dirección (f) única
onion cebolla
  spring onion cebolleta
only solamente
OPEC OPEP
open (adj) abierto

open (vb) *abrir*
open-air restaurant *restaurante (m) al aire libre*
open-air swimming pool *piscina al aire libre*
opening times (pl) *horas (fpl) de apertura*
opera *ópera*
opera house *teatro de la ópera*
operate (surgically) *operar*
operation (surgical) *operación (f) (médica)*
opposite (adv) *enfrente*
  opposite /the station/ *enfrente /de la estación/*
optician *oculista (m)*
or *o*
orange *naranja*
  orangeade *naranja gaseosa*
  orange juice *zumo de naranja*
  a bottle of orange juice *una botella de zumo de naranja*
  a glass of orange juice *un vaso de zumo de naranja*
orchestra *orquesta*
order /a steak/ *pedir /un bistec/*
ordinary *corriente (adj)*
original *original*
ornament *adorno*
other *otro*
  the other /train/ *el otro /tren/*
our *nuestro*
  our passport *nuestro pasaporte (m)*
  our sister *nuestra hermana (f)*
  our tickets *nuestros billetes (mpl)*
  our keys *nuestras llaves (fpl)*
ours *nuestro*
  it's ours *es nuestro (m) es nuestra (f)*
out *fuera (adv)*
  he's out *está fuera (de casa)*
out of date (eg clothes) *anticuado*
out of date (eg passport) *caducado*
out of order *no funciona*
outboard motor *motor (m) fuera bordo*
outside (adv) *fuera (=parte de fuera)*

outside (prep) *fuera de (=en la parte de fuera)*
  outside /the house/ *fuera de /la casa/*
oven *horno*
over (=above) *por encima de*
  fly over /the mountains/ *volar por encima de /las montañas/*
overcoat *abrigo*
overcooked *demasiado hecho*
overheated (of engine) *recalentado*
overland *por vía terrestre*
overtake *adelantar*
overweight (people) *gordo (para personas)*
  be overweight *ser/estar gordo*
  he's overweight *es/está gordo*
  be overweight (things) *pesar demasiado*
owe *deber*
  how much do I owe you? *¿cuánto le debo?*
  you owe me / / *me debe / /*
owner *propietario (de algo)*
oxygen *oxígeno*
oyster *ostra*
  a dozen oysters *una docena de ostras*

P

pack (vb) *empacar*
  pack /my suitcase/ *hacer /mi maleta/*
package holiday *vacaciones (fpl) en grupo*
packet *paquete (m) (=cajetilla)*
  a packet of /cigarettes/ (=20) *un paquete de /cigarrillos/*
packing materials (to prevent breakages) *embalaje (m)*
pad (of writing paper) *papel (m) de escribir*
  sketch-pad *bloc (m) de dibujo*
paddle (for canoe) *remo*
padlock (n) *candado*
page (of a book) *página*

pain *dolor (m)*
painful *doloroso*
painkiller *analgésico*
paint *pintura (paredes)*
  a tin of paint *un bote de pintura*
paintbrush -es *brocha*
  paintbrush *pincel (m)*
painting (n) *pintura (cuadro)*
  oil painting *pintura al óleo*
  watercolour *acuarela*
paints (pl) *pinturas (fpl)*
  box of paints *caja de pinturas*
pair *par (m)*
  a pair of / / *un par de / /*
palace *palacio*
pale (of people & things) *pálido*
pants (pl) *bragas (fpl)*
  a pair of pants *unas bragas*
panty-girdle *faja-pantalón (f)*
paper *papel (m)*
  airmail paper *papel de avión*
  a sheet of paper *una hoja de papel*
  carbon paper *papel carbón*
  drawing paper *papel de dibujo*
  lined paper *papel rayado*
  typing paper *papel de máquina*
  unlined paper *papel liso*
  wrapping paper *papel de envolver*
  writing paper *papel de escribir*
paper bag *bolsa de papel*
paper clip *clip (m)*
paperback *libro de bolsillo*
parcel *paquete (m) (envuelto)*
  by parcel post *paquete postal*
parent *padre (m)*
park (n) *parque (m)*
park (vb) *aparcar*
parking
  no parking *prohibido aparcar*
parking meter *parquímetro*
parliament *parlamento*
part *parte (f)*
  a part of / / *una parte de / /*
part (car) *pieza (coche)*
  spare parts *piezas (fpl) de recambio*
partner (business) *socio (negocios)*
partridge *perdiz (f)*

part-time work *trabajo de media jornada*
party -ies *fiesta (=reunión)*
  birthday party *fiesta de cumpleaños*
pass -es (n) (=pass to enter building)
  pase (m) (para entrar en algún sitio)
  mountain pass *puerto (de montaña)*
passage (on a boat) *pasaje (m)*
passenger *pasajero*
  transit passenger *pasajero en tránsito*
passport *pasaporte (m)*
past
  go past /the station/ *pasar por delante /de la estación/*
pastille *pastilla*
  throat pastille *pastilla de garganta*
pastry -ies (=cake) *pastel (m)*
patch (n) *pieza (=pedazo)*
patch (vb) *remendar*
pâté *paté (m)*
  liver pâté *paté de hígado*
path *sendero*
patient (adj) *paciente (adj)*
patient (n) *paciente (m&f) (n)*
  outpatient *paciente externo*
pattern *patrón (m)*
  dress pattern *patrón de vestido*
  knitting pattern *patrón de punto*
pavement *acera*
pay *pagar*
  by /credit card/ *con /tarjeta de crédito/*
  in advance *por adelantado*
  in cash *al contado*
  in /pounds/ *en /libras esterlinas/*
  the bill *la cuenta*
pea *guisante (m)*
peach -es *melocotón (m)*
peanut *cacahuete (m)*
  a packet of peanuts *un paquete de cacahuetes*
pear *pera*
pearl *perla*
pedestrian *peatón (m)*
  pedestrian crossing *paso de peatones*

peel (vb) *pelar*
peg (=clothes peg) *pinza (de la ropa)*
pen (=fountain pen) *pluma (de escribir)*
  ballpoint pen *bolígrafo*
pen friend *amigo por correspondencia*
pencil *lápiz (m) lápices (mpl)*
  pencil sharpener *sacapuntas (m)
  sacapuntas (mpl)*
penicillin *penicilina*
  I'm allergic to penicillin *soy alérgico
  a la penicilina*
penknife -ves *navaja*
people (pl) *gente (fs)*
pepper *pimienta*
pepper (=vegetable) *pimiento*
  green pepper *pimiento verde*
  red pepper *pimiento rojo*
peppermint (=flavour/drink) *menta*
  peppermint (sweet) *pastilla de menta*
per annum *por año*
per cent *por ciento*
percolator *cafetera exprés*
perfect (adj) *perfecto*
performance *representación (f)*
perfume *perfume (m)*
  a bottle of perfume *un frasco de
  perfume*
perhaps *quizás*
period (of time) *período*
period (=menstrual period) *período*
perm (=permanent wave) *permanente
  (f) (n)*
permanent *permanente (adj)*
permission *permiso (comentimiento)*
  permission to /enter/ *permiso para
  /entrar/*
permit (n) *permiso*
permit (vb) *permitir*
person *persona*
personal *personal*
pet *animal (m) doméstico*
petrol *gasolina*
  petrol can *bidón (m) de gasolina*
petrol station *estación (f) de servicio*
petticoat *combinación (f) (ropa)*
pheasant *faisán (m)*
phone (n) *teléfono*

external phone *teléfono exterior*
internal phone *teléfono interior*
may I use your phone please?
  ¿puedo usar su teléfono por favor?
photocopier *fotocopiadora*
photocopy (vb) *fotocopiar*
photocopy (n) **-ies** *fotocopia*
photograph/photo (infml)
  fotografía/foto (f)
  black and white photograph
  fotografía en blanco y negro
  colour photograph *fotografía en color*
  take a photograph *hacer una
  fotografía*
photographer *fotógrafo*
  photographer's studio *estudio de
  fotografía*
photographic *fotográfico*
phrase *frase (f)*
phrase book *libro de frases*
piano *piano*
pick (=gather flowers etc) *coger (flores
  etc)*
picnic *picnic (m)*
  go on a picnic *ir de picnic*
picture (drawing or painting) *cuadro*
piece *trozo*
  a piece of / / *un trozo de / /*
pig *cerdo (animal)*
pigeon *paloma*
piles (illness) *hemorroides (fpl)*
pill *pastilla (=píldora)*
  a bottle of pills *un frasco de pastillas*
  sleeping pills *pastillas para dormir*
  the Pill *la Píldora (pastilla)*
pillow *almohada*
  pillow case *funda de almohada*
pilot *piloto*
pin *alfiler (m)*
  drawing pin *chincheta*
pine (wood) *pino*
pineapple *piña*
  a slice of pineapple *una cortada de
  piña*
  pineapple juice *zumo de piña*
pink *rosa (adj)*
pint *pinta*

pipe (smoker's) *pipa*
  pipe cleaner *limpiador (m) de pipa*
place (exact location) *lugar (m)*
  place of birth *lugar de nacimiento*
  place of work *lugar de trabajo*
place (eg on a plane) *sitio (=asiento)*
plaice/plaice (pl) *platija*
plain (adj) *natural*
plain (adj) (=simple) *sencillo*
plan (n) *plan (m)*
plan (vb) *planear*
  planned (=already decided) *proyectado*
plane (n) (=aeroplane) *avión (m)*
  by plane *en avión*
plant (n) *planta*
plant (vb) *plantar*
plaster (for walls) *yeso*
  sticking plaster (for cuts) *esparadrapo*
plastic (adj) *plástico*
  plastic bag *bolsa de plástico*
plate (=dental plate) *placa de la dentadura postiza*
plate (=dinner plate) *plato (para comer)*
platform /eight/ *andén (m) /ocho/*
platinum *platino*
play (n) (at theatre) *obra de teatro*
play (vb) *jugar*
  play a game of / / *jugar una partida de / /*
  play rugby *jugar a rugby*
play (vb) (an instrument) *tocar (instrumento)*
playground *terreno de juegos*
playgroup *grupo de juegos*
pleasant *agradable*
please (request) *por favor*
  yes please (acceptance of offer) *sí, por favor*
pleased *contento (=satisfecho)*
  pleased with / / *contento con / /*
plenty *mucho*
  plenty of / / *mucho / /*
pliers (pl) *alicates (mpl)*
  a pair of pliers *unos alicates*
plimsolls (pl) *zapatillas (fpl) de tenis*

  a pair of plimsolls *un par de zapatillas de tenis*
plug (for sink) *tapón (m)*
plug (electric) *enchufe (m) (en aparato)*
  adaptor plug *adaptador (m)*
plug in *enchufar*
plum *ciruela*
plumber *fontanero*
plus *más (además de)*
p.m. *por la tarde*
pneumonia *pulmonía*
poach *escalfar*
pocket *bolsillo*
  pocket dictionary -ies *diccionario de bolsillo*
  pocket money *dinero de bolsillo*
pocketknife -ves *cuchillo de bolsillo*
point (n) (=a sharpened point) *punta*
point (vb) (=indicate) *señalar*
pointed *puntiagudo*
poison *veneno*
poisoning *envenenamiento*
  food poisoning *envenenamiento por ingestión de alimentos*
poisonous *venenoso*
poker (=game) *póker (m)*
  a game of poker *una partida de póker*
  play poker *jugar al póker*
police (pl) *policía (cuerpo de policía)*
  police station *comisaría de policía*
policeman/policemen (pl) *policía (miembro)*
polish (n) *pulimento*
  shoe polish *betún (m)*
polish (vb) *pulir*
polite *educado*
political *político*
politician *político*
politics (pl) *política (s)*
polo neck sweater *suéter (m) de cuello alto*
pond *estanque (m)*
pony -ies *pony (m)*
pony trekking *montar en pony*
  go pony trekking *ir a montar en pony*
pool (=swimming pool) *piscina*

poor (=not rich) *pobre*
poor (poor quality) *de mala calidad*
pop (music) *música popular*
popcorn *palomitas (fpl) de maíz*
popular *popular*
population *población (f)*
pork *cerdo (carne)*
pornographic *pornográfico*
port (=harbour) *puerto*
portable *portátil*
  portable television *televisión (f) portátil*
porter (hotel) *conserje (m)*
porter (railway) *mozo de estación*
portion *ración (f)*
  a portion of / / *una ración de / /*
portrait *retrato*
position *posición (f)*
possible *posible*
post (vb) *enviar por correo*
  post this airmail *enviar esto por correo aéreo*
  as printed matter *como papel impreso*
  express *urgente*
  parcel post *como paquete postal*
  registered *certificado*
  surface mail *por correo normal*
post office *correos (ms)*
postage *franqueo*
postal order *giro postal*
postal rate for /England/ *tarifa postal para /Inglaterra/*
postbox -es *buzón (m)*
postcard *tarjeta postal*
postcode *distrito postal*
poster *cartel (m)*
pot *puchero*
  a pot of tea *una tetera llena*
potato -es *patata*
potato peeler *pelador (m) de patatas*
pottery (substance) *alfarería*
poultry *aves (fpl)*
  chicken *pollo*
  duck *pato*
  turkey *pavo*
pound *libra*

pour *verter*
powder (face powder) *polvos (mpl) de tocador*
  baby powder *polvos de talco para niños*
  talcum powder *polvos de talco*
practice (=custom) *costumbre (f)*
practice (=training) *práctica*
practise (=put into practice) *practicar*
practise (=train) *entrenarse*
pram *cochecito de niño*
prawn *gamba (grande)*
precious *precioso*
  precious stone *piedra preciosa*
prefer *preferir*
pregnant *embarazada*
prepare *preparar*
prescribe *recetar*
prescription *receta (médica)*
present (adj) *presente (adj)*
present (n) (=gift) *regalo*
present (n) (time) *presente (m) (n)*
present (vb) *presentar*
president (of company) *presidente (m)*
press (vb) (eg button) *apretar*
press (vb) (ironing) *planchar*
pressure *presión (f)*
  blood pressure *tensión (f) sanguínea*
pressure cooker *olla a presión*
pretty *bonito*
price (n) *precio*
  price list *lista de precios*
priest *sacerdote (m)*
prince *príncipe (m)*
princess -es *princesa*
print (n) (photographic) *foto (f)*
print (vb) *imprimir*
printer *impresor (m)*
prison *cárcel (f)*
private *privado*
  private /bath/ */baño/ privado*
prize *premio*
probable *probable*
problem *problema (m)*
procession *procesión (f)*
produce (vb) *producir*
product *producto (n)*

programme (of events) *programa (m)*

promise (n) *promesa*

promise (vb) *prometer*

promotion *promoción (f)*

pronounce *pronunciar*

proof *prueba (=confirmación)*

property -ies (=belongings) *propiedad (f)*

prospectus -es *prospecto*

prostitute *prostituta*

protect *proteger*
protect me from / / *protegerme de / /*

protection *protección (f)*

protective *protector (adj)*

Protestant (adj) *protestante*
Protestant church *iglesia (f) protestante*

prove *demostrar*

provisions (pl) *provisiones (fpl)*

prune *ciruela pasa*

public *público*
public buildings (pl) *edificios (mpl) públicos*
public convenience *servicios (mpl) públicos*
public /garden/ */jardín/ (m) público*

pull *estirar*

pump *bomba (a presión)*
bicycle pump *bombín (m) de bicicleta*
foot pump *hinchador (m) de pie*
water pump *bomba de agua*

puncture *pinchazo*

punish *castigar*

punishment *castigo*

pupil *alumno*

pure *puro (adj)*

purple *morado*

purse *monedero*

pus *pus (m)*

push (vb) *empujar*

pushchair *sillita de niño*

put *poner*
put on /my coat/ *poner /mi abrigo/*

puzzle *acertijo*
jigsaw puzzle *rompecabezas (m) rompecabezas (mpl)*

pyjamas (pl) *pijama (ms)*
a pair of pyjamas *un pijama*

Q

quail (=bird) *codorniz (f) codornices (fpl)*

qualifications (pl) *títulos (mpl) (profesionales)*

qualified *titulado*

quality -ies *calidad (f)*

quarrel (n) *pelea*

quarter *cuarto*
a quarter of /an hour/ *un cuarto de /hora/*

queen *reina*

query (vb) *poner en duda*
I would like to query /the bill/ *quiero comprobar /la cuenta/*

question (n) *pregunta*

question (vb) *preguntar*

queue (n) *cola*

queue (vb) *hacer cola*

quick *rápido*
quick! *¡rápido!*

quickly *rapidamente*

quiet (adj) *tranquilo/callado*
quiet please! *¡silencio, por favor!*

quinine *quinina*

quite *bastante*

R

rabbi *rabino*

rabbit *conejo*

rabies *rabia*

race (n) (=contest) *carrera (competición)*
horse race *carrera de caballos*
motor race *carrera de coches*

race (vb) *hacer una carrera*

racecourse *circuito de carreras*

racehorse *caballo de carreras*

races (pl) (=the races) *carreras (fpl)*

racing *carreras (fpl)*
horse racing *carrera de caballos*
motor racing *carrera de coches*

racquet *raqueta*
  tennis racquet *raqueta de tenis*
  squash racquet *raqueta de squash*
radiator (car) *radiador (m)*
radio *radio (f)*
  car radio *radio del coche*
  portable radio *radio (f) portátil*
  transistor radio *radio transistor*
radish -es *rábano*
raft *balsa*
  life raft *balsa salvavidas*
rag (for cleaning) *trapo*
railway *ferrocarril (m)*
  railway station *estación (f) de ferrocarril*
  underground railway *metro*
rain (n) *lluvia*
rain (vb) *llover*
  it's raining *llueve*
raincoat *impermeable (m) (n)*
raisin *pasa*
rally -ies *rallye (m)*
  motor rally *rallye de coches*
range (=range of goods) *surtido*
range (=mountain range) *cordillera*
rare (=unusual) *raro*
rare (eg of steak) *poco hecho*
  medium-rare *normal*
rash -es *erupción (f)*
rasher of bacon *cortada de bacon*
raspberry -ies *frambuesa*
  a punnet of raspberries *una cesta de frambuesas*
rat *ratto*
rate (n) *tarifa*
  cheap rate (mail, telephone) *tarifa económica*
  exchange rate *tarifa de cambio*
  postal rate *tarifa postal*
  rate per day *tarifa diaria*
  rates (charges) *tarifas (fpl)*
rattle (baby's rattle) *sonajero*
rattle (noise) *repiqueteo*
raw *crudo*
razor *maquinilla de afeitar*
  electric razor *máquina de afeitar eléctrica*

razor blade *cuchilla de afeitar*
  a packet of razor blades *un paquete de cuchillas de afeitar*
reach (=attain) (vb) *alcanzar*
read *leer*
  read /a magazine/ *leer /una revista/*
ready *listo (a punto)*
  are you ready? *¿está listo? (m) ¿está lista? (f) ¿están listos? (mpl) ¿están listas? (fpl)*
  when will it be ready? *¿cuándo estará listo?*
real *real*
really *realmente*
rear /coach/ *último /coche/ (m)*
reason (n) *razón (f)*
reasonable *razonable*
receipt *recibo*
receive *recibir*
recent *reciente*
Reception (eg in a hotel) *Recepción (f)*
recharge (battery) *recargar*
recipe *receta (cocina)*
recognise *reconocer*
recommend *recomendar*
record (n) *disco*
  thirty-three r.p.m. record *disco de treinta y tres r.p.m.*
  forty-five r.p.m. record/single *disco de cuarenta y cinco r.p.m.*
  classical record *disco de música clásica*
  jazz record *disco de jazz*
  light music record *disco de música ligera*
  pop record *disco de música pop*
record (vb) *grabar (disco)*
record player *tocadiscos (m)*
  tocadiscos (mpl)
record shop *tienda de discos*
rectangular *rectangular*
red *rojo*
reduce (price) *rebajar (precio)*
  reduce the price *rebajar el precio*
reduction *rebaja (=descuento)*
reel (of cotton) *carrete (m) (de hilo)*
reel (recording tape) *cinta (de grabar)*

refill *recambio*
refrigerator/fridge (infml) *refrigerador (m)/nevera*
refund (n) *devolución (f)* (=reembolso)
refund (vb) *devolver* (=reembolsar)
regards
  give /Julie/ my regards *dele recuerdos a /Julie/ de mi parte*
register (at) (eg a club) *inscribirse*
registered (mail) *certificado (adj)*
registration number *número de registro*
regret (vb) *sentir*
regular *regular*
  regular /service/ */servicio/ regular*
regulations (pl) *reglamento (s)*
reimburse *reembolsar*
relations (pl) *parientes (mpl)*
relative (n) *pariente (m)*
reliable *digno de confianza*
religion *religión (f)*
religious *religioso*
remedy -ies *remedio*
remember *acordarse*
  I don't remember *no me acuerdo*
  I remember /the name/ *me acuerdo /del nombre/*
remove *quitar*
renew *renovar*
rent (n) (payment) *alquiler (m)*
rent /a villa/ *alquilar /un chalet/*
repair (n) *reparación (f)*
repair (vb) *reparar*
repairs (pl) *reparaciónes (fpl)*
  do repairs *hacer reparaciones*
  shoe repairs (=shop) *reparaciónes de zapatos*
  watch repairs (=shop) *reparaciónes de relojes*
repay *devolver (pagar)*
  repay me *devolver me*
  repay the money *devolver el dinero*
repeat *repetir*
replace *reponer*
reply -ies (n) *respuesta*
  reply-paid *respuesta pagada*
report (n) *informe (m)*

report (vb) *denunciar*
  report /a loss/ *denunciar /una pérdida/*
represent *representar*
reproduction (=painting) *reproducción (f)*
request (n) *petición (f)*
  make a request *hacer una petición*
research (n) *investigación (f)*
  market research *estudio de mercado*
reservation (hotel, restaurant, theatre) *reserva*
reserve (vb), **make a reservation** *reservar*
  reserved *reservado*
  reserved seat *asiento reservado*
responsible *responsable*
  responsible for/ / responsable de / /
rest (n) *descanso*
  have a rest *tomar un descanso*
rest (vb) *descansar*
restaurant *restaurante (m)*
  self-service restaurant *restaurante de auto-servicio*
restrictions (pl) *restricciones (fpl)*
result *resultado*
retired (adj) *jubilado*
  I'm retired *estoy jubilado*
return (ticket)
  day return *billete (m) de ida y vuelta en el día*
  return (ticket) *billete (m) de ida y vuelta*
return (=give back) *devolver (algo prestado)*
  return /this sweater/ *devolver/este suéter/*
return (=go back) *volver*
  return at / four-thirty/ *volver a /las cuatro y media/*
  return in /July/ *volver en /julio/*
  return on /Monday/ *volver el /lunes/*
reverse (vb) *hacer marcha atrás*
reverse (n) (gear) *marcha atrás*
  reverse the charges *revertir el cobro*
  I'd like to reverse the charges

quiero revertir el cobro

reward (n) *recompensa*

reward (vb) *recompensar*

rheumatism *reúma (m)*

rib (part of body) *costilla*

ribbon *cinta (de tela)*

  a piece of ribbon *un trozo de cinta*

  typewriter ribbon *cinto para máquina de escribir*

rice *arroz (m)*

rich *rico*

ride (vb) *montar*

  ride a bicycle *montar en bicicleta*

  ride a horse *montar a caballo*

  go for a ride (in a car) *dar una vuelta*

riding (=horse riding) *equitación (f)*

go riding *ir a montar a caballo*

right (=correct) *correcto*

right (=not left) *derecha*

right (direction) *a la derecha*

right-handed *que usa la mano derecha*

ring *sortija*

  /diamond/ ring *sortija de /diamantes/*

  engagement ring *sortija de compromiso*

  wedding ring *anillo de matrimonio*

ring (vb) **at the door** *tocar el timbre*

ring road *carretera de circunvalación*

rinse (n) (clothes) *aclarado*

  colour rinse (hair) *tinte (m)*

rinse (vb) *enjuagar*

ripe *maduro*

river *río*

road *carretera*

  main road *carretera principal*

  ring road *carretera de circunvalación*

  side road *carretera secundaria*

roast (vb) *asar*

  roast beef *rosbif (m)*

  roast chicken *pollo asado*

rock (n) *roca*

rod (=fishing rod) *caña de pescar*

roll (=bread roll) *panecillo*

roll of /toilet paper/ *rollo de /papel higiénico/*

roller skating *patinaje (m) sobre ruedas*

go roller skating *ir a patinar*

roof *techo (edificio)*

roof rack *baca*

room *habitación (f)*

  double room *habitación doble*

  quiet room *habitación tranquila*

  room service *servicio de habitación*

  room with a view *habitación con vistas*

  single room *habitación sencilla*

  twin-bedded room *habitación de dos camas*

  with /shower/ *con /ducha/*

  without /bath/ *sin /baño/*

rope *cuerda (gruesa)*

  tow rope *cuerda de remolque*

rose *rosa (n)*

  a bunch of roses *un ramo de rosas*

rotten *podrido*

rough (=not calm) *movido (no en calma)*

rough (=not smooth) *áspero (no suave)*

roughly (=approximately) *aproximadamente*

round (adj) *redondo*

roundabout (n) *cruce (m) giratorio*

route *ruta*

row (a boat) *remar*

row (of seats) *fila*

  the /first/ row *la /primera/ fila*

rowing boat *barco de remo*

rub *frotar*

rubber (=eraser) *goma de borrar*

rubber (substance) *goma*

  rubber boots *botas (fpl) de agua*

rubber band *goma elástica*

rubbish (=litter) *basura*

rucksack *mochila*

rude *maleducado*

rug *alfombrilla*

rugby *rugby (m)*

  a game of rugby *un partido de rugby*

ruler (for measuring) *regla (para medir)*

rules (pl) *reglas (fpl) (normas)*

rum *ron (m)*

run (vb) *correr*

run (vb) (colour) *desteñir*

does it run? ¿destiñe?
run over / / atropellar / /
run-resistant (tights etc) indesmallable
rush hour hora punta

S

saccharine sacarina
  saccharine tablet tableta de sacarina
sad triste
saddle silla de montar
safe (adj) seguro (adj) (=no peligroso)
safe (n) caja fuerte
safety belt cinturón (m) de seguridad
safety pin imperdible (m)
sail (n) vela
sail (vb) navegar
sailing navegación (f) a vela
  go sailing hacer navegación a vela
sailor marinero
saint santo
salad ensalada
  green salad ensalada de lechuga
  mixed salad ensalada mixta
  salad dressing aliño para ensalada
salary -ies sueldo
sale rebaja (saldo)
sales (of a company) ventas (fpl)
  sales representative representante
  (m&f)
sales manager jefe (m) de ventas
salmon/salmon (pl) salmón (m)
  smoked salmon salmón ahumado
salt (n) sal (f)
salted salado
same mismo
  the same as / / el mismo que / /
sand arena
sandals (pl) sandalias (fpl)
  a pair of sandals unas sandalias
sandwich -es sandwich (m)
  a /cheese/ sandwich un sandwich de
  /queso/
sandy arenoso
sanitary towels (pl) compresas (fpl)
sardine sardina

satin (adj) terso
satin (n) raso
satisfactory satisfactorio
Saturday sábado
  on Saturday el sábado
  on Saturdays los sábados
sauce salsa
saucepan cacerola
saucer platito
  a cup and saucer una taza y platito
sauna sauna
sausage salchicha
save (money) ahorrar
save (=rescue) salvar
savoury (=not sweet) salado
say (something) decir
scale (on a map) escala
  large scale a gran escala
  small scale a pequeña escala
scales (pl) (=weighing machine)
  balanza (s)
scallop vieira
scar cicatriz (f) cicatrices (pl)
scarf -ves bufanda
  /silk/ scarf bufanda de /seda/
scenery paisaje (m) (decorado)
schedule horario
school escuela
  language school escuela de idiomas
schoolboy escolar (m)
schoolgirl escolar (f)
science ciencia
scissors (pl) tijeras (fpl)
  a pair of scissors unas tijeras
scooter (=child's scooter) patinete (m)
  motor scooter moto (f)
score /a goal/ marcar /un gol/
scratch (vb) arañar
scratch -es (n) arañazo
scream (n) chillido
screen (=film screen) pantalla
screen (=movable partition) biombo
screw tornillo
screwdriver destornillador (m)
sculpture escultura
sea mar (m)
  by sea por mar

seafood mariscos (mpl)
search (vb) registrar
search -es (n) búsqueda
seasick
  be seasick marearse (querer devolver)
  I feel seasick estoy mareado
season estación (f) (del año)
season ticket billete (m) de temporada
seasoning condimento
seat asiento
  at the back al final
  at the front delante
  at the theatre en el teatro
  by the exit junto a la salida
  by the window al lado de la ventanilla
  in a non-smoker (train) en un departamento de no fumadores
  in the non-smoking section (aeroplane) en la sección de no fumadores
  in a smoker (train) en un departamento de fumadores
  in the smoking section (aeroplane) en la sección de fumadores
  in the middle en el centro
  on a coach en un autocar
  on a train en el tren
second (of time) segundo
second-hand usado
  a second-hand car un coche usado
secret (adj) secreto (adj)
secret (n) secreto (n)
secretary -ies secretaria
security seguridad (f)
  security check, security control control (m) de seguridad
sedative calmante (m)
see ver
  I see (= understand) veo
  see /the manager/ ver /al director/
  see /the menu/ ver /el menú/
  see you! ¡hasta la vista!
  see you soon! ¡hasta pronto!
self-addressed envelope sobre (m) con la propia dirección

sell vender
Sellotape (tdmk) papel (m) de celo
send enviar
  send /a message/ enviar /un recado/
  send / / to me enviarme / /
  send it by / / mail enviarlo por correo / /
separate (adj) separado
September septiembre (m)
septic séptico
serve servir
service (church) servicio religioso
service servicio
  room service servicio de habitación
  twenty-four hour service servicio permanente
service (vb) (car) revisar
service (n) (car) revisión (f)
serviette servilleta
set (n) juego (piezas)
  dinner set vajilla
  tea service juego de té
set (vb) (hair) marcar (pelo)
  shampoo and set (n) lavado y marcado
several varios
sew coser
sewing costura
  do some sewing hacer costura
sex -es sexo
shade (colour) tono
shade sombra
  in the shade a la sombra
shake (vb) agitar
  shake hands estrechar la mano
shampoo (n) champú (m)
  a bottle of shampoo un frasco de champú
  a sachet of shampoo una bolsa de champú
  .shampoo and blow dry lavado y brushing
  shampoo and set lavado y marcado
shampoo (vb) dar un champú
shape (n) forma
share (vb) ccmpartir

sharp (of things) *afilado*
sharpen *afilar*
shave (n) *afeitado*
shave (vb) *afeitar*
shaving brush -es *brocha de afeitar*
shaving cream *crema de afeitar*
  a tube of shaving cream *un tubo de crema de afeitar*
shaving soap *jabón (m) de afeitar*
  a stick of shaving soap *una barra de jabón de afeitar*
shawl *chal (m)*
she *ella*
sheath (=Durex) *preservativo*
  a packet of sheaths *un paquete de preservativos*
sheep/sheep (pl) *oveja*
sheepskin *piel (f) de carnero*
  sheepskin /rug/ */alfombra/ de piel de carnero*
sheet (bed linen) *sábana*
sheet (of paper) *hoja*
shelf -ves *estante (m)*
  bookshelf *estantería*
shell (sea-shell) *concha*
shellfish (s)/**shellfish** (pl) *mariscos (mpl)*
sheltered *protegido*
sherry *jerez (m)*
  a bottle of sherry *una botella de jerez*
  a sherry *un jerez*
shiny *brillante*
ship (n) *barco*
ship (vb) *transportar por barco*
shirt *camisa*
  casual shirt *camisa de diario*
  /cotton/ shirt *camisa de /algodón/*
  formal shirt *camisa de vestir*
  short-sleeved shirt *camisa de manga corta*
shock (n) *susto*
  electric shock *calambre (m) (descarga elétrica)*
  state of shock *estado de shock*
shock absorber (car) *amortiguador (m)*
shockproof (eg of watch) *antichoque*

shoebrush -es *cepillo de zapatos*
shoelaces (pl) *cordones (mpl) de zapatos*
  a pair of shoelaces *unos cordones de zapatos*
shoepolish *betún (m)*
shoes (pl) *zapatos (mpl)*
  a pair of shoes *un par de zapatos*
  boys' shoes *zapatos de niño*
  girls' shoes *zapatos de niña*
  flat-heeled shoes *zapatos de tacón bajo*
  high-heeled shoes *zapatos de tacón alto*
  ladies' shoes *zapatos de señora*
  men's shoes *zapatos de caballero*
  walking shoes *zapatos cómodos para andar*
shoeshop *zapatería*
shop *tienda*
shop assistant *dependiente (m)*
shopping *compras (fpl)*
  go shopping *ir de compras*
  shopping bag *bolso de compras*
  shopping centre *zona comercial*
shore *costa*
short (people) *bajo (estatura)*
short *corto*
short circuit *corto circuito*
shorten *acortar*
shorts (pl) *pantalones (mpl) cortos*
  a pair of shorts *unos pantalones cortos*
shot (n) *disparo*
shoulder *hombro*
shout (n) *grito*
shout (vb) *gritar*
show *espectáculo*
  fashion show *desfile (m) de modelos*
  floor show *espectáculo (cabaret)*
  strip show *espectáculo de strip-tease*
  variety show *espectáculo de variedades*
show (vb) *enseñar* (=mostrar)
  show /it/ to me *enseñarme/lo/*
shower (=shower bath) *ducha*
  shower cap *gorro de ducha*

shrimp *gamba (pequeña)*
shut (adj) *cerrado*
shut (vb) *cerrar*
shutters (pl) *persianas (fpl)*
shy *tímido*
sick *enfermo*
  I feel sick *estoy mareado*
side (n) (in game) *equipo (conjunto)*
side (n) (of object) *lado (de objeto)*
sights (pl) (of a town) *monumentos (mpl) (de una ciudad)*
sightseeing *visita a monumentos*
  go sightseeing *visitar los monumentos*
sign (n) *indicación (f)*
sign /a cheque/ *firmar /un cheque/*
  sign here *firme aquí*
signal (n) *señal (f)*
signal (vb) *hacer señas*
signature *firma*
signpost *poste (m) indicador*
silence *silencio*
silent *silencioso*
silk (adj) *de seda*
silk (n) *seda*
silver (adj) *de plata*
silver (n) *plata*
similar *similar*
simple *sencillo*
sincere *sincero*
sing *cantar*
singer *cantante (m&f)*
single (=not married) *soltero*
  single bed *cama sencilla*
  single ticket *billete (m) de ida*
sink (n) *pila (cocina)*
sink (vb) *hundir*
sister *hermana*
sister-in-law/sisters-in-law (pl) *cuñada*
sit (seat) *sentarse*
  please sit down *siéntese, por favor*
site *solar (m)*
  campsite *camping (m)*
  caravan site *camping (m)*
size *tamaño*
  large size *tamaño grande*
  medium size *tamaño medio*

  small size *tamaño pequeño*
  what size? *¿qué talla?*
size (shoes) *número (zapatos)*
skating *patinaje (m)*
  go skating *hacer patinaje*
  ice-skating *patinaje sobre hielo*
  roller-skating *patinaje sobre ruedas*
sketch -es (n) *boceto*
sketchpad *bloc (m) de dibujo*
ski lift *telesilla*
ski-boots (pl) *botas (fpl) de esquí*
  a pair of ski-boots *un par de botas de esquí*
skid (n) *patinazo*
skid (vb) (car) *patinar (coche)*
skiing *esquí (m)*
  go skiing *ir a esquiar*
  water-skiing *esquí acuático*
skin *piel (f)*
skin diving *buceo (n)*
  go skin diving *bucear con equipo*
skirt *falda*
  long skirt *falda larga*
  short skirt *falda corta*
skis (pl) *esquís (mpl)*
  a pair of skis *un par de esquís*
  water skis *esquís acuáticos*
sky -ies *cielo*
sleep (n) *sueño*
sleep (vb) *dormir*
  he's asleep *duerme*
sleeper (on a train) *coche (m) cama*
sleeping bag *saco de dormir*
sleeping berth *litera (barco)*
sleeping car *coche (m) cama*
sleeping pill *somnífero*
sleepy
  be sleepy *tener sueño*
  I'm sleepy *tengo sueño*
sleeves (pl) *mangas (fpl)*
  long sleeves *mangas largas*
  short sleeves *mangas cortas*
  sleeveless *sin mangas*
slice (n) *cortada*
  a slice of /   / *una cortada de /   /*
slice (vb) *cortar a rebanadas*
slide viewer *visor (m) de diapositivas*

slides (pl) *diapositivas (fpl)*
  colour slides *diapositivas en color*
slippers (pl) *zapatillas (fpl)*
  a pair of slippers *un par de zapatillas*
slippery *resbaladizo*
slope *cuesta*
slot machine *máquina tragaperras*
slow *lento*
  slow train *tren (m) lento*
slower *más despacio*
slowly *lentamente*
small (size) *pequeño*
smart (appearance) *elegante*
smell (n) *olor (m)*
smell (vb) *oler*
  it smells /good/ *huele /bien/*
smoke (n) *humo*
smoke /a cigarette/ *fumar /un cigarrillo/*
smoked (of fish & meat etc) *ahumado*
  smoked /ham/ */jamón/ ahumado*
smoker *fumador (m)*
  non-smoker *no fumador*
smooth *suave (al tacto)*
snack *bocadillo*
snack-bar *snack-bar (m)*
snake *serpiente (f)*
  snakebite *mordedura de serpiente*
sneeze (vb) *estornudar*
snorkel (n) *tubo (natación)*
  snorkel mask *máscara de respiración*
  snorkel tube *tubo de respiración*
snorkel (vb) *respirar con tubo*
snow (n) *nieve (f)*
snow (vb) *nevar*
  it's snowing *nieva*
so (=therefore) *así que*
soak (vb) *remojar*
soap *jabón (m)*
  a bar of soap *una pastilla de jabón*
  shaving soap *jabón de afeitar*
  soap flakes *escamas (fpl) de jabón*
soapy *jabonoso*
sober *sobrio*
socket *enchufe (m) (de pared)*
  electric razor socket *enchufe para máquina de afeitar*

light socket *enchufe de luz*
/three/-pin socket *enchufe de /tres/ clavijas*
socks (pl) *calcetines (mpl)*
  a pair of socks *un par de calcetines*
  short socks *calcetines cortos*
  long socks *calcetines largos*
  /woollen/ socks *calcetines de /lana/*
soda (water) *soda*
  a bottle of soda (water) *una botella de soda*
  a glass of soda (water) *un vaso de soda*
soft (=not hard) *blando*
sold *vendido*
sold out *agotado*
soldier *soldado*
sole (=fish) *lenguado*
sole (of shoe) *suela*
solid *sólido*
somebody, someone *alguien*
something *algo*
  something to drink *algo de beber*
  something to eat *algo de comer*
sometimes *a veces*
somewhere *en alguna parte*
son *hijo*
song *canción (f)*
  folk song *canción folklórica*
  pop song *canción pop*
son-in-law /sons-in-law (pl) *yerno*
soon *pronto*
sore (adj) *dolorido*
  sore throat *dolor (m) de garganta*
sorry? (= pardon?) *¿cómo?*
sorry! (apology) *¡perdón!*
sound (n) *sonido*
soup *sopa*
  /chicken/ soup *sopa de /pollo/*
sour *amargo (agrio)*
south *sur (m)*
  southeast *sureste (m)*
  southwest *suroeste (m)*
souvenir *recuerdo (objeto)*
  souvenir shop *tienda de recuerdos*
space (room) *sitio (=espacio)*
spade *pala (playa)*

spanner *llave (f) inglesa*
  adjustable spanner *llave inglesa ajustable*
spare (adj) *de recambio*
  spare parts (pl) *piezas (fpl) de recambio*
spare time *tiempo libre*
sparking plug (car) *bujía*
speak *hablar* (=*dirigir la palabra*)
  speak /English/ *hablar /inglés/*
  do you speak /English/? *¿habla /inglés/?*
  I don't speak /Spanish/ *no hablo /español/*
  may I speak /to the manager/ please? *¿puedo hablar /con el gerente/ por favor?*
special *especial*
speed *velocidad (f)*
speedboat *lancha rápida*
spell *deletrear*
spend (money) *gastar*
spend (time) *pasar (tiempo)*
spice *especia*
spicy *con especias*
spider *araña*
spilt *derramado*
spinach (s) *espinacas (fpl)*
spine (part of body) *columna vertebral*
spirits (pl) (=alcohol) *bebida alcohólica*
spit (vb) *escupir*
splendid *espléndido*
spoil (vb) *estropear*
sponge (bath sponge) *esponja*
spoon *cuchara*
spoonful *cucharada*
  a spoonful of / / *una cucharada de / /*
sport *deporte (m)*
sports car *coche (m) deportivo*
spot (=blemish) *grano (en cara etc)*
spot (=dot) *punto*
sprain (n) *dislocación (f)*
sprained *dislocado*
spring (=season) *primavera*
  in spring *en primavera*
spring (=wire coil) *muelle (m) (colchón)*

spring onion *cebolleta*
sprout (=Brussels sprout) *col (f) de Bruselas*
square (=scarf) *pañuelo (complemento)*
  a /silk/ square *un pañuelo de /seda/*
square (shape) *cuadrado*
square (place) *plaza (en ciudad)*
  main square *plaza principal*
squash *squash (m)*
  a game of squash *una partida de squash*
  play squash *jugar a squash*
squeeze (vb) *exprimir*
stable (for horses) *establo*
stadium *estadio*
staff (=employees) *plantilla*
stage (in a theatre) *escenario*
stain *mancha*
  stain remover *quitamanchas (m) quitamanchas (mpl)*
stained *manchado*
stainless steel *acero inoxidable*
  stainless steel /cutlery/ */cubertería/ de acero inoxidable*
staircase *escalera*
stairs (pl) *escaleras (fpl)*
stale (bread, cheese etc) *duro (no fresco)*
stamp (n) *sello*
  a /ten/ peseta stamp *un sello de /diez/ pesetas*
stand (vb) *estar de pie*
standard (adj) *standard*
stapler *grapadora*
staples (n) (pl) *grapas (fpl)*
star *estrella*
  film star *estrella de cine*
starch (vb) *almidonar*
starch -es (n) *almidón (m)*
start *comienzo*
start (vb) *comenzar*
  start /the journey/ *comenzar /el viaje/*
start (eg a car) *arrancar*
  it won't start *no arranca*
starter (=hors d'oeuvre) *entremés (m)*
starter motor (car) *motor (m) de arranque (coche)*

state (n) *estado*
station (=railway station) *estación (f)*
  bus station *estación de autobuses*
  coach station *estación de autocares*
  underground station *estación de metro*
stationery *artículos (mpl) de papelería*
statue *estátua*
stay (somewhere) *hospedarse*
  where are you staying? *¿dónde se hospeda?*
stay at / / *quedarse en / /*
  for a night *una noche*
  for /two/ nights */dos/ noches*
  for a week *una semana*
  for /two/ weeks */dos/ semanas*
  till / / *hasta / /*
  from / / till / / *desde / / hasta / /*
steak *bistec (m)*
  medium *no muy hecho*
  rare *poco hecho*
  well-done *muy hecho*
steal *robar*
steam (vb) *cocer al vapor*
steel *acero*
  stainless steel *acier inoxidable*
steep *empinado*
steer (vb) *conducir*
steering (n) (car) *dirección (f) (coche)*
step (n) (movement) *paso (movimiento)*
step (n) (part of staircase) *escalón (m)*
stereo *estéreo*
  stereo equipment *equipo estéreo*
stern (of boat) *popa*
steward (plane or boat) *camarero (avión, barco)*
stewardess -es (plane or boat) *azafata*
stick (n) *palo*
sticking plaster *esparadrapo*
sticky *pegajoso*
sticky tape (eg Sellotape (tdmk)) *papel (m) de celo*
stiff *rígido*
sting (n) *picadura*
  /bee/ sting *picadura de /abeja/*

sting (vb) *picar (insectos)*
stir (vb) *remover*
stock (n) (of things) *stock (m)*
stockings (pl) *medias (fpl)*
  fifteen/thirty denier *medias finas*
  a pair of stockings *un par de medias*
  /nylon/ stockings *medias de /nylon/*
stolen *robado*
stomach *estómago*
  I've got a stomach ache *tengo dolor de estómago*
  I've got a stomach upset *tengo un trastorno estomacal*
stone (substance) *piedra*
  precious stone *piedra preciosa*
stone (of fruit) *hueso (frutas)*
stool *banqueta*
stop (n) *parada*
  bus stop *parada de autobús*
  tram stop *parada de tranvía*
stop (vb) *parar*
stop at / / *pararse en / /*
store (=department store) *grandes almacenes (mpl)*
storm *tormenta*
stormy *tormentoso*
story -ies *historia (cuento)*
straight *recto*
stranger (n) *extraño (n)*
strap *correa*
  watch-strap *correa de reloj*
strapless *sin tirantes*
straw (=drinking straw) *pajita*
strawberry -ies *fresa*
  a punnet of strawberries *una cesta de fresas*
streak (n) (of hair) *mechón (m)*
streak (vb) (of hair)
  I'd like my hair streaked *quiero que me hagan mechas*
stream (n) *riachuelo*
street *calle (f)*
  main street *calle principal*
stretcher *camilla*
strike (n) *huelga*
  be on strike *estar en huelga*
strike (vb) (of clock) *dar la hora*

string *cordón (m)*
  a ball of string *un ovillo de cordón*
  a piece of string *un trozo de cordón*
strip show *espectáculo de strip-tease*
striped *rayado*
strong (physically) *fuerte (físicamente)*
  strong /coffee/ */café/ fuerte*
student *estudiante (m&f)*
studio *estudio (TV, arte)*
study *estudiar*
  study at / / *estudiar en / /*
  study /Spanish/ *estudiar /español/*
stuffing (material) *relleno*
stuffing (food) *relleno*
stupid *estúpido*
style *estilo*
stylus *aguja*
  diamond *diamante*
  sapphire *zafiro*
subscribe to / / *suscribirse a / /*
subscription *suscripción (f)*
substance *sustancia*
suburb *barrio periférico*
subway *paso subterráneo*
suede (n) *ante (m)*
  suede /jacket/ */chaqueta/ de ante*
suffer *padecer*
  suffer from /headaches/ *padecer de /dolores de cabeza/*
sugar *azúcar (m)*
  a spoonful of sugar *una cucharada de azúcar*
sugar lump *terrón (m) de azúcar*
suggest *sugerir*
suit (n) *traje (m) de chaqueta*
suit (vb) *sentar bien*
suitable *apropiado*
suitcase *maleta*
suite (=hotel suite) *suite (f)*
summer *verano*
  in summer *en verano*
sun *sol (m)*
  in the sun *al sol*
sunbathe *tomar el sol*
sunburn *quemadura del sol*
sunburnt *quemado por el sol*
Sunday *domingo*

on Sunday *el domingo*
on Sundays *los domingos*
sunglasses (pl) *gafas (fpl) de sol*
  a pair of sunglasses *unas gafas de sol*
  polaroid sunglasses *gafas de sol polaroid*
sunny *soleado*
sunrise *amanecer (m)*
sunset *anochecer (m)*
sunshade *sombrilla*
sunstroke *insolación (f)*
suntan (n) *bronceado (n)*
  suntan oil *aceite (m) bronceador*
suntanned *bronceado (adj)*
supermarket *supermercado*
supper *cena*
  have supper *cenar*
supply (vb) *proveer*
supply -ies (n) *provisiones (fpl)*
suppository -ies *supositorio*
sure *seguro*
  he's sure *está seguro*
surface (n) *superficie (f)*
  surface mail *correo ordinario*
surfboard *tabla de surf*
surfing *surfing (m)*
  go surfing *hacer surfing*
surgery -ies (=place) *consulta*
  doctor's surgery *consulta del médico*
surname *apellido*
surplus -es *excedente (m)*
surprise (n) *sorpresa*
surprised *sorprendido*
  surprised at /the result/ *sorprendido /del resultado/*
surveyor *ingeniero topógrafo*
survive *sobrevivir*
suspect (vb) *sospechar*
suspender belt *liguero*
suspension (car) *suspensión (f)*
swallow (vb) *tragar*
sweat (n) *sudor (m)*
sweat (vb) *sudar*
sweater *suéter (m)*
  /cashmere/ sweater *suéter de /cachemir/*

long-sleeved sweater *suéter de manga larga*
short-sleeved sweater *suéter de manga corta*
sleeveless sweater *suéter sin mangas*
sweep (vb) *barrer*
sweet (=not savoury) (adj) *dulce*
sweet (n) (=confectionery) *caramelo*
sweet (n)(=dessert) *postre (m)*
swelling *hinchazón (m)*
swim (n) *baño (eg de mar)*
    have a swim *bañarse*
swim (vb) *nadar*
swimming *natación (f)*
    go swimming *ir a bañarse*
    swimming costume *traje (m) de baño (para mujeres)*
    swimming trunks (pl) *traje (m) de baño (para hombres)*
swimming cap *gorro de baño*
swimming pool *piscina*
    heated swimming pool *piscina caliente*
    indoor swimming pool *piscina cubierta*
    open air swimming pool *piscina al aire libre*
    public swimming pool *piscina pública*
swing (n) (children's swing) *columpio*
switch -es (=light switch) *interruptor (m)*
switch off *apagar*
switch on *encender (luz)*
switchboard (company) *centralita*
swollen *hinchado*
symptom *síntoma (m)*
synagogue *sinagoga*
synthetic *sintético*

T

table *mesa*
table tennis *tenis (m) de mesa*
    a game of table tennis *una partida de tenis de mesa*
    play table tennis *jugar al tenis de*
mesa
tablecloth *mantel (m)*
tablemat *salvamanteles (m) salvamanteles (mpl)*
tailor *sastre (m)*
take *tomar*
    I'll take it (in shop) *me lo llevo*
take (time) *tardar*
take away (vb) *llevar (a otro lugar)*
    take-away meal *comida para llevar*
take off /a coat/ *quitarse /un abrigo/*
take out (tooth) *sacar*
talcum powder *polvos (mpl) de talco*
talk (n) (discussion, chat) *charla*
talk (vb) *hablar (=conversar)*
    talk to me about /   / *hablarme de /   /*
tall *alto (persona)*
tame (adj) *domado*
tampons (pl) *tampones (mpl)*
    a box of tampons (eg Tampax (tdmk)) *una caja de tampons (eg Tampax (tdmk))*
tank *depósito (líquidos)*
    water tank *depósito de agua*
tap *grifo*
    cold tap *grifo de agua fría*
    hot tap *grifo de agua caliente*
tape (n) *cinta (grabada)*
    cassette tape *cinta cassette*
tape measure *cinta métrica*
tape recorder *magnetófono*
    cassette recorder *cassette (f)*
    open reel recorder *magnetófono*
tartan
    tartan skirt *falda escocesa*
taste (n) *gusto*
    good/bad taste *buen/mal gusto*
taste (n) (of food) *sabor (m)*
taste (vb) (=have a certain taste) *saber a*
taste (vb) (perceive with tongue) *probar (sabor)*
tasty *sabroso*
tax -es *impuesto (en general)*
    airport tax *impuesto de aeropuerto*
    income tax *impuesto sobre la renta*

tax free *libre de impuesto*
taxi *taxi (m)*
  by taxi *en taxi*
  taxi rank *parada de taxi*
taxi driver *conductor (m) de taxi*
tea (meal) *merienda*
  have tea *merendar*
tea *té (m)*
  a cup of tea *una taza de té*
  a pot of tea *una tetera con té*
  China tea *té chino*
  Indian tea *té indio*
tea towel *toalla de secar platos*
teabag *bolsa de té*
teach *enseñar (enseñanza)*
  teach (me) **/Spanish/** *enseñar (me) /español/*
  he teaches (me) **/Spanish/** *(me) enseña /español/*
teacher *profesor (m) profesora (f)*
team *equipo (conjunto)*
teapot *tetera*
tear (n) (= hole in material) *roto*
tear (vb) (material) *romper*
teaspoon *cucharadita*
  a teaspoonful of / / *una cucharadita de / /*
teat *teta*
teenager *adolescente (m&f)*
teetotal *abstemio*
telegram *telegrama (m)*
  send a telegram *enviar un telegrama*
  telegram form *impreso de telegrama*
telephone (vb) *telefonear*
  telephone Reception *telefonear a Recepción*
  telephone the exchange *telefonear a la central*
  telephone the operator *telefonear a la operadora*
  telephone this number *telefonear a este número*
telephone/phone (n) *teléfono*
  telephone directory -ies *guía (m) de teléfonos*
  on the phone *al teléfono*

  call box -es *cabina de teléfono*
  telephone call *llamada telefónica*
  to be on the phone (have a phone) *tener teléfono*
television/TV (infml) *televisión (f)/tele (f)*
  on television/on TV *en la televisión/en la tele*
  portable television *televisión portátil*
  television aerial *antena de televisión*
  television channel *canal (m) de televisión*
  television programme *programa (m) de televisión*
  television set *aparato de televisión*
  television channel *canal (m) de televisión*
  television programme *programa (m) de televisión*
telex (vb) *poner un télex*
tell me (something) **about / /** *contarme (algo) de / /*
  he told /me/ about it */me/ lo contó*
temperature (atmosphere, body) *temperatura*
  I've got a temperature *tengo fiebre*
temple *templo*
temporary *temporal (adj)*
tender (eg of meat) *tierno*
tennis *tenis (m)*
  a game of tennis *un partido de tenis*
  play tennis *jugar a tenis*
tent *tienda de campaña*
term (= expression) *término*
term (= period of time) *trimestre (m)*
terminal *terminal (f)*
  air terminal *terminal del aeropuerto*
terminus *estación (f) terminal*
  bus terminus *estación terminal de autobuses*
  railway terminus *estación terminal de ferrocarril*
terms (pl) *condiciones (fpl) (términos)*
terrace *terraza*
terrible *terrible*
test (n) *prueba (= comprobación)*
test (vb) *probar (= comprobar)*

textbook *libro de texto*
thank you *gracias*
  no thank you *no gracias*
thank you for / / (vb) *agradecerle / /*
  thank you for your hospitality *le agradezco su hospitalidad*
that one *ése (m) ésa (f)*
the *el (m) la (f) los (mpl) las (fpl)*
theatre *teatro*
  theatre programme *programa (m) de teatro*
theft *robo*
their *su (m&f) sus (pl)*
  their passport *su pasaporte (m)*
  their sister *su hermana (f)*
  their tickets *sus billetes (mpl)*
  their keys *sus llaves (fpl)*
theirs
  it's theirs *es suyo (m) es suya (f)*
them
  for them *para ellos (mpl) para ellas (fpl)*
then *entonces*
there *allí*
  over there *allí*
there is (s) **there are** (pl) *hay*
  are there /any restaurants/ near here? *¿hay /restaurantes/ por aquí?*
  there's /some beer/ *hay /cerveza/*
  there aren't /any hotels/ near here *no hay /hoteles/ por aquí*
thermometer *termómetro*
  Centigrade thermometer *termómetro en centigrados*
  Fahrenheit thermometer *termómetro en fahrenheit*
  clinical thermometer *termómetro clínico*
these *estos (mpl) estas (fpl) (adj)*
  these ones *estos (mpl) estas (fpl) (pron)*
they *ellos (mpl) /ellas (fpl)*
thick *espeso*
thigh *muslo*
thin (coat etc) *ligero (abrigo etc)*
thin (of person) *delgado*

thing *cosa*
things (=belongings) *posesiones (fpl)*
think about /something/ *pensar en /algo/*
thirsty
  be thirsty *tener sed*
  I'm thirsty *tengo sed*
this
  this one *éste (m) ésta (f) (pron)*
those *esos (mpl) esas (fpl)*
  those ones *ésos (mpl) ésas (fpl)*
thousand *mil (m) mil (mpl)*
  thousands of / / *miles de / /*
thread *hilo*
  a reel of thread *una bobina de hilo*
throat *garganta*
  sore throat *dolor de garganta*
  throat pastille *pastilla para la garganta*
through (prep)
  through the countryside *a través del campo*
  through /the streets/ *por /las calles/*
thumb *pulgar (m)*
thunderstorm *truenos (mpl)*
Thursday *jueves (m)*
  on Thursday *el jueves*
  on Thursdays *los jueves*
ticket *billete (m) (eg de avión)*
  child's ticket *billete de niño*
  day return *billete de ida y vuelta en el día*
  first class ticket *billete de primera clase*
  group ticket *billete de grupo*
  return ticket *billete de ida y vuelta*
  season ticket *billete de temporada*
  second class ticket *billete de segunda clase*
  single *billete de ida*
ticket office *taquilla*
tide *marea*
  high tide *marea alta*
  low tide *marea baja*
tidy (adj) *ordenado*
tidy (vb) *poner en orden*

tie (n) *corbata*
tie (vb) *atar*
tiepin *alfiler (m) de corbata*
tight *apretado*
tights (pl) *leotardos (mpl)*
 a pair of tights *unos leotardos*
till (= until) *hasta*
time *tiempo (hora)*
 the time (clock) *la hora*
 /six/ times */seis / veces*
 have a good time *pasarlo bien*
 in time *con tiempo*
 on time *a tiempo*
 what time is it? *¿qué hora es?*
timetable *horario*
 bus timetable *horario de autobuses*
 coach timetable *horario de autocaros*
 train timetable *horario de trenes*
tin *lata*
 a tin of / / *una lata de / /*
tin opener *abrelatas (m) abrelatas (mpl)*
tint (n) (= hair tint) *tinte (m)*
tint (vb) *tintar*
tip (n) (money) *propina*
tip (vb) (money) *dar una propina*
 tip the waiter/ *dar una propina /al camarero/*
tired *cansado (persona)*
tiring *cansado (que causa)*
tissues (pl) **/Kleenex** (tdmk) *pañuelos. (mpl) de celulosa/ Kleenex*
 a box of tissues *una caja de pañuelos de celulosa*
title *título (libro, etc)*
to
 to /the station/ *a /la estación/*
toast (vb) *tostar*
toast (n) *tostada*
 a slice of toast *una tostada*
tobacco *tabaco*
tobacconist's *tabacalera*
today *hoy*
toe *dedo del pie*
toenail *uña del dedo del pie*
together *juntos*
toilet *servicios (mpl)*
toilet paper *papel (m) higiénico*

 a roll of toilet paper *un rollo de papel higiénico*
toilet water *agua de colonia*
tomato -es *tomate (m)*
 tomato sauce *salsa de tomate*
tomato juice *zumo de tomate*
 a bottle of tomato juice *una botella de zumo de tomate*
 a can of tomato juice *una lata de zumo de tomate*
 a glass of tomato juice *un vaso de zumo de tomate*
tomorrow *mañana*
ton *tonelada*
tongue *lengua*
tonic (water) *tónica*
tonight *esta noche*
tonsillitis *amigdalitis (f)*
too (= more than can be endured) *demasiado (adv)*
 too /big/ *demasiado /grande/*
 too many *demasiados (mpl) demasiadas (fpl)*
 too much *demasiado (adj)*
tool *herramienta*
tooth/teeth (pl) *diente (m)*
 wisdom tooth *muela del juicio*
toothache (s) *dolor (m) de muelas*
toothbrush -es *cepillo de dientes*
toothpaste *pasta de dientes*
 a tube of toothpaste *un tubo de pasta de dientes*
toothpick *palillo*
top *parte (f) superior*
 the top of / / *la parte superior de / /*
torch -es *linterna*
tortoiseshell (adj) *de carey*
total (adj) *total (adj)*
total (n) *total (m) (n)*
touch (vb) *tocar (tacto)*
tough (meat etc) *duro (carne)*
tour *gira*
 conducted tour *gira con guía*
tourist *turista (m&f)*
 tourist class *clase (f) turista*
 tourist office *oficina de turismo*

tow (vb) *remolcar*
tow rope *cuerda de remolcar*
towel (=bath towel) *toalla*
towelling (material) *tela de rizo*
tower *torre* (f)
town *ciudad* (f)
  town centre *centro ciudad*
  town hall *ayuntamiento*
toxic *tóxico*
toy *juguete* (m)
  toy shop *tienda de juguetes*
track *pista*
track (=race track) *pista de carreras*
traditional *tradicional*
traffic *tráfico*
traffic jam *embotellamiento*
traffic lights (pl) *semáforos* (mpl)
trailer *remolque* (m)
train *tren* (m)
  boat train *tren de enlace con puerto*
  express train *Talgo*
  fast train *tren rápido*
  slow train *tren lento*
  train driver *maquinista* (m)
training (of personnel) *formación* (f)
tram *tranvía* (m)
  by tram *en tranvía*
  the tram for / / *el tranvía para / /*
  tram stop *parada de tranvía*
  tram terminus *final* (m) *de trayecto de tranvía*
tranquilliser *tranquilizante* (m)
transfer (vb) *transferir*
transformer *transformador* (m)
transistor (transistor radio) *transistor* (m)
transit passenger *pasajero en tránsito*
  in transit *en tránsito*
translate *traducir*
translation *traducción* (f)
transmission (car) *transmisión* (f)
transparent *transparente*
transport (n) *transporte* (m)
  public transport *transporte público*
trap (n) *trampa*
trap (vb) *atrapar*
travel (vb) *viajar*

by air *en avión*
by boat, by bus *en barco, en autobús*
by coach, by car *en autocar, en coche*
by hovercraft *en hovercraft*
by sea *por mar*
by train, by tram, by underground *en tren, en tranvía, en metro*
on foot *a pie*
on the ferry *en ferry*
overland *por tierra*
to / / a / /
travel agent's *agencia de viajes*
traveller's cheque *cheque* (m) *de viajero*
tray *bandeja*
treat (medically) *tratar*
treatment *tratamiento*
tree *árbol* (m)
triangular *triangular*
trim (vb) *recortar*
trim (n) (haircut) *recorte* (m)
trip (n) *viaje* (m)
  coach trip *viaje en autocar*
  have a good trip! *¡buen viaje!*
tripod *trípode* (m)
trolley (=luggage trolley) *carrito*
tropical *tropical*
trot (vb) *trotar*
trouble *problema* (m)
  I'm in trouble *tengo problemas*
trousers (pl) *pantalones* (mpl)
  a pair of trousers *un par de pantalones*
trout/trout (pl) *trucha*
true *verdadero*
trunk (of tree) *tronco*
trunk (for luggage) *baúl* (m)
trust (vb) *confiar*
  I trust /her/ *confío en /ella/*
truth *verdad* (f)
  tell the truth *decir la verdad*
try (vb) *probar*
  try on /this sweater/ *probarse /este suéter/*
  try /this ice-cream/ *probar /este helado/*

T-shirt *camiseta (ropa sport)*
tube *tubo (pieza cilíndrica)*
 a tube of / / *un tubo de / /*
tube (for a tyre) *cámara de aire*
tubeless (tyre) *(neumático) sin cámara*
Tuesday *martes (m)*
 on Tuesday *el martes*
 on Tuesdays *los martes*
tulip *tulipán (m)*
 a bunch of tulips *un ramo de
 tulipanes*
tunnel (n) *túnel (m)*
turkey *pavo*
turn off (switch) *apagar*
turn on (switch) *encender*
turnip *nabo*
turntable (on record player) *plato
 (tocadiscos)*
turpentine *aguarrás (m)*
tweed *tweed (m)*
tweezers (pl) *pinzas (fpl) de depilar*
 a pair of tweezers *unas pinzas de
 depilar*
twice *dos veces*
twin *gemelo*
 twin beds *dos camas sencillas*
type (vb) *escribir a máquina*
typewriter *máquina de escribir*
typhoid *fiebre (f) tifoidea*
typical *típico*
typist *mecanógrafo (m) mecanógrafa (f)*
tyre *neumático*
 flat tyre *rueda pinchada*
 tyre pressure *presión (f) de los
 neumáticos*

U

ugly *feo*
ulcer *úlcera*
umbrella *paraguas (m) paraguas (mpl)*
 beach umbrella *sombrilla*
umpire *árbitro*
UN *ONU*
uncle *tío*
uncomfortable *incómodo*
unconscious *inconsciente*

under *debajo*
 under /the chair/ *debajo /de la silla/*
undercooked *poco hecho*
underground (underground railway
 train) *metro (tren)*
 by underground *en metro*
underpants (pl) (for men) *calzoncillos
 (mpl)*
 a pair of underpants *unos
 calzoncillos*
understand *entender*
 I don't understand *no entiendo*
underwear *ropa interior*
 children's underwear *ropa interior de
 niños*
 men's underwear *ropa interior de
 caballeros*
 women's underwear *ropa interior de
 señoras*
unemployed (adj) *en paro*
unemployment *paro*
unfashionable *pasado de moda*
unfasten *desabrochar*
unfortunately *desagraciadamente*
unfriendly *poco amistoso*
uniform (n) *uniforme (m)*
 in uniform *de uniforme*
unique *único*
university -ies *universidad (f)*
unlocked *no cerrado con llave*
unlucky
 be unlucky *ser desafortunado*
 he's unlucky *es desafortunado*
unpack *deshacer las maletas*
unpleasant *desagradable*
unripe *verde (=no maduro)*
untie *desatar*
until *hasta*
 until /Friday/ *hasta /el viernes/*
unusual *poco corriente*
up *arriba (posición)*
 are you going up? *¿sube usted?*
 be up (=out of bed) *estar levantado*
upset (n)
 I've got a stomach upset *tengo
 trastornos de estómago*
upset (adj) *molesto (estar)*

upside-down al revés
upstairs arriba (piso)
urgent urgente (adj)
urinate orinar
urine orina
us nosotros (acusativo)
 for us para nosotros
use (vb) usar
 use /your phone/ usar /su teléfono/
useful útil (provechoso)
usually generalmente
utensil utensilio

V

V -necked sweater suéter (m) de pico
vacancy -ies (job) vacante (f)
vacancy -ies (room) plaza libre
vacant libre (=desocupado)
vaccinate vacunar
vaccination vacunación (f)
vaccine vacuna
vacuum cleaner aspirador (m)
vacuum flask termo
valid válido
 valid /passport/ /pasaporte/ (m) válido
valley -ies valle (f)
valuable valioso
valuables (pl) objetos (mpl) de valor
value (n) valor (m)
value (vb) valorar
van furgoneta
 luggage van furgón (m) de equipaje
vanilla vainilla
variety -ies variedad (f)
various varios
varnish (vb) (eg boat) barnizar
varnish -es (n) barniz (m)
 nail varnish esmalte (m) de uñas
vase (=flower vase) florero
vaseline vaselina
 a tube of vaseline un tube de vaselina
VAT IVA (m)
veal ternera
vegetables (pl) verduras (fpl)

 fresh vegetables verduras frescas
 mixed vegetables panaché de verduras
vegetarian vegetariano
vehicle vehículo
vein vena
velvet terciopelo
venereal disease (VD) enfermedad (f) venérea
venison venado
ventilator ventilador (m)
very muy
vest camiseta (ropa interior)
 cotton vest camiseta de algodón
 woollen vest camiseta de lana
VHF UHF
via via
 travel via /Rome/ viajar via /Roma/
vicar pastor (m)
view (n) vista
viewfinder objetivo
villa (=holiday villa) chalet (m)
village pueblecito
vinegar vinagre (m)
 a bottle of vinegar una botella de vinagre
 oil and vinegar aceite y vinagre
vineyard viña
violin violín (m)
visa visado
visibility visibilidad (f)
visit /a museum/ visitar /un museo/
visitor visitante (m&f)
vitamin pills (pl) vitaminas (fpl)
 a bottle of vitamin pills un frasco de vitaminas
vodka vodka (m)
 a bottle of vodka una botella de vodka
 a vodka un vodka
voice voz (f)
volt voltio
 / a hundred and ten/ volts /ciento diez/ voltios
voltage voltaje (m)
 high voltage alto voltaje
 low voltage bajo voltaje

volume *volumen (m)*
vomit (n) *vómito*
vomit (vb) *vomitar*
voucher *vale (m)*
  hotel voucher *vale para hotel*
voyage (n) *viaje (m) (por mar)*

W

waist *cintura*
waistcoat *chaleco*
wait /for me/ *esperar/me/*
  please wait /for me/ *espére/me/,
  por favor*
waiter *camarero (restaurante)*
waiting room *sala de espera
  (=consulta)*
waitress -es *camarera (restaurante)*
wake /me/ up *despertar/me/*
walk (n) *paseo (andar)*
  go for a walk *dar un paseo*
walk (vb) *andar*
walking *andando*
  do some walking *ir andando*
walking stick *bastón (m)*
wall (=inside wall) *pared (f)*
wallet *cartera*
walnut (nut) *nuez (f) nueces (fpl)*
walnut (wood) *nogal (m)*
want *querer*
  want /a room/ *querer /una
  habitación/*
  want to /buy/ it *querer /comprar/lo*
war *guerra*
ward (in hospital) *sala (de hospital)*
wardrobe *armario (ropa)*
warm (adj) *caliente (templado)*
warm (vb) *calentar*
warn *advertir*
warning *advertencia*
wash (vb) *lavar*
wash -es (n) *lavado*
  have a wash *lavarse*
wash up *fregar (los platos)*
washbasin *lavabo*
washing machine *lavadora*
washing powder *detergente (m)*

wasp *avispa*
  wasp sting *picadura de avispa*
waste (vb) *malgastar*
wastepaper basket *papelera*
watch (vb) *mirar*
watch -es (n) *reloj (m) (de pulsera)*
  face (of watch) *esfera*
  hand (of watch) *aguja*
  watch strap *correa de reloj*
watch /TV/ *mirar /la tele/*
watchmaker's *relojería*
water *agua*
  cold water *agua fría*
  distilled water *agua destilada*
  drinking water *agua potable*
  hot water *agua caliente*
  running water *agua corriente*
water skiing *esquí (m) acuático*
  go water skiing *hacer esquí acuático*
watercolour (=painting) *acuarela*
waterproof (adj) *impermeable (adj)*
watt *watio*
  /a hundred/ watts */cien/ watios*
wave (radio) *onda*
  long wave *onda larga*
  medium wave *onda media*
  short wave *onda corta*
  VHF *UHF*
wave (sea) *ola*
wax *cera*
way (n) (to a place) *camino*
  that way *por allí*
  this way *por aquí*
  which way? *¿por dónde?*
we *nosotros (sujeto)*
weak (physically) *débil*
wear (vb) (clothes) *llevar (ropa)*
weather *tiempo (clima)*
  weather conditions (pl) *estado del
  tiempo*
  weather forecast (s) *predicción (f)
  del tiempo*
  what's the weather like? *¿qué
  tiempo hace?*
wedding *boda*
Wednesday *miércoles (m)*
  on Wednesday *el miércoles*

on Wednesdays *los miércoles*
week *semana*
  this week *esta semana*
  last week *la semana pasada*
  next week *la semana próxima*
weekend *fin (m) de semana*
weekly (adj) *semanal*
  twice weekly *dos veces por semana*
weigh *pesar*
weight *peso*
  weight limit *límite (m) de peso*
welcome (n) *bienvenida*
welcome (vb) *dar la bienvenida*
  welcome to / / *bienvenido a / /*
  you're welcome (in reply to 'thank
  you') *de nada (respuesta a 'gracias')*
well (=all right) *bien (adv)*
  well done! (congratulation) *¡bien
  hecho!*
  well-done (eg of steak) *muy hecho*
well (n) *pozo*
Wellingtons (pl) *botas (fpl) de agua*
west *oeste (m)*
Western (=film) *película del oeste*
wet *mojado*
  I'm wet *estoy mojado*
  it's wet (weather) *el tiempo está
  lluvioso*
  /this towel/ is wet */esta toalla/ está
  mojada*
what? *¿qué?*
  at what time? *¿qué hora?*
  what about /Mary/? *¿qué hay de
  /Mary/?*
  what's /your address/? *¿cuál es /su
  dirección/?*
wheel *rueda*
wheelchair *silla de ruedas*
when? *¿cuándo?*
  when do /the shops/ open?
  ¿cuándo abren /las tiendas/?
where? *¿dónde?*
  where are you from? *¿de dónde es?*
which? *¿qué?*
  which /plane/? *¿qué /avión/?*
  which one?/which ones? *¿cuál?
  (m&f) ¿cuáles? (pl)*

whisky -ies *whisky (m) (escocés)*
  a bottle of whisky *una botella de
  whisky*
  a whisky *un whisky*
whistle (n) *silbato*
white *blanco*
  white coffee *café (m) con leche*
who? *¿quién?*
whole *entero*
  a whole /month/ */un mes/ entero*
  the whole /month/ */el mes/ entero*
whose? *¿de quién?*
  whose is it? *¿de quién es?*
why? *¿por qué?*
wick (lamp, lighter) *mecha*
wide *ancho*
widow *viuda*
widower *viudo*
width *anchura*
wife/wives (pl) *esposa*
wig *peluca*
wild (=not tame) *salvaje*
  wild animal *animal (m) salvaje*
win (vb) *ganar (en juego)*
wind (n) *viento*
wind (vb) (clock) *remontar*
window *ventana*
  French window *ventana francesa*
  shop window *escaparate (m)*
window (car) *ventanilla*
windy *de viento (=ventoso)*
  it's windy *hace viento*
wine *vino*
  a bottle of wine *una botella de vino*
  a carafe of wine *una jarra de vino*
  a glass of wine *un vaso de vino*
  a half bottle of wine *media botella de
  vino*
  dry wine *vino seco*
  red wine *vino tinto*
  rosé *vino rosado*
  sparkling wine *vino espumoso*
  sweet wine *vino dulce*
  white wine *vino blanco*
wine glass -es *vaso de vino*
wine list *carta de vinos*
wine merchant's *tienda de vinos*

wing (bird or plane) *ala*
wing (car) *aleta (coche)*
winter *invierno*
 in winter *en invierno*
wipe (vb) *limpiar (=secar)*
wire *alambre (m)*
 a piece of wire *un trozo de alambre*
with *con*
without *sin*
witness -es (n) *testigo (m&f)*
woman/women (pl) *mujer (f)*
wonderful *maravilloso*
wood (group of trees) *bosque (m)
 (grupo de árboles)*
wood (substance) *madera*
wooden *de madera*
wool *lana*
woollen *de lana*
word *palabra*
work (n) *trabajo (ocupación)*
 do some work *hacer un poco de
 trabajo*
work (vb) (of machines) *funcionar*
 it doesn't work *no funciona*
work (vb) (of people) *trabajar*
world (the world) *mundo*
worn-out *gastado*
worried *preocupado*
worse (in health) *peor*
 he's worse *está peor*
worse (things) *peor*
 worse than / / *peor que / /*
 it's worse *es peor*
worst *el peor*
 the worst /hotel/ *el peor /hotel/*
 the worst /room/ *la peor
 /habitación/*
worth
 be worth *valer*
 it's worth /500/ pesetas *vale
 /quinientas/ pesetas*
would like
 I'd like to /go swimming/ *me
 gustaría /ir a bañarme/*
 would you like /a drink/? *¿le
 gustaría /tomar una copa/?*
wound (=injury) *herida (n)*

wrap (vb) *envolver*
 gift-wrap (vb) *envolver para regalo*
wreath -es (funeral wreath) *corona de
 flores*
wreck (n) *naufragio*
wrist *muñeca (brazo)*
write *escribir*
writing paper *papel (m) de escribir*
wrong *equivocado*
 be wrong *estar equivocado*
 I'm wrong *estoy equivocado*
 wrong number *número equivocado*

X

x-ray *rayo x*

Y

yacht *yate (m)*
year *año*
 last year *el año pasado*
 next year *el año próximo*
 this year *este año*
yearly *anualmente*
yellow *amarillo*
yes *sí (afirmación)*
yesterday *ayer*
yet
 not yet *todavía no*
yoghurt *yogur (m)*
 a carton of yoghurt *un yogur*
 plain yoghurt *yogur natural*
 fruit yoghurt *yogur de fruta*
you *usted (s) ustedes (pl) / tú (infml) (s)
 vosotros (infml) (pl)*
 for you *para usted (s) para ustedes
 (pl)/ para ti (infml)(s) para vosotros
 (infml) (pl)*
young *joven*
young man/young men (pl) *hombre
 (m) joven/ hombres jóvenes (mpl)*
young woman/young women (pl) *mujer (f)
 joven/ mujeres jóvenes (fpl)*
your *su (s) sus (pl)/ tu (infml) (s) tus
 (infml) (pl)*
 your passport *su pasaporte (m)*

your sister *su hermana (f)*
your tickets *sus billetes (mpl)*
your keys *sus llaves (pl)*
yours
  it's yours *es suyo (m) es suya (f)*
youth hostel *albergue (m) de juventud*

Z

zero *cero*
  above zero *sobre cero*
  below zero *bajo cero*
zip (n) *cremallera*
zoo *zoo (m)*
zoom lens -es *lente (f) zoom*

English foods   La comida inglesa

Cooking methods   Métodos culinarios

baked	cocido al horno
boiled	hervido
braised	braseado
creamed	a la crema
devilled	condimentado con picantes
dressed	aliñado
fresh	fresco/natural
fried	frito
grilled	a la parrilla
in batter	rebozado
in sauce	en salsa
in vinegar	en vinagre/a la vinegreta
jugged	cocido en cazuela tapada
mashed	en puré
medium	no muy hecho

melted	fundido
overcooked	demasiado hecho
pickled	escabechado
poached	escalfado
rare	poco hecho
raw	crudo
roast	asado
scrambled	revuelto
smoked	ahumado
steamed	al vapor
stewed	guisado
stuffed	relleno
toasted	tostado
undercooked	no bastante hecho
well done	muy hecho

Food and drink

Comida y bebida

Recuerde:
Quiero / / , por favor
I'd like/ /please

à la carte	a la carta
ale	cerveza
brown a.	c. negra
light a.	c. rubia
pale a.	c. clara
almonds	almendras
anchovies	anchoas
apple	manzana
a. crumble	m. cubierta de harina, mantequilla y azúcar
a. pie	pastel de m.
a. tart	tarta de m.
apricot	albaricoque
artichoke	alcachofa

asparagus	espárragos
a. tips	puntas de e.
assortment	surtido
avocado pear	aguacate
bacon	bacón
a rasher of b.	una cortada de b.
baked alaska	bizcocho con helado y merengue
baked beans	alubias guisadas
banana	plátano
b. split	p. partido (p., helado y nata)
beans	alubias/judías
broad b.	habas gruesas
French b.	judías verdes enamas
haricot b.	judías pequeñas y blancas
kidney b.	alubías pintas
runner b.	judías verdes
beef	carne de vaca
beefburger	hamburguesa de ternera
beer	cerveza
bitter	c. armarga
draught b.	c. de barril
beverages	bebidas
biscuits	galletas
biscuits and cheese	galletas con queso
bitter lemon	limón Schweppes
blue cheese	queso azul
brandy	coñac, brandy
bread	pan
breakfast	desayuno
broad beans	habas gruesas
broccoli	brécoles
broth	caldo
brown ale	cerveza negra

brussels sprouts	coles de bruselas
bun	bollo
butter	mantequilla
butterscotch	dulce de azúcar terciado con mantequilla
cabbage	col
red c.	c. roja
cake	pastel
fruit c.	p. de fruta
sponge c.	p. de bizcocho, muy ligero
caramel cream	flan
carrot	zanahoria
cauliflower	coliflor
caviar	caviar
celery	apio
cereal	cereales (para desayuno)
Chateaubriand steak	filete chateaubriand
cheese	queso
blue c.	q. azul
Caerphilly	q. galés blanco y cremoso
Cheddar c.	cheddar (tipo manchego) no fuerte
Cheshire c.	chesire (tipo manchego) no fuerte
cottage c.	requesón
cream c.	q. cremoso
Roquefort	q. roquefort
Stilton	q. azul
Wensleydale	q. blanco no muy fuerte
cheeseboard	quesera
cheesecake	tarta de queso
cherry	cereza
chestnut	castaña
chicken	pollo

c. soup	sopa de p.
China tea	té chino
chips	patatas fritas
chives	cebollinos
chocolate	chocolate
milk c.	ch. con leche
plain c.	ch. sin leche
chop	chuleta
lamb c.	ch. de cordero
pork c.	ch. de cerdo
chowder	sopa de pescado, verduras y carne
Christmas cake	pastel con mucha fruta seca y cubierto con mazapán y garapiña
Christmas pudding	budín hecho con frutos secos y coñac
cider	sidra
clam	almeja
clotted cream	nata cuajada
cocktail	cóctel
coconut	coco
cod	bacalao
coffee	café
coleslaw	ensalada de col
coq-au-vin	pollo al vino
cordial	concentrado de zumo de frutas (muy dulce y se añade al agua)
corn on the cob	mazorca
cornflakes	copos de maíz tostado
cottage cheese	requesón
cottage pie	carne picada con puré de patatas
courgettes	pequeños calabacines

•course	plato
three-course meal	comida de 3 platos
• cover charge	precio del cubierto
crab	cangrejo
crayfish	cangrejo de agua dulce
cream	nata
clotted c.	n. cuajada
double c.	n. espesa
fresh c.	n. fresca
single c.	n. líquida
whipped c.	n. montada
cream cheese	queso cremoso
crêpes Suzette	crêpes soucete
crisps	patatas fritas (en paquete)
croquette	croqueta
c. potatoes	croquetas de patata
• crumble	cubierta de mantequilla, harina y azúcar
cucumber	pepino
currant bread	pan de pasas
c. bun	bollo de pasas
• custard	natillas
cutlet	costilla
lamb c.	c. de cordero
date	dátil
dinner	cena
double cream	nata espesa
doughnut	donut
Dover sole	lenguado Dover
dressing	aliño
duck	pato
eel	anguilà
jellied e.	a. en gelatina
egg	huevo

e. mayonnaise	huevo pasado por agua, con mayonesa
escalope	escalope
veal e.	e. de ternera
escargots	caracoles
fillet	filete
cod f.	f. de bacalao
f. of plaice	f. de platija
f. steak	solomillo
filling	relleno
fish	pescado
fish cake	pastel de pescado
flan	tartaleta de fruta o queso
fool	puré de fruta con nata
frankfurter	salchicha de Frankfurt
French beans	judías verdes
French dressing	aliño de aceite, vinagre y sal
fricassée	carne guisada con salsa blanca
f. of chicken	g. de pollo con salsa blanca
f. of veal	g. de ternera con salsa blanca
fritters	buñuelos
fruit	fruta
fruit cake	pastel de fruta
fruit cocktail	ensalada de frutas
fruit salad	macedonia de frutas
fudge	dulce de azúcar, leche y mantequilla
Gaelic coffee	café con whisky escocés y nata
game	caza
gammon	jamón cocido
garlic	ajo
garnished with	aderezado con
gâteau	pastel (con nata)
gin	ginebra

ginger	jengibre
goose	ganso
gooseberry	grosella
grapes	uvas
grapefruit	pomelo
g. juice	zumo de p.
g. segments	gajos de p.
gravy	salsa espesa de carne
green pepper	pimiento verde
green salad	ensalada de lechuga
haddock	eglefino (tipo bacalao pero más pequeño)
hake	merluza
halibut	halibut (pescado grande y plano)
ham	jamón
hamburger	hamburguesa
hare	liebre
haricot beans	judías pequeñas y blancas
heart	corazón
herbs	hierbas
herring	arenque
honey	miel
hors d'oeuvres	entremeses
horseradish sauce	salsa de rábano picante
hot dog	perro caliente
hotpot	estofado de cordero, patatas y cebollas
ice	hielo
ice-cream	helado
i. sundae	h. con fruta, nueces y chocolate
icing	garapiña
Indian tea	té índio

Irish coffee	café con whisky irlandés y nata
Irish stew	estofado de carne con patatas, cebollas y zanahoria
jacket potatoes	patatas asadas al horno
jam	mermelada
j. tart	tarta de m.
jellied eel	anguila en gelatina
jelly (fruit)	jalea
juice	zumo
grapefruit j.	z. de pomelo
orange j.	z. de naranja
tomato j.	z. de tomate
kebab	trozos de carne y verduras asados en brocheta
kedgeree	arroz blanco con huevo duro, nata y pescado
ketchup	catsup
kidney	riñon
king prawn	gamba grande
kipper	arenque ahumado
knickerbocker glory	helado con jugo dulce, nueces y frutas
lager	cerveza rubia
lamb	cordero
l. chop	chuleta de c.
l. cutlet	costilla de c.
leg of l.	pierna de c.
Lancashire hotpot	estofado de cordero con cebollas, patatas y zanahorias
lasagne	lasaña
leek	puerro
lemon	limón
l. juice	zumo de l.

lemon meringue pie	pastel de limón cubierto de merengue
lemon sole	lenguado al limón
lentil soup	sopa de lentejas
lettuce	lechuga
light ale	cerveza clara
lime juice	zumo de lima
liqueur	licor
liver	hígado
l. sausage	salchicha de hígado
lobster	langosta
loin	lomo
l. of lamb	l. de cordero
l. of pork	l. de cerdo
lunch	almuerzo
macaroni	macarrones
m. cheese	m. con queso
mackerel	caballa
marmalade	mermelada de naranja
marrow	calabacín
Martini (vermouth)	martini (vermut)
mayonnaise	mayonesa
meal	comida
meat	carne
meatball	albóndiga
melon	melón
menu	carta/menú
meringue	merengue
milk	leche
m. shake	batido de l.
mince	carne picada
mincemeat	conserva de picadillo de fruta
mince pies	pasteles de picadillo de fruta
minestrone	minestrone

mint	menta
m. jelly	gelatina de m.
m. sauce	salsa de m.
minute steak	bistec al minuto
mixed grill	parrillada de carne
mixed salad	ensalada mixta
mock turtle soup	sopa de carne de sabor parecido a la tortuga
moussaka	musaka: plato griego de carne, berenjenas y queso
muesli	mezcla de cereales, frutos secos tomado como desayuno
muffin	panecillo, que se come caliente y con mantequilla
mullet	salmonete
mushroom	champiñon
mussels	mejillones
mustard	mostaza
English m.	m. fuerte
French m.	m. suave
mutton	carnero
new potatoes	patatas nuevas
noodles	tallarines
nut	nuez
oatmeal	harina de avena
oil	aceite
corn o.	a. de maíz
olive o.	a. de oliva
olive	aceituna
omelette	tortilla
onion	cebolla
orange	naranja
o. juice	zumo de n. fresca
o. squash	zumo de n. embotellado

oyster	ostra
pale ale	cerveza clara
pancake	tortita delgada hecha en sartén
paprika	pimienta (húngara)
parsley	perejil
parsnip	chirivía
pastries	pasteles
pastry	pastas
flaky p.	p. de hojaldre
puff p.	p. de crema
shortcake p.	p. inglesa de pasteles
peas	guisantes
peach	melocotón
p. melba	helado con m., nata, y mermelada
pear	pera
pepper	pimiento
green p.	p. verde
red p.	p. rojo
peppermint	menta
pheasant	faisán
pickles	conservas en vinagre o en escabeche
pie	pastel
pilchard (tinned)	sardina pequeña (en lata)
pineapple	piña
plaice	platija
plum	ciruela
pomegranate	granada
popcorn	palomitas
pork	cerdo
fillet of p.	solomillo de c.
loin of p.	lomo de c.
p. chop	chuleta de c.

porridge	sopa de avena
potato	patata
croquette potatoes	croquetas de patata
jacket potatoes	asadas a la americana
mashed potatoes	patatas en puré
new potatoes	patatas nuevas
potato salad	ensalada de patatas
potted shrimps	gambas en bote
poultry	ave
prawn	gamba
p. cocktail	cóctel de g.
profiteroles	bollos pequeños con nata servidos con salsa de chocolate caliente
prune	ciruela pasa
pudding	budín/postre
puff pastry	hojaldre
puffed wheat	trigo hinchado y tostado
purée	puré
rabbit	conejo
radish	rábano
ragoût	guisado
r. of lamb	g. de cordero
raspberry	frambuesa
red cabbage	col roja
redcurrant	grosella roja
rhubarb	ruibarbo
rib	costilla
r. of beef	c. de vaca
rice	arroz
brown r.	a. con su envoltura natural
r. pudding	a. con leche
roll	bollo
Roquefort cheese	queso rochefort

rum	ron
rump steak	churrasco
runner beans	judías verdes
sage	salvia
s. & onion stuffing	relleno de s. y cebolla
salad	ensalada
green s.	e. de lechuga
mixed s.	e. mixta
potato s.	e. de patata
s. cream	mayonesa
s. dressing	aliño
tomato s.	e. de tomate
salt	sal
salmon	salmón
sandwich	bocadillo
sardine	sardina
sauce	salsa
apple s.	s. de manzana
bread s.	s. de pan
mint s.	s. de menta
tartare s.	s. tártara
white s.	s. blanca
Worcester s.	s. worcester
sausage	salchicha
s. roll	empanada de s.
scallop	vieira
scampi	cigalas
scone	pasta de harina, leche y margarina (para merendar)
Scotch broth	sopa espesa con verduras, carne y cebada
Scotch egg	huevo duro hecho dentro de pasta de embutido
seafood	mariscos

semolina pudding	budín hecho al horno con maíz, azúcar y leche
service charge	tarife por servicio (restaurante)
shandy	cerveza con limonada
shepherds pie	carne picada con puré de patatas
sherry	jerez
shrimps	gambas
s. cocktail	cóctel de g.
single cream	nata liquida
snacks	bocadillos
snails	caracoles
soda water	agua de soda
sole	lenguado
Dover s.	l. de Dover
fillet of s.	filete de l.
lemon s.	l. al limon
sorbet	sorbete
soup	sopa
soup of the day	sopa del día
sour cream	nata cortada
soy sauce	salsa de soja
spaghetti	espaguettis
spinach	espinacas
sponge cake	bizcocho
squash	jugo
starters	aperitivo/primer plato
steak	filete
Chateaubriand	chateaubriand
fillet	solomillo
minute	al minuto
rump	churrasco
sirloin	solomillo
T-bone	chuleta
steak and kidney pie	pastel de ternera y riñones

steak and kidney pudding	budín hecho con sebo y relleno de ternera y riñones
stew	guisado
Stilton (blue cheese)	queso stilton (= queso azul)
stout	cerveza negra
strawberry	fresa
stuffing	relleno
sugar	azúcar
sundae	helado con nueces y chocolate, fruta y zumo dulce
supper	cena
swede	nabo sueco
sweet	postre/dulce
sweetbread	lechecillas
swiss roll	pastel de bizcocho relleno de mermelada o nata
tabasco sauce	salsa tabasco
table d'hôte	menú del dia
tangerine	mandarina
tart	tarta
tartare sauce	salsa tártara
tea	té
China t.	t. chino
Indian t.	t. indio
cup of t.	taza de t.
pot of t.	tetera de t.
toast	tostada
tomato	tomate
t. juice	zumo de t.
t. salad	ensalada de t.
tongue	lengua
tonic water	agua tónica
treacle	almíbar
t. tart	tarta de a.

trifle	bizcocho con jerez, mermelada y frutas, cubierto con jalea, natillas y nata montada
tripe	callos
trout	trucha
tuna	atún
turbot	rodaballo
turkey	pavo
turnip	nabo
T-bone steak	chuleta de vaca
vanilla	vainilla
veal	ternera
vegetables	verduras
vermouth	vermut
venison	venado
vinaigrette	salsa vinagreta
vinegar	vinagre
waffle	buñuelo
walnut	nuez
water	agua
watercress	berro
water melon	sandía
Welsh rarebit	tostada con queso fundido y mostaza
whisky	whisky
whitebait	boquerones
white sauce	salsa blanca
wine list	carta de vinos
Worcester sauce	salsa worcester
yoghurt	yogur
Yorkshire pudding	budín de harina, leche y huevo, hecho al horno (generalmente se como con rosbif)

English signs   Señalizaciones inglesas

'A' FILM	Espectáculo solo para mayores y menores acompañados
AA (AUTOMOBILE ASSOCIATION)	Asociación automovilística
'AA' FILM	Autorizada mayores de 14 años
ABROAD	Al extranjero (cartas)
AC (ALTERNATING CURRENT)	Corriente alterna
ACCESSORIES	Accesorios
ACCIDENT	Accidente
ACCOMMODATION	Alojamiento
ACCOUNTS	Departamento de cuentas
ADDITIONAL CHARGE	Sobrecarga
ADMISSION (FREE)	Entrada (libre)
ADMISSIONS	Ingresos (hospital)
ADVANCE BOOKING	Reserva anticipada

AFTERNOON TEAS	Meriendas
AGENCY	Agencia
AIR	Aire (garaje)
AIRLINE INFORMATION	Información de vuelos
AIRMAIL	Correo aéreo
AIRPORT BUS	Autobús del aeropuerto
AIR TERMINAL	Terminal aérea
ALARM SIGNAL	Señal de alarma
PULL CHAIN IN AN EMERGENCY	En caso de alarma tire de la cadena (tren)
ALL-NIGHT CINEMA	Cine sesión contínua toda la noche
ALL TICKETS TO BE SHOWN	Todos los billetes han de ser sometidos a inspección
ALLOW TIME FOR COIN TO DROP	Deje tiempo para que caiga la moneda (en autobús etc)
ALTERNATIVE ROUTE	Ruta alternativa
AMBULANCE	Ambulancia
AMPHITHEATRE	Anfiteatro
ANNEXE	Anexo
ANTIQUES	Antigüedades
ARRIVALS	Llegadas
ASSEMBLY POINT	Punto de reunión
AT ANY TIME (NO PARKING SIGN)	A cualquier hora (señal de prohibición de aparcamiento)
ATTENDANT	Empleado
AUTOMATIC	Automático
AUTOMATIC BARRIERS	Barreras automáticas (metro)
BAGGAGE OFFICE	Sala de equipajes
BANK	Banco
BARGAINS	Gangas
BASEMENT (B) (on lift)	Sótano (S) (en ascensor)
BED AND BREAKFAST (B & B)	Alojamiento y desayuno
BENDS FOR /1 MILE/	Curvas durante /una milla/

BEWARE OF THE DOG!	¡Cuidado con el perro!
BOARDING NOW	Embarcando ahora
BOATS FOR HIRE	Alquiler de botes
BOOKABLE	Se puede reservar
BOOK HERE	Reserve aquí sus entradas
BOOKING OFFICE	Despacho de billetes por adelantado
BOX OFFICE	Taquilla
BUFFET	Cantina
BUREAU DE CHANGE	Oficina de cambio
BUSINESS ADDRESS	Razón comercial
BUS LANE	Carril reservado a autobuses
BUS STOP	Parada de autobús
BUSES ONLY	Sólo bus
CAFETERIA	Cafetería
CALL	Llame (timbre)
CAMERAS AND FILMS	Máquinas fotográficas y carretes
CAMPING PROHIBITED	Prohibido acampar
CANCELLED	Anulado
CAR ACCESSORIES	Accesorios de automóvil
CAR FERRY BOOKINGS	Reserva de plazas de automóvil para el ferry
CAR HIRE	Alquiler de coches
CAR PARK (FULL)	Aparcamiento (completo)
CAR WASH	Lavado de automóviles
CASH DESK	Caja
CASHIER	Cajero
CASUALTY	Emergencias
CASUAL WEAR	Ropa de sport
CATALOGUES	Catálogos
CAUTION	Precaución
CENTRE	Centro
CHAMBERMAID	Camarera

CHANGE	Cambio
CHANGING ROOM	Vestuario
CHANNEL	Canal
CHARGES	Costes
CHECK-IN (DESK)	(Mostrador de) facturación
CHECK OUT (HERE)	Notifique aquí la partida (mostrador de hotel)
CHEMIST	Farmacia
CHILD(REN)	Niño(s)
CHILDREN CROSSING	Cruce de escolares
CHILDREN'S DEPARTMENT	Departamento de niños
CHILDREN UNDER 3 MUST BE CARRIED	Los niños menores de 3 años deben ser llevados en brazos
CHINA AND GLASS	Porcelana y cristal
CHURCH	Iglesia
CIRCUS	Circo
CLEARANCE (SALE)	Liquidación
CLOAKROOM	Guardarropa
CLOSED CIRCUIT SECURITY SYSTEM IN OPERATION	Sistema de seguridad de circuito cerrado en funcionamiento
CLOSED (FOR LUNCH)	Cerrado (durante hora de almuerzo)
CLOSE DOOR (FIRMLY)	Sírvase cerrar (bien) la puerta
CLOSING DOWN (SALE)	Liquidación total por cese negocio
CLOSING HOURS	Horas de cierre
COACH DEPARTURES	Salida de autocares
COACH FARES	Tarifas de autocares
COACH STATION	Estación de autocares
COCKTAIL BAR	Coctelería
COCKTAIL LOUNGE	Salón para cócteles
COFFEE BAR	Cafetería
COFFEE HOUSE	Cafetería
COIN CHANGE	Máquina para cambio de monedas

COINS	Monedas
COLD (C)	Frío (F) (en grifos)
COLD DRINKS	Bebidas frescas
COLLECTION TIMES	Horas de recogida (en buzones)
COLOUR PROCESSING	Revelado en color
CO. LTD.	S.A. (Sociedad Anónima)
CONCEALED ENTRANCE	Entrada disimulada
CONDUCTED COACH TOURS	Excursiones en autocar con guía
CONTINENTAL DEPARTURES	Salidas al continente
CONTINUOUS PERFORMANCES	Sesión contínua
CONTROLLED ZONE	Zona controlada
CONVENIENCES	Servicios
CO-ORDINATES	Coordinados (ropa)
COPYING SERVICE	Servicio de fotocopia (offset)
COUNTRY	Correo interior (buzón)
COURTESY SERVICE	Servicio gratis para clientes
CRÊCHE	Guardería infantil
CROSS NOW	Pasen (peatones)
CUL-DE-SAC	Callejón sin salida
CUSTOMERS MUST TAKE A BASKET	Se ruega a los clientes que cojan una cesta (supermercado)
CUSTOMS (DECLARATION)	Aduana (declaración)
CUTLERY	Cubiertos (auto-servicio)
CYCLISTS ONLY	Sólo bicicletas
DANGER	Peligro
DANGEROUS CORNER	Curva peligrosa
DANGEROUS CURRENTS	Corrientes peligrosas
DAY BELL	Timbre para servicio
DAY TOURS	Excursiones diurnas
DC (DIRECT CURRENT)	CD (corriente directa)
DEAD SLOW	Muy despacio
DELAYED	Lleva retraso
DELIVERIES	Reparto a domicilio

DENTAL SURGERY	Clínica dental
DENTIST	Dentista
DEPARTMENT	Departamento (de una tienda)
DEPARTURE LOUNGE	Sala de espera para viajeros: salidas
DEPARTURES	Salidas
DEPARTURE TIMES	Horario de salidas
DEPOSITS	Libretas de ahorro
DESTINATION	Destino
DETAILS AVAILABLE ON REQUEST	Pida información aqui
DETOUR	Desvío
DISCO	Discoteca
DISPENSING CHEMISTS	Farmacia
DISPOSABLE BAG	Bolsa para usar y tirar
DIVERSION	Desvío
DOCKS	Muelles (puerto)
DO NOT DISTURB	No molestar
DO NOT ENTER	Se prohibe la entrada
DO NOT FEED (THE ANIMALS)	Se prohibe dar de comer (a los animales)
DO NOT OBSTRUCT ENTRANCE	Vado permanente
DO NOT SMOKE	Se prohibe fumar
DO NOT SPEAK TO THE DRIVER	Se prohibe hablar con el conductor
DO NOT STAND NEAR THE STAIRS	No permanezca junto a las escaleras
DO NOT TOUCH	No tocar
DOOR OPEN/SHUT	Puerta abierta/cerrada (ascensor)
DOORS OPEN /1.00 P.M./	Local abierto al público /a las trece horas/
DOWN	Abajo
DRINKING WATER	Agua potable

DRY CLEANING	Limpieza en seco
DUAL CARRIAGEWAY (AHEAD)	Carretera de dos carriles (más adelante)
DUMPING PROHIBITED	Se prohíbe echar escombros
DUTY FREE SHOP	Tienda libre de impuestos
EASTBOUND	Dirección: este (metro)
EAT BY . . .	Debe consumirse antes del . . . (alimentos perecederos)
ELECTRICAL GOODS	Electro domésticos
EMBARKATION	Embarque
EMERGENCY	Emergencia
EMERGENCY DOOR TO NEXT CAR	Puerta de emergencia para pasar al coche siguiente (metro)
EMERGENCY EXIT	Salida de emergencia
EMERGENCY SWITCH	Interruptor de emergencia (escalera mecánica)
EMERGENCY TREATMENT	Cura de emergencia
EMPTY	Vacío
END	Fin
END OF BUS LANE	Fin de carril de autobús
ENGAGED	Ocupado (servicios)
ENQUIRIES	Información
ENTRANCE	Entrada
ESCALATOR	Escalera mecánica
EVENING(S) ONLY	Sólo noche(s)
EVENING PERFORMANCE	Sesión de noche (teatro)
EXACT CHANGE	Cambio exacto
EXACT FARE	Tarifa exacta
EXCEPT FOR ACCESS	Prohibida la entrada a toda persona ajena
EXCESS BAGGAGE CHARGE	Suplemento por exceso de equipaje
EXCESS FARES	Suplemento del billete

EXCESS PERIOD	Período suplementario (en parquímetros)
EXIT	Salida
EXIT ONLY	Sólo salida
EXPORT FACILITIES AVAILABLE	Facilidades de exportación disponibles
EXPRESS DELIVERY	Entrega rápida
EXTRA CHARGES/EXTRAS	Sobretasas (taxímetro)
FARE STAGE	Parada de reajuste de tarifas (el autobús se para automaticamente siempre en una parada de reajuste de tarifas)
FASHIONS	Modas
FASTEN SEAT BELTS	Abrochense los cinturones de seguridad
FAST FIT EXHAUST SERVICE	Colocación rápida de tubo de escape (garaje)
FILLING STATION	Estación de servicio
FINE	Multa
FIRE ESCAPE	Escalera de emergencia
FIRE (EXIT)	Salida de incendios
FIRST CLASS	Primera clase
FISH AND CHIPS	Pescado con patatas fritas
FISH BAR	Restaurante especializado en pescados
FLIGHT	Vuelo
FLORIST	Florista
FOOD HALL	Departamento de alimentación
FOOTPATH	Sendero
FOOTWEAR	Calzado
FOR HIRE	Para alquilar
FRAGILE, WITH CARE	Frágil (en paquetes)
FREE	Gratis

FREE SERVICE	Servicio gratis
FUEL	Combustible
FULL	Completo
FULLY LICENSED	Local autorizado para venta de bebidas alcohólicas
FURNISHING FABRICS	Tejidos para mobiliario y decoración
FURNITURE DEPARTMENT	Departamento de muebles
GARAGE (IN CONSTANT USE)	Garaje (en uso continuo)
GARAGE PARKING	Aparcamiento de garaje
GATE	Puerta
GATES CLOSE AT …	Las puertas se cierran a …
GENTLEMEN/GENTS	Caballeros
GET IN LANE	Colóquese en su carril
GIFT SHOP	Tienda de artículos de regalo
GIVE WAY	Ceda el paso
GOLF CLUB/COURSE	Club/campo de golf
GOODS TO DECLARE	Artículos que declarar
GRILLS	Parrilla
GRIT FOR ROADS	Gravilla para carretera
GROUND FLOOR (G)	Planta baja (B)
GUARD DOG	Perro guardián
GUEST HOUSE	Casa de huéspedes
GUIDE	Guía
HABERDASHERY	Paquetería
HAIRDRESSING SALON	Peluquería
HALF-DAY TOURS	Excursiones de medio día
HALF-PRICE	Mitad de precio
HALT	Stop
HAND BAGGAGE	Equipaje de mano
HARD SHOULDER	Arcén (autopista)
HARDWARE	Quincallería
HAVE YOU LEFT YOUR KEY?	¿Ha devuelto su llave? (hotel)
HEADROOM	Altura máxima (en puentes de altura limitada)

HEATER	Calentador
HEEL BAR	Reparación rápida de calzado
HEIGHT LIMIT	Límite de altura
HIGHLY INFLAMMABLE	Altamente inflamable
HIGH VOLTAGE	Alta tensión
HILL 20%/1 IN 5	Pendiente 20%
HOLD	Sujete las puertas (ascensor)
HOSPITAL	Hospital
HOSTEL ACCOMMODATION	Albergue (alojamiento)
HOT (H)	Caliente (C) (en grifos)
HOT DRINKS	Bebidas calientes
HOTEL ENTRANCE	Entrada de hotel
HOTEL MANAGEMENT	Dirección de hotel
HOTEL RESERVATIONS	Reservas de hotel
HOT MEALS SERVED ALL DAY	Se sirven comidas calientes durante todo el día
HOURS OF BUSINESS	Horario comercial
24 HOUR SERVICE	24 horas
HOUSEHOLD DEPARTMENT	Departamento del hogar
ICES	Helados
IMMIGRATION	Control de pasaportes
IMMUNISATION	Vacunación
IN	Entrada (en puertas)
IN EMERGENCY BREAK GLASS	En caso de emergencia rompa el cristal (alarma de incendio)
INFLAMMABLE	Inflamable
INFORMATION	Información
INFORMATION DESK	Mostrador de información
INN FOOD	Comidas y bebidas
IN-PATIENTS	Pacientes residentes
INQUIRIES	Información
INSERT COIN	Introduzca moneda
INSERT /5P/ HERE	Introduzca /5 p/ aquí
INTERMISSION	Intermedio

INTERNATIONAL	Internacional (salidas en aeropuertos)
INTERNATIONAL TRAVELLERS' AID	Ayuda Internacional de Viajeros
INVISIBLE MENDING	Zurcido invisible
JEWELLERY	Joyas
JUNCTION (JCT)	Cruce
KEEP AWAY FROM CHILDREN	Manténgase fuera del alcance de los niños
KEEP CLEAR	Manténgase apartado
KEEP DOORS CLOSED	Mantenga cerradas los puertas
KEEP IN LANE	Circule por su carril
KEEP LEFT	Circule por su izquierda
KEEP OFF THE GRASS	No pisar el césped
KEEP OUT	Prohibida la entrada
KEEP RIGHT	Circule por su derecha
KEEP SHUT	Mantengase cerrado
KEYS (CUT HERE)	Llaves (se hacen)
KNITWEAR	Prendas de punto
KOSHER	Kosher (alimentos preparados según las normas religiosas judías)
LADIES/LADIES ROOM	Señoras/lavabos de señoras
LADIES HAIRDRESSING	Peluquería de señoras
LADIES ONLY	Sólo señoras
LANDED	Aterrizado (aeropuerto)
LANE CLOSED	Carril cerrado
2-LANE TRAFFIC	Circulación por dos carriles
LAST NAME	Apellido
LAST TRAIN	Último tren
LATE PERFORMANCE	Sesión de noche (teatro)
LATE SHOPPING (e.g. THURSDAYS 7 p.m.)	Horario comercial prolongado (por ej. los jueves hasta las siete)

LATE SHOW	Actuación de última hora
LAUNDERETTE/LAUNDROMAT	Autoservicio de lavandería
LAUNDRY	Lavandería
LAYBY	Zona de aparcamiento
LEAVE BY CENTRE DOORS	Descienda del vehículo por las puertas centrales
LEFT LUGGAGE	Consigna
LEFT LUGGAGE LOCKERS	Depósito de equipajes (casillas)
LETTERS	Cartas
LEVEL CROSSING	Paso a nivel
LIBRARY	Biblioteca
LICENSED BAR/RESTAURANT	Bar/restaurante autorizado para servir bebidas alcohólicas
LICENSING HOURS	Horas durante las cuales se autoriza servir bebidas alcohólicas
LIFEBELTS	Cinturónes salvavidas
LIFT(S)	Ascensor
LIGHT REFRESHMENTS	Meriendas
LINE	Línea (metro)
LITTER	Basura
LOADING AND UNLOADING ONLY	Sólo carga y descarga
LONG VEHICLE	Vehículo largo
LOOK LEFT/RIGHT	Mire a su izquierda/derecha
LOOSE CHIPPINGS	Astillas sueltas
LOST PROPERTY OFFICE	Oficina de objetos perdidos
LOUNGE	Salón
LOUNGE BAR	Bar (de más categoría, en pubs)
LOW BRIDGE	Puente de baja altura
LOWER DECK (BUS)	Piso bajo (autobús)
LOWER SALES FLOOR	Planta baja (centro comercial)
LOW FLYING AIRCRAFT	Aviones en vuelo bajo
LTD (= LIMITED)	Sociedad anónima
LUGGAGE	Equipaje

MADE IN . . .	Fabricado en . . .
MAGAZINES	Revistas
MAIL	Correo
MAIN LINE STATION	Estación de ferrocarril de red principal
MAIN ROAD	Carretera principal
MAJOR ROAD AHEAD	Carretera principal más delante
MATINÉE	Matinal (teatro)
MAXIMUM 2 HOURS (parking meter)	Máximo 2 horas (parquímetros)
MAX. LOAD	Carga máxima
MEMBERS ONLY	Reservado socios
MEN	Caballeros
MEN ONLY	Sólo caballeros
MENSWEAR	Ropa de caballero
MEN WORKING	Atención obras
MENU	Carta/menú
MESSAGES	Recados
METER ZONE	Zona de parquímetros
MEZZANINE FLOOR	Entresuelo
MIND THE GAP	Cuidado con no introducir el pié entre coche y andén (metro)
MIND THE STEP	Atención al escalón
MIND YOUR HEAD	Cuidado con la cabeza
MINICABS	Taxis (reserva por teléfono)
MINIMUM CHARGE	Tarifa mínima
MONEY ORDERS	Giros/transferencias bancartas
MON–SAT	Lunes–sábado
MORNING COFFEE	Se sirven cafés por la mañana
MOTOR CYCLES ONLY	Sólo motos (aparcamiento)
MOTOR VEHICLES PROHIBITED	Prohibida la entrada a vehículos de motor
MOTORWAY	Autopista
MOTORWAYS MERGE	Enlace de autopistas

English	Spanish
N (NIGHT) (BUSES)	Autobuses nocturnos
NATIONAL (AIRPORT DEPARTURES)	Nacionales (salidas de aeropuerto)
NCP (NATIONAL CAR PARKS)	Aparcamiento público. propriedad municipal
NEW PATIENTS	Pacientes nuevos
NEXT COACH DEPARTS AT …	El próximo autocar sale a …
NIGHT BELL	Timbre para servicio nocturno
NIGHT CHARGE	Tarifa nocturna (taxi)
NO ACCESS	Prohibido el paso
NO ADMITTANCE/ADMISSION (EXCEPT ON BUSINESS)	Prohibida la entrada (excepto por razones comerciales)
NO ADVANCE BOOKING	No se hacen reservas
NO BATHING	Prohibido bañarse
NO CAMPING	Prohibido acampar
NO CARAVANS	No se admiten caravanas
NO CHANGE AVAILABLE FROM DRIVER	El conductor no devuelve cambio
NO CHARGE SUNDAYS AND BANK HOLIDAYS	Aparcamiento gratuito los domingos y fiestas oficiales (parquímetros)
NO COLLECTIONS SUNDAY. CHRISTMAS DAY. BANK AND PUBLIC HOLIDAYS	No hay recogida los domingos, día de Navidad y fiestas oficiales
NO CREDIT	No se fía
NO CYCLING	Prohibido montar en bicicleta
NO DOGS	No se admiten perros
NO ENTRY	Prohibida la entrada
NO L DRIVERS	Prohibida la entrada a conductores en prácticas (autopista)
NO LEFT TURN	Prohibido girar a la izquierda
NO LITTER	Prohibido tirar basura
NO LOADING (MON–SAT 8 A.M.–6.30 P.M.)	Prohibido cargar (lunes–sábado 8–18.30)

NO OVERTAKING	Prohibido adelantar
NO PARKING	Prohibido aparcar
NO PARKING BEYOND THIS POINT	Prohibido aparcar más allá de esta señal
NO PASSING	Prohibido adelantar
NO PEDESTRIANS	Prohibido el acceso a peatones
NO PERSON UNDER 18 YEARS OF AGE ALLOWED ON THESE PREMISES	No se permite la entrada en este local a personas menores de 18 años
NO PRAMS OR PUSHCHAIRS	No se admiten coches o sillas de niños
NO RIGHT TURN	Prohibido girar a la derecha
NORTHBOUND (UNDERGROUND)	Dirección: norte (metro)
NO SERVICE	No hay servicio
NO SMOKING	Prohibido fumar
NO STANDING	Prohibido viajar de pie (piso superior de los autobuses)
NO STOPPING	Prohibido detenerse
NO SWIMMING	Prohibido bañarse
NOTHING TO DECLARE	Nada que declarar
NO THOROUGHFARE	Prohibido el paso
NO THROUGH ROAD	Callejón sin salida
NOTICE	Aviso
NOT IN USE	Fuera de servicio
NO TRAILERS	No se admiten remolques
NO TRESPASSING	Propiedad privada: prohibida la entrada
NOT TO BE TAKEN AWAY	No debe llevarse
NOT TRANSFERABLE	Intransferible (billete)
NO U TURNS	Prohibido girar en dirección contraria
NO VACANCIES	No quedan habitaciones
NO WAITING	Prohibido estacionarse
NO WAY OUT	No hay salida

NOW BEING SERVED	Se sirve ahora (desayunos, comida etc.)
NURSERY	Víveres de plantas
NURSERY	Habitación de los niños
OAP (OLD AGE PENSIONER)	Pensionista
OCCUPIED	Ocupado
OCTANE	Octano
OFF	Apagado
OFFENCE (PARKING O.)	Infracción (i. de tráfico)
OFF LICENCE	Tienda autorizada para vender bebidas alcohólicas
OIL	Aceite
ON	Encendido
ONE WAY	Dirección única
ON SALE HERE	De venta aquí
OPEN (EVERYDAY)/(TILL)	Abierto (diariamente)/(hasta)
OPEN TO NON-RESIDENTS	Abierto a los no residentes
OPENING HOURS	Horario comercial
(OPHTHALMIC) OPTICIAN	Óptico (oftalmólogo)
OUT	Salida
OUTPATIENTS	Pacientes externos
OVERSEAS TELEPHONE CALLS	Conferencias internacionales
OVERSEAS VISITORS RECEPTION	Recepción de visitantes extranjeros
PACKETS	Paquetes
PAPERBACKS	Libros de bolsillo
PARKING (P)	Aparcamiento
PARTS	Accesorios (garaje)
PASSENGERS ARE ADVISED/ REQUESTED NOT TO LEAVE LUGGAGE UNATTENDED	Se aconseja/ruega a los pasajeros no dejar su equipaje desatendido
PASSENGERS ARE ALLOWED ONE ITEM OF LUGGAGE IN THE AIRCRAFT CABIN	Se permite a los pasajeros llevar un artículo de equipaje dentro del avión

PASSENGERS MUST KEEP THEIR BAGGAGE WITH THEM AT ALL TIMES	Los pasajeros deben llevar consigo su equipaje en todo momento
PASSPORTS	Pasaportes
PAY AS YOU ENTER	Pague el entrar
PAY ATTENDANT	Pague al encargado
PAY HERE	Pague aquí
PEDESTRIAN CROSSING	Paso de peatones
PEDESTRIAN PUSH BUTTON	Pulse el botón para cruzar
PEDESTRIAN PRECINCT	Zona peatonal
PEDESTRIANS ONLY	Sólo peatones
PENALTY (FOR IMPROPER USE)	Multa (por uso indebido)
PERFORMANCE ENDS . . .	La actuación termina . . .
PERFUMERY	Perfumería
PERMIT HOLDERS ONLY	Sólo poseedores de permiso
PETROL	Gasolina
PETROL STATION	Estación de servicio
PHONE	Teléfono
3-PIECE (SUIT)	(Conjunto) de tres piezas
PLACE IN BIN PROVIDED	Depositar en recipiente adecuado
PLATFORM	Andén
PLATFORM TICKETS	Billetes de andén
PLEASE . . .	Por favor . . .
PLEASE DRIVE CAREFULLY	Conduzca con cuidado
PLEASE FORWARD	Por favor, haga seguir a destinatario (en cartas)
PLEASE LIFT HAND BAGGAGE CLEAR OF GATES	Sírvase levantar el equipaje de mano por encima de las puertas (torniquete, metro)
PLEASE RECLAIM YOUR BAGGAGE ON LEAVING THE COACH	Sírvase pedir su equipaje al bajar del autocar
PLEASE RING THE BELL	Sírvase tocar el timbre

PLEASE SHOW YOUR TICKET (AT THE BARRIER)	Sírvase enseñar su billete (en control de billetes)
PLEASE STAND ON THE RIGHT	Manténgase a la derecha
PLEASE TAKE A BASKET	Sírvase coger una cesta (super-mercado)
POISON	Veneno
POLICE	Policía
POLICE NOTICE	Comunicación policial
PORTER	Portero
POSITION CLOSED	Puesto cerrado
POSTE RESTANTE	Lista de correos
POSTING BOX	Buzón
POST OFFICE	Correos
POWDER ROOM	Servicio y tocador de señoras
PRESS BUTTON (FOR ASSISTANCE)	Pulse botón (para que le atiendan)
PRESS BUTTONS FIRMLY AND WAIT FOR CROSS SIGNAL	Pulse el botón con fuerza y espere la señal para cruzar
PRESS RETURN COIN BUTTON HERE	Pulse botón para devolución de moneda
PRESS TO REJECT	Pulse para devolución
PRICES SLASHED	Precios drasticamente reducidos
PRIVATE	Particular
PRIVATE PARKING ONLY	Sólo aparcamiento particular
PRIVATE ROAD	Camino particular
PROHIBITED	Prohibido
PUBLIC BAR	Sección más economica y popular de un pub
PUBLIC CONVENIENCES	Lavabos
PUBLIC HOLIDAY CHARGE	Tarifa suplementaria de festivos (taxi)
PUBLIC LIBRARY	Biblioteca pública
PULL	Tirar
PUSH	Empujar

PUSH BAR TO OPEN	Empujar manivela para abrir
PUSHCHAIRS MUST BE FOLDED	Las sillas de niños deben plegarse (escaleras mecánicas)
PUSH ONCE	Pulsar una vez (timbre en autobús)
PUT IN /THREE/ /10P/ PIECES	Introducir /tres/ monedas de /10p/
QUEUE HERE/Q HERE	Formar cola aquí
QUEUING	Cola
QUEUE OTHER SIDE	Formar cola al otro lado
QUEUE THIS SIDE	Formar cola a este lado
QUIET	Silencio
RAC (ROYAL AUTOMOBILE CLUB)	Real Automovil Club
RAILAIR LINK	Tren para aeropuerto
RAIL–DRIVE	Servicio de ferrocarril y barco para coches
RAMP AHEAD	Rampa más adelante
RATES OF EXCHANGE	Cambio de moneda
RECEPTION	Recepción
RECORDED DELIVERY	Certificado (correos)
RECORDS	Discos
RED CROSS	Cruz Roja
REDUCED (FOR CLEARANCE)	Precio rebajado (por saldo)
REDUCE SPEED NOW	Reduzca velocidad
REDUCTIONS	Descuentos
REFRESHMENTS	Refrescos
REGISTERED LETTERS	Cartas certificadas
REGISTERED LUGGAGE	Equipaje facturado
REJECT COINS	Monedas no admitidas
RENTALS	Alquileres
REPAIRS	Reparaciones
REPLACE IN HOLDER	Vuelva a colocarlo en el soporte

REQUEST (R) (BUS STOP)	Parada discrecional (el autobús sólo se detiene si se pide parado)
RESERVATIONS	Reservas
RESERVED	Reservado
RESIDENTS' LOUNGE	Sala de residentes
RESIDENTS ONLY	Sólo residentes
RESTAURANT	Restaurante
RESTAURANT CAR	Coche restaurante
RETURN CARS ONLY	Sólo automóviles devueltos
RETURN TO SEAT	Vuelva a su asiento
RING FOR ATTENDANT	Llame para que acuda empleado
RING FOR SERVICE	Llame para servicio
RING ROAD	Circunvalación
ROAD CLEAR	Carretera libre de obstáculos
ROAD WORKS AHEAD	Obras mas adelante
ROOM SERVICE	Servicio de habitación
ROOMS TO LET	Habitaciones para alquilar
ROUNDABOUT	Sentido de giro obligatorio
ROW	Fila (teatro)
SAFETY CURTAIN	Telón de seguridad
SALE	Rebajas
SALES AND SERVICE	Ventas y entretenimiento (garaje)
SALOON BAR	Bar-salón
SANDWICH BAR	Snack-bar
SCHEDULED TIME	Hora oficial
SCHOOL	Escuela
SEALINK	Servicio de ferry
SEAT	Asiento (teatro)
SEAT RESERVATIONS	Reserva de asientos
SECOND CLASS	Segunda clase
SECURITY CHECKS IN OPERATION	Controles de seguridad en funcionamiento

SELF-DRIVE CAR HIRE	Alquiler de coches sin conductor
SELF-SERVE/SELF-SERVICE	Auto servicio
SELL BY . . .	Debe venderse antes del . . . (alimentos perecederos)
SEPARATE PERFORMANCES	Sesiones independientes
SEPARATES	Prendas sueltas (en tienda de ropas)
SERVICES (S)	Servicios
SERVICE AREA	Área de servicio (autopista)
SERVICE (NOT) INCLUDED	Servicio (no) incluido
SHAVERS ONLY	Sólo máquinas de afeitar
SHOE DEPARTMENT	Departamento de calzados
SHOE REPAIRS	Reparación de calzado
SHOPLIFTERS WILL BE PROSECUTED	Las personas culpables de hurto serán responsables ante la ley
SHOPPING HOURS	Horario comercial
SHOW TICKETS PLEASE	Sírvase enseñar billetes
SHUT (THE DOOR/THE GATE)	Sírvase cerrar (la puerta/verja)
SINGLE FILE TRAFFIC	Tráfico de un sólo carril
SINGLE TRACK WITH PASSING PLACES	Carril único con zonas de adelantamento
SLOW	Despacio
SNACKS	Bocadillos
SOLD OUT	Agotado
SOUTHBOUND	Dirección: sur (metro)
SPARE PARTS	Piezas de recambio
SPEAK HERE	Hable aquí
SPECIAL OFFER	Oferta especial
STAFF ONLY	Sólo empleados
STAGE DOOR	Puerta reservada para empleados y actores
STAIRS	Escaleras
STAMPS	Sellos
STAND CLEAR OF THE DOORS	No acercarse a las puertas
STANDING ROOM ONLY	Sólo para estar de pié

STEAK BAR	Restaurante especializado en filetes
STEEP GRADIENT/HILL	Pendiente muy empinada
STREET LEVEL (lift)	Planta baja (ascensor)
SUBURBAN SERVICES	Servicios de cercanías
SUBWAY	Paso subterráneo
SURGERY	Consulta médica
SURGERY HOURS	Horas de consulta
SURNAME	Apellido
SUSPENDED	Temporalmente suspendido
SWEETS AND CIGARETTES	Caramelos y tabaco
SWIMMING POOL	Piscina
SWITCH OFF ENGINE	Apague el motor (garaje)
TAKE-AWAY	Comidas para llevar
TAKE TICKET – KEEP IT PLEASE	Coja su billete – sírvase guardarlo
TARIFF	Tarifa
TAXI QUEUE	Taxis en cordón
TAXI RANK	Parada de taxis
TAXIS ONLY	Sólo taxis
TEAS	Té/meriendas
TELEGRAMS	Telegramas
TELEPHONE	Teléfono
TELEPHONE DIRECTORIES	Listín de teléfonos
TELEVISION (TV)	Televisión TVE (tele)
TELEX SERVICE	Servicio de telex
TEMPORARY ROAD SURFACE	Calzada provisional
THEATRE	Teatro
THERE ARE NO TICKETS. YOUR COIN RELEASES THE GATE	No hay billetes. Su moneda abrirá la puerta (Autobuses)
THESE ARTICLES WILL BE CARRIED FREE	Estos artículos serán transportados gratuitamente
THIS PERFORMANCE	Esta sesión

THIS SIDE UP/DOWN	Manténgase en posición hacia arriba/abajo
THIS WAY	Siga por aquí
TICKET HOLDERS ONLY	Entrada sólo con billete
TICKETS	Billetes
TILL CLOSED	Caja cerrada
TIMETABLE	Horario
TOBACCONIST	Estanco
TO COACHES	A los autocares
TODAY'S PERFORMANCE(S)	Sesion(es) de hoy
TO EAT HERE OR TAKE AWAY	Para consumir aquí o para llevar
TOILETRIES	Artículos de baño
TOILETS	Lavabos/servicios/aseos
TO LET	Para alquilar
TOLL BRIDGE	Puente de peaje
TOLL GATE	Puesto de peaje
TO OPEN IN EMERGENCY TURN TAP AND PULL HANDLES	Para abrir en emergencia abra válvula y tire de las manillas
TO STOP THE BUS RING THE BELL ONCE	Para que pare el autobús toque el timbre una vez
TO THE BOATS	A los barcos
TOURIST TICKETS	Billetes turísticos
TOWN CENTRE	Centro ciudad
TOY DEPARTMENT	Departamento de juguetes
TRAFFIC SIGNALS AHEAD	Señales de tráfico más adelante
TRANSFER PASSENGERS TRANSIT PASSENGERS	Pasajeros en tránsito
TRAVEL AGENCY TRAVEL OFFICE	Oficina de viajes
TRAYS	Bandejas
TRESPASSERS WILL BE PROSECUTED	Propiedad privada prohibida la entrada
TUNNEL	Túnel
TURN HANDLE	Gire la manilla

TWIN TOWN	Ciudad gemela
TWO-WAY TRAFFIC	Tráfico en dos direcciones
'U' FILM	Película tolerada para menores
UNACCOMPANIED BAGGAGE	Equipaje no acompañado
UNDERGROUND	Metro
UNDERGROUND STATION	Estación de metro
UNDERWEAR	Ropa interior
UNRESERVED	Sin reserva
UNSUITABLE FOR LONG VEHICLES	No apropiado para vehículos largos
UP	Arriba
UPPER DECK	Piso superior (autobús)
URBAN CLEARWAY	Autopista zona urbana
USED BLADES	Hojas de afeitar usadas
USED TICKETS	Billetes usados
USE OTHER DOOR	Por la otra puerta
VACANCIES	Vacantes
VACANT	Libre
VAT (VALUE ADDED TAX)	I.V.A.
VIP LOUNGE	Salón de V.I.Ps
WAIT (HERE)	Espere (aquí)
WAITING AREA	Zona de espera
WAITING LIMITED TO 30 MINUTES IN ANY HOUR	Espera limitada a treinta minutos a cualquier hora
WAITING ROOM	Sala de espera
WARD	Sala (hospital)
WARNING	Advertencia
WASH ROOM	Lavabos
WASHING CREAM	Jabón líquido
WATCH YOUR STEP	Cuidado con el escalón
WAY IN	Entrada
WAY OUT	Salida

WEEKEND CHARGE	Tarifa de fin de semana (taxi)
WEIGHT LIMIT	Límite de peso
WELCOME TO ...	Bienvenido a ...
WESTBOUND	Dirección oeste (metro)
WET PAINT	Recien pintado
WHERE TO STAY	Donde hospedarse
WHILE YOU/U WAIT	Al momento, llaves, reparaciones etc.
... WILL ARRIVE ...	Llegará (terminal aérea)
WINE BAR	Bodega
WINES AND SPIRITS	Vinos y licores
WOMEN	Señoras
YELLOW TICKETS THROUGH GATE: OTHER TICKETS THROUGH TICKET COLLECTOR'S GATE	Pasajeros con billetes amarillos por la puerta. Pasajeros con otros billetes, por el revisor
YHA YOUTH HOSTEL	YHA Albergue de juventud
YOU MAY TELEPHONE FROM HERE	Teléfono aquí
X FILM (Adults only)	Peliculas autorizadas para mayores de 18 años
X RAY	Rayos X
Z BEND	Curva Z
ZONE ENDS	Fin de zona

Motoring key

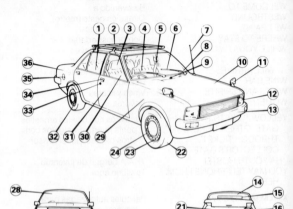

1	back seat	el asiento trasero
2	roof rack	la baca
3	head restraint	el apoyacabezas
4	passenger's seat	el asiento delantero
5	seat belt	el cinturón de seguridad
6	windscreen wiper blade	el canto de goma del limpiaparabrisas
7	aerial	la antena
8	windscreen wiper arm	el brazo de limpiaparabrisas
9	windscreen washer	el lavacristales
10	bonnet	el capó
11	exterior mirror	el retrovisor exterior
12	headlight	el faro
13	bumper	el parachoques
14	rear window	la luneta trasera
15	rear window heater	la luneta térmica trasera
16	spare wheel	la rueda de recambio
17	fuel tank	el depósito de gasolina
18	hazard warning light	el intermitente de emergencia
19	brake light	la luz de frenos
20	rear light	la luz trasera
21	boot	el maletero
22	tyre	el neumático
23	front wheel	la rueda delantera
24	hubcap	el tapacubos
25	sidelight	la luz de posición
26	number plate	la placa de matrícula
27	registration number	la matrícula
28	windscreen	el parabrisas
29	front wing	el guardabarros delantero
30	driver's seat	el asiento del conductor
31	door	la puerta
32	rear wheel	la rueda trasera
33	lock	la cerradura
34	door handle	la manecilla de la puerta
35	petrol filler cap	el tapón del depósito
36	rear wing	el guardabarros trasero

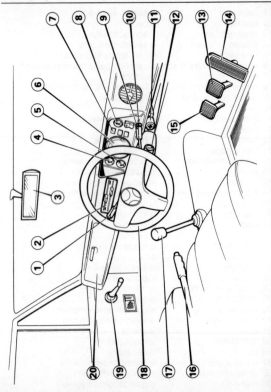

1 dipswitch — el conmutador para luces
2 heater — la calefacción
3 interior mirror — el retrovisor
4 water temperature gauge — el termómetro del agua
5 ammeter — el amperímetro
6 speedometer — el indicador de velocidad
7 oil pressure warning light — el testigo de la presión del aceite
8 fuel gauge — el indicador del nivel de la gasolina

9 horn — la bocina
10 direction indicator — el intermitente
11 choke — el stárter/el dispositivo de arranque en frío

12 ignition switch — el encendido
13 brake pedal — el pedal de freno
14 accelerator — el acelerador
15 clutch pedal — el pedal de embrague
16 handbrake — el freno de mano
17 gear lever (selector) — la palanca de velocidades
18 steering wheel — el volante
19 window winder — la manivela para abrir la ventanilla

20 glove compartment — la guantera

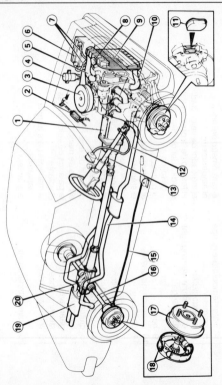

1	gearbox	la caja de cambios
2	fusebox	la caja de fusibles
3	air filter	el filtro de aire
4	ignition coil	la bobina de encendido
5	radiator hose (top)	el tubo flexible superior
6	battery	la batería
7	leads (battery) (pl)	los hilos conductores
8	filler cap (radiator)	el tapón del radiador
9	radiator	el radiador
10	radiator hose (bottom)	el tubo flexible inferior
11	disc brake pad	el forro de freno de disco
12	speedometer cable	el cable de velocímetro
13	steering column	la columna de dirección
14	exhaust pipe	el tubo de escape
15	handbrake cable	el cable de freno de mano
16	rear brake	el eje trasero
17	brake drum	el tambor de freno
18	brake shoe	la zapata de freno
19	silencer	el silencioso
20	differential	el diferencial

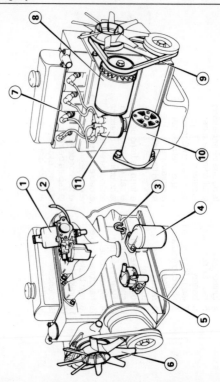

1 carburettor — el carburador
2 cable — el cable
3 oil dip stick — la varilla del nivel de aceite
4 oil filter — el filtro de aceite
5 fuel pump — la bomba de gasolina
6 fan — el ventilador
7 sparking plug — la bujía
8 alternator — la dínamo
9 fan belt — la correa del ventilador
10 starter motor — el motor de arranque
11 distributor — el distribuidor

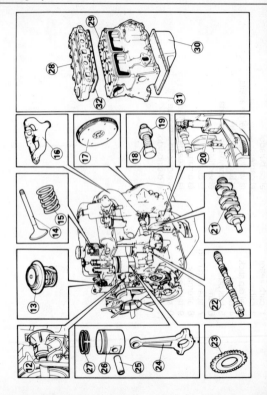

12	water pump	la bomba de agua
13	thermostat	el termostato
14	valve	la válvula
15	spring	el resorte
16	manifold, inlet and exhaust	el colector de admisión y escape
17	flywheel	el volante
18	bolt	el tornillo
19	nut	la tuerca
20	oil pump	la bomba de aceite
21	crankshaft	el eje cigüeñal
22	camshaft	el eje de levas
23	sprocket	las ruedas de cadena
24	connecting rod	la biela
25	gudgeon pin	el bulón de pistón
26	piston	el pistón
27	piston rings (pl)	los aros de pistón
28	cylinder head	la culata de cilindros
29	cylinder	el cilindro
30	oil sump	el colector de aceite
31	cylinder block	el bloque de cilindros
32	gasket	la junta

Numbers, days and months

Numbers

0	cero	43	cuarenta y tres
1	uno	54	cincuenta y cuatro
2	dos	65	sesenta y cinco
3	tres	76	setenta y seis
4	cuatro	87	ochenta y siete
5	cinco	98	noventa y ocho
6	seis	100	cien
7	siete	101	ciento uno
8	ocho	211	doscientos once
9	nueve	322	trescientos vientidós
10	diez	433	cuatrocientos trienta y tres
11	once	544	quinientos cuarenta y cuatro
12	doce	655	seiscientos cincuenta y cinco
13	trece	766	setecientos sesenta y seis
14	catorce	877	ochocientos setenta y siete
15	quince	988	novecientos ochenta y ocho
16	dieciséis	1000	mil
17	diecisiete	1001	mil uno
18	dieciocho	2112	dos mil ciento doce
19	diecinueve	3223	tres mil doscientos veintitrés
20	veinte	4334	cuatro mil trescientos treinta y
21	veintiuno		cuatro
32	treinta y dos	10,000	diez mil

0.1 = 0,1 cero coma uno (literally 'nought comma one')
Change '–cientos' to '–cientas' with pesetas eg 'doscientas once pesetas'.

The days of the week

Monday	Lunes
Tuesday	Martes
Wednesday	Miércoles
Thursday	Jueves
Friday	Viernes
Saturday	Sábado
Sunday	Domingo

The months of the year

January	Enero
February	Febrero
March	Marzo
April	Abril
May	Mayo
June	Junio
July	Julio
August	Agosto
September	Septiembre
October	Octubre
November	Noviembre
December	Diciembre

Equivalents

Spanish money

Pesetas = ptas   1 pta = 100 céntimos   72 ptas = setenta y dos
pesetas

Coins (monedas)
1 peseta (pta) (una peseta)
5 pesetas (ptas) (cinco
   pesetas) (un duro)
25 pesetas (ptas) (veinticinco
   pesetas) (cinco duros)
50 pesetas (ptas) (cincuenta
   pesetas) (diez duros)

Notes (billetes)
100 pesetas (ptas) (cien
   pesetas) (veinte duros)
500 pesetas (ptas) (quinientas
   pesetas)
1000 pesetas (ptas) (mil
   pesetas)
5000 pesetas (ptas) (cinco mil
   pesetas)

In a bank you will be asked:

How would you like the money?   ¿Cómo quiere los billetes?
In /hundreds/   En billetes de /cien/
In /five hundreds/   En billetes de /quinientas/
In /thousands/   En billetes de /mil/
In /five thousands/   En billetes de /cinco mil/

Distances

1 mile = 1.6 kilometres   1.6 kilómetros = 1 milla

Miles	10	20	30	40	50	60	70	80	90	100	Millas
Kilometres	16	32	48	64	80	97	113	128	145	160	Kilómetros

Lengths and sizes

Some approximate equivalents:

British		**Metric**
1 inch		= 2.5 centímetros
6 inches		= 15 centímetros
1 foot	= 12 inches	= 30 centímetros
2 feet	= 24 inches	= 60 centímetros
1 yard	= 3 feet or 36 inches	= 91 centímetros
1 yard 3 inches		= 1 metro

General clothes sizes (including chest/hip measurements)

GB	USA	Europe	ins	cms
8	6	36	30/32	76/81
10	8	38	32/34	81/86
12	10	40	34/36	86/91
14	12	42	36/38	91/97
16	14	44	38/40	97/102
18	16	46	40/42	102/107
20	18	48	42/44	107/112
22	20	50	44/46	112/117
24	22	52	46/48	117/122
26	24	54	48/50	122/127

Waist measurements

(ins) GB/USA 22 24 26 28 30 32 34 36 38 40 42 44 46 48 48
(cms) Europe 56 61 66 71 76 81 86 91 97 102 107 112 117 122 127

Collar measurements

(ins) GB/USA 14 $14\frac{1}{2}$ 15 $15\frac{1}{2}$ 16 $16\frac{1}{2}$ 17 $17\frac{1}{2}$
(cms) Europe 36 37 38 39 40 41 42 43

Shoes

GB	3	$3\frac{1}{2}$	4	$4\frac{1}{2}$	5	$5\frac{1}{2}$	6	$6\frac{1}{2}$	7	$7\frac{1}{2}$	8	$8\frac{1}{2}$	9	10	11	12
USA		$4\frac{1}{2}$ 5		$5\frac{1}{2}$ 6		$6\frac{1}{2}$ 7		$7\frac{1}{2}$ 8		$8\frac{1}{2}$ 9		$9\frac{1}{2}$ 10		$10\frac{1}{2}$ $11\frac{1}{2}$	$12\frac{1}{2}$	$13\frac{1}{2}$
Europe	36		37		38		39		40		41		42	43	44	45

Hats

GB	$6\frac{5}{8}$	$6\frac{3}{8}$	$6\frac{7}{8}$	7	$7\frac{1}{8}$	$7\frac{1}{4}$	$7\frac{3}{8}$	$7\frac{1}{2}$	$7\frac{5}{8}$
USA	$6\frac{3}{4}$	$6\frac{7}{8}$	7	$7\frac{1}{8}$	$7\frac{1}{4}$	$7\frac{3}{8}$	$7\frac{1}{2}$	$7\frac{5}{8}$	$7\frac{3}{4}$
Europe	54	55	56	57	58	59	60	61	62

Glove sizes are the same in every country.

Weights

Some approximate equivalents:
Gramos (g) (Grams) and *kilogramos* (kg) (kilograms)
1000 *gramos* (1000 g) = 1 *kilogramo* (kilo/kg)

1 oz. (onza)	=	25 gramos (g)
4 ozs. (onzas)	=	100/125 gramos
8 ozs.	=	225 gramos
1 pound (16 ozs.) (libra)	=	450 gramos
1 pound 2 ozs.	=	500 gramos (½ kilogramo)
2 pounds 4 ozs.	=	1 kilogramo (1 kilo/kg)
1 stone	=	6 kilogramos

Body weight

Body weight in Spanish-speaking countries is measured in kilograms (*kilogramos*).
Some approximate equivalents:

Pounds	Stones	Kilograms
28	2	12½
42	3	19
56	4	25
70	5	32
84	6	38
98	7	45
112	8	51
126	9	57½
140	10	63
154	11	70
168	12	76
182	13	83
196	14	90

Liquid measure

In Spanish-speaking countries all liquids are measured in litres.
Most bottles contain one litre but liquids such as milk, oil and soft
drinks are also sold in 1½ litre bottles.
Some approximate equivalents:
1 pint = 0.57 litres (*litros*)   1 gallon = 4.55 litres

GB Measures	Litres
1 pint	= 0.5
(20 fluid ounces (fl. ozs.))	
1.7 pints	= 1
1.1 gallons	= 5
2.2 gallons	= 10
3.3 gallons	= 15
4.4 gallons	= 20
5.5 gallons	= 25
6.6 gallons	= 30
7.7 gallons	= 35
8.8 gallons	= 40
9.9 gallons	= 45

Temperature

	Fahrenheit (F)	**Centigrade** (C)
Boiling point	212°	100°
	104°	40°
Body temperature	98.4°	36.9°
	86°	30°
	68°	20°
	59°	15°
	50°	10°
Freezing point	32°	0°
	23°	− 5°
	0°	−18°

(Convert Fahrenheit to Centigrade by subtracting 32 and multiplying by 5/9. Convert Centigrade to Fahrenheit by multiplying by 9/5 and adding 32.) In Spain, all temperatures are measured in Centigrade (*centigrados*).

Tyre pressures

lb/sq in	kg/cm²	lb/sq in	kg/cm²	lb/sq in	kg/cm²
20	= 1.40	24	= 1.68	30	= 2.10
21	= 1.47	26	= 1.82	34	= 2.39
22	= 1.54	28	= 1.96	40	= 2.81

Countries, currencies, nationalities and languages

Country, area or continent	Main unit of currency	Description & nationality (feminine form given in brackets)	Main language(s)
Africa	África	—	Africano (–na)	—
Albania	Albania	Lek	Albano (–na)	Tosk
Algeria	Argelia	Dinar	Argelino (–na)	Árabe/Francés
Argentina	Argentina	Peso	Argentino (–na)	Español
Asia	Asia	—	Asiático (–ca)	—
Australia	Australia	Dollar	Australiano (–na)	Inglés
Austria	Austria	Schilling	Austríaco (–ca)	Alemán
Bahrain	Bahrain	Dinar	Bahraini (m&f)	Árabe
Belgium	Bélgica	Franc	Belga (m&f)	Flamenco/Francés
Bolivia	Bolivia	Peso	Boliviano (–na)	Español
Brazil	Brasil	Cruzeiro	Brasileño (–ña)	Portugués
Bulgaria	Bulgaria	Lev	Búlgaro (–ra)	Búlgaro
Burma	Birmania	Kyat	Birmano (–na)	Birmano
Canada	Canadá	Dollar	Canadiense (m&f)	Inglés/Francés
Chile	Chile	Escudo	Chileno (–na)	Español
China	China	Yuan	Chino (–na)	Chino
Colombia	Colombia	Peso	Colombiano (–na)	Español
Costa Rica	Costa Rica	Colón	Costarriqueño (–ña)	Español

Country, area or continent		Main unit of currency	Description & nationality (feminine form given in brackets)	Main language(s)
Cuba	Cuba	Peso	Cubano (–na)	Español
Cyprus	Chipre	Pound	Chipriota (m&f)	Griego/Turco
Czechoslovakia	Checoslovaquia	Koruna	Checoslovaco (–ca)	Checo/Eslovaco
Denmark	Dinamarca	Krone	Danés (–sa)	Danés
Ecuador	Ecuador	Sucre	Ecuatoriano (–na)	Español
Egypt	Egipto	Pound	Egipcio (–ia)	Árabe
Eire	Eire	Punt	Irlandés (–sa)	Inglés/Gaélico
England	Inglaterra	Pound	Inglés (–sa)	Inglés
Ethiopia	Etiopía	Dollar	Etíope (m&f)	Amharic
Europe	Europa	—	Europeo (–ea)	
Finland	Finlandia	Markka	Finlandés (–sa)	Finlandés
France	Francia	Franc	Francés (–sa)	Francés
Germany	Alemania		Alemán (–na)	Alemán
West G.	A. occidental	Deutschmark	Alemán (–na)	Alemán
East G.	A. oriental	Ostmark	Alemán (–na)	Alemán
Ghana	Ghana	New Cedi	Ghaneano (–na)	Inglés/Akan
Greece	Grecia	Drachma	Griego (–ga)	Griego
Guatemala	Guatemala	Quetzal	Guatemalteco (–ca)	Español
Guyana	Guyana	Dollar	Guyanés (–sa)	Inglés
Holland (The Netherlands)	Holanda (los Países Bajos)	Guilder	Holandés (–sa)	Holandés

Hong Kong	Hong Kong	Dollar	de Hong Kong (m&f)	Chino/Inglés
Hungary	Hungría	Forint	Húngaro (–ra)	Húngaro
Iceland	Islandia	Krona	Islandés (–sa)	Islandés
India	India	Rupee	Indio (–ia)	Indostánico/Inglés
Indonesia	Indonesia	Rupiah	Indonesio (–ia)	Bahasa Indonesia
Iran	Irán	Rial	Iranio (–ia)/ Iraní (m&f)	Farsi
Iraq	Irak	Dinar	Iraquí (m&f)	Árabe
Israel	Israel	Pound	Israelí (m&f)	Hebreo
Italy	Italia	Lira	Italiano (–na)	Italiano
Jamaica	Jamaica	Dollar	Jamaicano (–na)	Inglés
Japan	Japón	Yen	Japonés (–sa)	Japonés
Jordan	Jordania	Dinar	Jordano (–na)	Árabe
Kenya	Kenia	Shilling	Keniata (m&f)	Suajile
Kuwait	Kuwait	Dinar	Kuwaití (m&f)	Árabe
Lebanon	El Líbano	Pound	Libanés (–sa)	Árabe
Libya	Libia	Dinar	Libio (–ia)	Árabe
Luxemburg	Luxemburgo	Franc	Luxemburgués (–sa)	Francés/Alemán
Malaysia	Malasia	Dollar	Malasio (–ia)	Malayo/Chino
Malta	Malta	Pound	Maltés (–sa)	Maltés/Inglés
Mexico	Méjico	Peso	Mejicano (–na)	Español
Morocco	Marruecos	Dirham	Marroquí (m&f)	Árabe
New Zealand	Nueva Zelanda	Dollar	Neozelandés (–sa)	Inglés

Country, area or continent		Main unit of currency	Description & nationality (feminine form given in brackets)	Main language(s)
Nicaragua	Nicaragua	Córdoba	Nicaragüense (m&f)	Español
Nigeria	Nigeria	Naira	Nigeriano (–na)	Hausa/Ibo/ Yoruba/Inglés
Northern Ireland	Irlanda del Norte	Pound	Irlandés (–sa)	Inglés
Norway	Noruega	Krone	Noruego (–ga)	Noruego
Pakistan	Pakistán	Rupee	Pakistaní (m&f)	Urdu
Paraguay	Paraguay	Guaraní	Paraguayo (–ya)	Español
Peru	El Perú	Sol	Peruano (–na)	Español
Poland	Polonia	Zloty	Polaco (–ca)	Polaco
Portugal	Portugal	Escudo	Portugués (–sa)	Portugués
Rumania	Rumania	Leu	Rumano (–na)	Rumano
Saudi Arabia	Arabia Saudita	Riyal	Saudita (m&f)	Árabe
Scotland	Escocia	Pound	Escocés (–sa)	Inglés/Gaélico
Singapore	Singapur	Dollar	de Singapur (m&f)	Malayo/Chino/ Inglés
South Africa	Africa del Sur	Rand	Sudafricano (–na)	Africaans/Inglés
Spain	España	Peseta	Español (–la)	Español
Sudan	El Sudán	Pound	Sudanés (–sa)	Árabe
Sweden	Suecia	Krona	Sueco (–ca)	Sueco
Switzerland	Suiza	Franc	Suizo (–za)	Francés/Alemán/ Italiano
Syria	Siria	Pound	Sirio (–ia)	Árabe

Tanzania	Tanzania	Shilling	Tanzano (–na)	Suajili
Thailand	Tailandia	Baht	Tailandés (–sa)	Tailandés/Tai
Tunisia	Túnez	Dinar	Tunecino (–na)	Árabe/Francés
Turkey	Turquia	Lira	Turco (–ca)	Turco
Union of Soviet Socialist Republics (USSR) Russia	Unión de Repúblicas Socialistas Soviéticas (URSS) Rusia	Rouble	Ruso (–sa)	Ruso
United Kingdom (UK) (= England, Northern Ireland, Scotland, Wales, Channel Islands)	El Reino Unido (= Inglaterra, Irlanda del norte, Escocia, Gales, Las Islas Normandas)	Pound Sterling	Británico (–ca)	Inglés
United States of America (USA)	Los Estados Unidos de América (EE.UU)	Dollar	Americano (–na)	Inglés
Uruguay	Uruguay	Peso	Uruguayo (–ya)	Español
Venezuela	Venezuela	Bolivar	Venezolano (–na)	Español
Vietnam	Vietnam	Dong	Vietnamita (m&f)	Vietnamita
Wales	Gales	Pound	Galés (–sa)	Galés/Inglés
Yugoslavia	Yugoslavia	Dinar	Yugoslavo (–va)	Yugoslavo/Serbo-croato
Zaire	Zaire	Zaire	Zaireno (–na)	Francés/Lingala
Zimbabwe	Zimbabwe	Dollar	Zimbabwense (m&f)	Inglés/Shona/Ndebele

Travel hints

Useful addresses

Oficina Municipal de Turismo, Plaza Mayor 3, Madrid (266 54 77)
Oficina Central de Correos (Central Post Office) Plaza de Cibeles, Madrid (open 9 a.m.–12 p.m.).
Oficinas de RENFE (Spanish Rail Service) Information office (Madrid 733 30 00).

Social behaviour

People usually shake hands on meeting and on saying goodbye. Women often kiss each other on both cheeks.
Spanish surnames can be confusing! A married woman is referred to as 'señora de' /husband's name/, and a man as 'señor' /surname/.
Girls and single women are referred to as 'señorita' /surname/.
The habit of clapping to call the waiter is disappearing. Say 'Camarero, por favor' ('Waiter, please') or simply catch his eye.
Queueing can be a little confusing. At least try to keep your place. To find out where the end of the queue is, ask '¿Quién es el último?'
Gift bringing: one often sends flowers or gives chocolates or a bottle of wine in return for hospitality. Christmas presents are given on January 6th (Epiphany).

Accommodation

Contact the local 'Oficina de Turismo' (Tourist Office).
Accommodation ranges from:
Hoteles Gran Lujo (4/5-star luxury hotels).
Paradores (Hotels situated in places of interest or restored historical buildings). Slightly more expensive than 'hoteles' but worth it.
Hoteles (2/3-star hotels).
Hostales (2/3-star hostels).
Habitaciones sin/con desayuno (Bed/Bed and breakfast). Spanish

breakfast is not cooked.
Hostales/Residencias (Student-type accommodation). Look in
newspapers for rooms to let.

Getting around

Rush hours are from 7.45–9.30 a.m. and from 7–8 p.m. on
weekdays.
Maps can be bought from stationers and bookshops. There is a
street map of most large towns, 'Guía Urbana de / /' which is very
comprehensive.

By taxi In Madrid and other cities you can stop a taxi in the street
when you see the 'Libre' sign on its windscreen (during the day) or its
green light (at night). There are taxi ranks in all central areas and at
railway stations. The fare is shown on the meter but there may be
some extras to pay. You can also phone for a taxi. Look under 'Taxis'
in the telephone directory.

By bus Put out your hand to stop a bus at a bus stop. In some buses
you enter at the front and pay the driver. In others you enter at the
back and pay the conductor. There are flat rate fares in towns
('bonobús'). (The 'Microbuses' are more expensive.) Keep your ticket
in case an inspector asks for it. Ring once to stop the bus. Check
when the last bus goes, as services stop any time between 10p.m.–
1a.m.

By underground Buy your ticket from the booking office or
automatic machine. The fare is the same wherever you are going.
Cheap day returns and weekly or monthly season tickets are also
available. Remember to keep your ticket; it is very rarely asked for
but you might be unlucky! Carriages are one-class and non-
smoking. Check that the train is going the right way and make sure
your stop is shown on the list. There is a shortage of change in Spain
so passengers are requested to tender the right amount whenever
possible.

By train *(RENFE)* First and second class. Most people travel second class but for extra space and comfort, travel first class. Make sure a 'Reserva' (reserved seat) is included in your ticket; if it is not, pay a little extra for one – it's worth it. 'TALGO' and 'TER' are fast trains; 'Expresos' are not. There are 'RENFE' offices in most towns. Buy your ticket there, or at the station.

By coach Private companies usually run the coach services. Coaches often depart from an 'Estación de autobuses' (bus station) and are slightly cheaper than trains.

By air A 'Puente aéreo' (shuttle service) operates between Madrid and Barcelona. Flights depart approximately every hour from either city starting at 7a.m. Last flight from Madrid at 11p.m.; from Barcelona at 10.30p.m.

Changing money

Banks (bancos) are open from 9a.m.–2p.m. every day except Sundays and public holidays. 'Cajas de Ahorros' (savings banks), 'Cambios' and larger hotels also change money.

Alternatively, you may change money at 'El Corte Inglés' department stores. Both 'El Corte Inglés' and 'Galerías Preciados', another large department store, accept foreign currency for purchases.

Shopping

Shops are usually open from 9a.m.–1.30p.m. and from 4.30p.m.–7.30p.m. Department stores are usually open from 10a.m.–8p.m. In summer they close slightly later. Many food shops, and many, but not all large supermarkets, close on Saturday afternoon. In Madrid 'VIPs' (chain stores) are open until later.

Post Offices (Correos) Most post offices are open from 9a.m.-2p.m. but some are also open from 4–6p.m. 'The Oficina Central de Correos' (Central Post Office), Plaza de Cibeles, Madrid, is open from 9a.m.–12p.m. and has a 24 hour telegram service. Stamps can also be bought at 'Estancos' (tobacconists) which keep the same hours as shops.

Food and drink

Eating out You can choose between 'cafeterías', 'bares', snack bars, self-services and restaurants. In restaurants, lunch is served from about 1.30p.m. until 3.30p.m. Dinner is served from 9p.m. to about 11p.m. You may find it difficult to eat earlier but you should be able to get a 'merienda' (snack–ie cake), and 'tapas' (a selection of snacks) are available in bars.

Drinking hours Bars are open all day and close at about 1a.m. Children are allowed in if accompanied by an adult.

Tipping Tip waiters, taxi drivers, hairdressers between 5 and 10%. Give about 5 pesetas to usherettes and cloakroom and public lavatory attendants.

Entertainments

To find out what's on consult the entertainments column (Espectáculos) of daily (morning and evening) newspapers. In Madrid the 'Guía del Ocio' gives detailed information of everything going on in town.

Booking There are no booking agencies. Buy your tickets at the theatre or cinema box office. Matinées start at about 11.30a.m. Evening sessions between 7 and 10p.m.

Museums and art galleries are usually open 10a.m.–5 p.m. in winter and 10a.m.–6p.m. in summer. On Sundays they are open till 2p.m.

1 ✈ **Madrid—Barajas** (NE of city)
Bus every 15 mins (05.10—01.10) to Plaza de la Hispanidad/Plaza de Colón (30 mins) 11km.

2 ✈ **Barcelona** (SW of city)
Train every 15 mins (06.00—22.45) to main station (11 mins) 12km.

3 ✈ **Palma** (N of city)
Bus every 30 mins (06.30—23.00) to Avenida Juan March Ordinas (15 mins) 13km.

4 ✈ **Valencia** (W of city)
Bus to bus station (15 mins) 12km.

5 ✈ **Málaga—Garcia Morato** (NW of city)
Bus to centre 8km.

6 ✈ **Tenerife—Los Rodeos** (SW of Sta Cruz)
Bus to Avenida de Anaga/Edificio Cacitsa (30 mins) 13km.

7 ✈ **Las Palmas—Gando** (SE of city)
Bus every 30 mins (05.30—22.00) to Avenida Maritima (30 mins) 25km.

Español – Inglés

Spanish – English

Para ayudarle a desenvolverse

Palabras básicas

Si se aprende éstos de memoria usted notará que se desenvuelve con más facilidad.

Por favor	Please [*pliis*]
Gracias	Thank you [**zenk***iu*]
Sí	Yes [*yes*]
No	No [*nou*]
Sí, por favor	Yes please [**yes** *pliis*]
No, gracias	No thank you [*nou* **zenk***iu*]
¿Como?	Sorry? [**sorr***i*]
¡Perdone!	Excuse me! [*ex***kius** *mi*]
¡Lo siento!	I'm sorry [*aim* **sorr***i*]
Está bien	That's all right [**dats** *ol rait*]
¡Bien!	Good! [*gud*]
No entiendo	I don't understand [*ai dount ande***stand**]
Hola	Hello [*jelou]
Me llamo _____	My name's _____ [*mai neims _____*]
Adiós	Goodbye [*gud***bai**]
Buenos días	Good morning [*gud* **moon***in*]
Buenas tardes	Good afternoon [*gud afte***nun**]
Buenas tardes (después de las 6)	Good evening [*gud* **iv***inin*]
Buenas noches	Good night [*gud* **nait**]
¿Cómo está?	How are you? [*jau **aa** *yu?*]
Bien, gracias	Fine thanks [**fain** *zanks*]
¡Salud!	Cheers! [*chies*]
Me alegro de haberle conocido	It was nice to meet you [*it uos nais tu* **miit** *yu*]

*Recuerde: la '*j*' tiene que ser <u>muy</u> suave

¿Podría repetirlo, por favor?

Más despacio, por favor
¿Cuánto es?
¿Cuánto valen?

Could you repeat that please?
[*cud yu ri**piit** dat pliis*]

Slower please [***sloua** pliis*]
How much is it? [**jau **mach** is it?*]
How much are they? [**jau **mach**
aa dei?*]

Estructuras clave

Una vez se haya aprendido de memoria estas frases modelo, usted
podrá hacer sus propias frases usando las palabras del diccionario.

¿Dónde está el /banco (más
cercano)/ , por favor?

Where's the /(nearest) bank/
please? [*uers de niarest **bank**
pliis*]

¿Hay un /aparcamiento/ por
aquí?

Is there a /car park/ near here? [*is
dea a **caa** paak nia *jia*]

¿Hay /restaurantes/ por
aquí?

Are there any restaurants near here?
[*aa dea eni **res**torants nia *jia*]

Me gustaría /ir a bañarme/

I'd like to /go swimming/ [*aid laik tu
gou **sui**min*]

¿Le gustaría /ir de compras/ ?

Would you like to /go shopping/ ?
[*u-ud yu laik tu gou **sho**pin*]

¿Tiene un /plano de la ciudad/,
por favor?

Have you got a /streetmap/ please?
[**javyu got e **striit**map pliis*]

¿Tiene /sobres/, por favor?

Have you got any /envelopes/
please? [**javyu got eni **enve**loups
pliis*]

No tengo /cambio/

I haven't got any /change/ [*ai *javent
got eni **cheinch**]

Necesito un /medico/

I need a /doctor/ [*ai niid e **doc**ta*]

Necesito /cheques de
viajero/

I need some /traveller's cheques/ [*ai
niid sam **trav**elers cheks*]

*Recuerde: la 'j' tiene que ser muy suave

Quiero una /habitación/ . por favor	I'd like a /room/ please [aid laik e **rum** pliis]
Quiero /sellos/ , por favor	I'd like some /stamps/ please [aid laik sam **stams** pliis]
¿Quiere un /café/ ?	Would you like a /coffee/ ? [u-ud yu laik e **co**fi]
¿Quiere /bombones/ ?	Would you like some /chocolates/ ? [u-ud yu laik sam **choc**olats]
Podría /llamarme/ un /taxi/ . por favor	Could you /call/ a /taxi/ for me please [cud yu col e **ta**xi fo mi pliis]
¿Cuándo sale el /(próximo) tren/ para /Brighton/ ?	When does the /(next) train/ to /Brighton/ leave? [uen das de next trein tu **brai**ton **liiv**]
¿Cuándo abren (cierran) los /bancos/ ?	When do the /banks/ open (close)? [uen du de banks **ou**pen (**clous**)]
¿Le gusta este /color/ ?	Do you like this /colour/ ? [du yu laik dis **ca**la]
¿Le gustan estos /zapatos/ ?	Do you like these /shoes/ ? [du yu laik diis **shus**]
Me gusta este /estilo/	I like this /style/ [ai laik dis **stail**]
No me gusta esta /forma/	I don't like this /shape/ [ai dount laik dis **sheip**]

Conversaciones

Ahora que se ha aprendido lo básico. y las frases modelo, aquí tiene unos ejemplos de conversaciones en las que puede tomar parte.

Presentaciones

Good morning Mr Baker. This is Pilar Soto	Buenos días, Mr Baker. Le presento a Pilar Soto
How do you do	¡Encantado!
How do you do	¡Encantada!

Si se encuentra con alguien que conoce

Good evening	Buenas tardes
Good evening Mr Allen	Buenas tardes, Mr Allen
How are you?	¿Cómo está?
Fine thanks. And you?	Bien gracias. ¿Y usted?
Fine thanks	Bien gracias

Para encontrar el camino

Excuse me	¡Perdone!
Yes?	¿Sí?
Where's the Hotel Bristol please?	¿Dónde esta el Hotel Bristol, por favor?
Straight on, then right	Todo recto, y a la derecha
Thank you	Gracias
Not at all	De nada

En la estación

A single to Cambridge please	Un billete de ida para Cambridge, por favor
£3.40 (three pounds forty)	3 libras 40
When does the next train leave?	¿Cuándo sale el próximo tren?
At four fifteen	A las 16.15
When does the train arrive in Cambridge?	¿Cuándo llega el tren a Cambridge?
At five thirty-six	A las 17.36
Thank you	Gracias

En el hotel – quiere una habitación

Good afternoon. Can I help you?	Buenas tardes. Desea alguna cosa?
Good afternoon. I'd like a double room please	Buenas tardes. Quiero una habitación doble, por favor
For how many nights	¿Para cuántas noches?
For two nights please	Para dos noches, por favor

Would you like a room with or without bath?	¿Quiere una habitación con baño o sin baño?
With bath please	Con baño, por favor
Yes, that's fine	Sí, está bien
How much is it please?	¿Cuánto es, por favor?
Twenty pounds a night	20 libras la noche
Yes. OK, thanks	Sí. Está bien, gracias

Si compra algo

Good morning. Can I help you?	Buenos días. ¿Desea alguna cosa?
Good morning. Have you got any coffee?	Buenos días. ¿Tiene café?
Yes. How much would you like?	Sí. ¿Cuánto quiere?
I'd like a pound please	Quiero una libra, por favor
Good. Anything else?	Bien. ¿Algo más?
Yes. I'd like some apples please	Sí. Quiero manzanas, por favor
How many?	¿Cuántas?
Four please	4, por favor
OK. Two pounds thirty please	De acuerdo. 2 libras 30, por favor
Thank you	Gracias

Para elegir una cosa

Good afternoon. Can I help you?	Buenos días. ¿Desea aguna cosa?
I'd like a T-shirt please	Quiero una camiseta, por favor
What size would you like?	¿Qué talla quiere?
Twelve please	12, por favor
Do you like this one?	¿Le gusta ésta?
No. I don't like that colour. Have you got a red one?	No. No me gusta este color. ¿La tiene en rojo?
Yes, of course	Sí, por supuesto
How much is it please?	¿Cuánto es, por favor?
Two pounds fifty	2 libras 50
I'll take it. Thank you	Me la llevo. Gracias

Algunas advertencias

El algunos puntos la gramática inglesa es mucho más sencilla que la española. Por ejemplo:

1 Usted y tú, ustedes y vosotros: '*You*'

Sólo existe una forma '*you*' para 'usted' y 'tú', y también para 'vosotros' y 'ustedes'.

2 ¿Masculino o femenino?

No hay diferencia entre nombre masculino y femenino en inglés, y por lo tanto el artículo no varía.
El artículo definido es '*the*' (el/la/los/las): *the ticket* (el billete)
the suitcases (las maletas)
El artículo indefinido es '*a*' (un/una), pero '*an*' antes de una palabra que comience por vocal: *a ticket* (une billete)
an apple (una manzana)

3 Plural

El plural de la mayoría de los sustantivos en inglés se forma simplemente añadiendo una '*s*' al singular. Los plurales que no siguen esta regla se indican del siguiente modo:
address –es (dirección)
baby –ies (bebé)
knife –ves (cuchillo)
sheep/sheep (pl) (oveja) donde el singular y el plural tienen la misma forma.

4 Adjetivos

Los adjetivos son invariables: no tienen género ni número.
Por ejemplo:
a red car (un coche rojo)

a <u>red</u> shirt (una camisa roja)
<u>red</u> umbrellas (paraguas rojos)
<u>red</u> T-shirts (camisetas rojas)

5 Comparaciones

Se pueden formar comparaciones añadiendo '*er*' a la terminación de los adjetivos de una o dos sílabas.

I'd like something bigger	Quiero algo más grande
I'd like something heavier	Quiero algo más pesado

Nótese que '*big*' se convierte en '*bigger*' (con adjetivos de un sílaba la consonante – en este caso '*g*' – se dobla); '*heavy*' se convierte en '*heavier*' (los adjetivos que terminan en '*–y*' cambian la '*y*' en '*i*' antes de '*–er*').

'*More*' (más): Si un adjetivo tiene mas de dos sílabas, el comparativo se forma con '*more*' (más):

I'd like something more comfortable	Quiero algo más cómodo

'*Less*' (menos) puede emplearse delante de todos los adjetivos:

I'd like something less expensive	Quiero algo menos caro

Comparativos irregulares:

good – better	bueno – más bueno/mejor
bad – worse	malo – más malo/peor
much/many – more	mucho/muchos – más
little – less	poco – menos

6 Notas sobre cantidad

El diccionario le permitirá precisar cantidades exactas. Por ejemplo, si busca 'cerilla' (*match*) también encontrará 'una caja de cerillas' (*a box of matches*). Así que usted podría decir:

I'd like some matches please	Quiero cerillas, por favor (general)
I'd like a box of matches please	Quiero una caja de cerillas, por favor (exacto)

La cantidad también se puede precisar exactamente en términos de

volumen o peso, por ejemplo, cuatro galones de gasolina, una libra
de tomates etc. Vea Equivalencias, p.288

Recuerde estos seis 'términos de cantidad' y será capaz de pedir
casi cualquier cosa:

a bottle of /beer/	una botella de /cerveza/
a glass of /milk/	un vaso de /leche/
a packet of /cigarettes/	un paquete de /cigarrillos/
a piece of /cake/	un trozo de /pastel/
a slice of /ham/	una cortada de /jamón/
a tin of /tomatoes/	una lata de /tomates/

7 Verbos

En este diccionario sólo encontrará generalmente la forma del
infinitivo del verbo, por ejemplo: *'close'* (cerrar)

8 Tener, o poseer algo: *'Have got'*

Cuando el verbo *'have'* significa 'tener o poseer algo', en inglés se le
suele añadir la partícula *'got'* (especialmente en Inglaterra).
Entonces el verbo se usa en la forma abreviada, pero la partícula
'got' no cambia.

I've got an appointment	Tengo una cita
I haven't got enough money	No tengo bastante dinero
Have you got the key?	¿Tiene la llave?

¿Como pronunciar el inglés?

Las consonantes

k, ch, p, t, m, n, f, l se pronuncian de una forma igual a la del castellano

ll	sueno como 'l' sencilla
b, v	hay que distinguirlas claramente, para evitar confusiones
h	es aspirada, se parece a la 'j' castellana, pero es mucho más suave
g	en algunos casos se pronuncia como la 'g' castellana cuando va seguida de 'a', 'o', 'u', por ej. en 'go' (ir) en otros, se pronuncia como 'ch' suave, por ej. en 'gin' (ginebra), George (Jorge)
j	Equivale a una 'ch' suave, por ej. 'jam' (mermelada), John (Juan)
th	suena como 'd' en palabras como 'that' (eso) suena como 'z' en palabras como 'three' (tres)
c	equivale siempre a 'k' delante de 'a', 'o', 'u' se pronuncia como 's' delante de 'e', 'i'
r, rr	no hay diferencia entre ellas y su sonido es similar al de la 'r' castellana intervocalica, como en 'pero', por ejemplo
w, wh	suenan como la 'u' castellana
–ing	(terminación) se pronuncia como 'in' (pero nasal)
sch	equivale a 'sk', por ejemplo en 'school' (escuela)
qu	equivale a 'ku', por ejemplo 'square' (plaza)

Las vocales

Las vocales ingleses son mucho mas complicadas para los españoles, porque cada una de ellas varia de sonido en diferentes palabras, por ejemplo:

Vocal inglesa:		Ejemplo:	Pronunciación:	como en:
a		man (hombre)	[a]	cama
a		father (padre)	[a]	parte (pero más larga)
a		*cake (pastel)		
pero también:	ai	main (principal)	[ei]	aceite
	ay	day (día)		
air		hair (pelo)		
pero también:	ear	wear (llevar)	[er]	hacer
	ere	there (allí)		
e		bed (cama)		
pero también:	ea	head (cabeza)	[e]	leche
	u	bury (enterrar)		
ee		meet (encontrarse)	[i]	sí
ear		hear (oír)	[ir]	salir
pero también:	ere	here (aquí)		
		thin (delgado)	[i]	inglés
		time (tiempo)	[ay]	hay
o		not (no)	[o]	los
o		note (nota)	[ou]	yo + uso
pero también:	oa	coat (abrigo)		
o		for (por/para)		
pero también:	au	Paul (Pablo)		
	aw	law (ley)	[o]	por
	a	fall (caer)		
	ou	four (cuatro)		
oo		moon (luna)	[u]	útil

* la 'e' final no se pronuncia pero hace que la vocal anterior se diptongue

Vocal inglesa:		Ejemplo:	Pronunciación:	como en:
oo		foot (pie)		
pero también:	u	full (lleno)	[u]	urgente (pe
	ou	would (gustaría)		más corta)
u		uniform (uniforme)		
pero también:	iew	view (vista)	[yu]	Yugoslavia
u		but (pero)	[a]	día
pero también:	o	love (amor)		
u		burn (quemar)		
pero también:	ear	learn (aprender)		gustaría (pe
	or	world (mundo)	[a]	
	er	her (la/su)		más larga)
	ir	girl (chica)		
ou		mouse (ratón)	[au]	autobús
oy		boy (chico)	[oy]	voy
pero también:	oi	spoil (estropear)		

Abreviaturas

Abbreviations

(adj)	adjetivo	adjective
(adv)	adverbio	adverb
(n)	nombre (sustantivo)	noun
(prep)	preposición	preposition
(pron)	pronombre	pronoun
(vb)	verbo	verb
(m)	masculino	masculine
(f)	femenino	feminine
(s)	singular	singular
(pl)	plural	plural
(infml)	familiar	informal
(tdmk)	marca de fábrica	trademark
(eg)	por ejemplo	for example
(etc)	etcétera	et cetera

Diccionario
A – Z
Dictionary

NB When looking up a Spanish word please note that in the Spanish alphabet '**ch**' follows '**c**', '**ll**' follows '**l**', and '**ñ**' follows '**n**'

A

a
a /la estación/ to /the station/
a /las siete y media/ at /seven-thirty/
a menudo often
abajo (posición) below (adv)
abajo (= ascensor) down
¿va Vd. abajo? are you going down?
abajo (piso) downstairs
abeja bee
picadura de abeja bee sting
abierto open (adj)
abogado lawyer
abrebotellas (m) abrebotellas (mpl)
bottle-opener
abrelatas (m) abrelatas (mpl) tin
opener
abrigo coat, overcoat
abril (m) April
abrir open (vb)
abrochar fasten
abstemio teetotal
abuela grandmother
abuelo grandfather
aburrido boring, dull
estar aburrido bored (to be bored)
estoy aburrido I'm bored
acantilado cliff
accidente (m) accident
aceite (m) (motor) oil (lubricating)
aceite (m) diesel derv, diesel oil
un bidón de aceite a can of oil
filtro de aceite oil filter
bomba de aceite oil pump
aceite (m) (cocina) oil (salad)
aceite de oliva olive oil
aceite vegetal vegetable oil
aceite (m) bronceador suntan oil
aceitoso oily
aceituna olive
aceituna negra black olive
aceituna verde green olive
aceptar accept
acera pavement

acerca about (= concerning)
acerca de /su problema/ about /your
problem/
acero steel
acero inoxidable stainless steel
/cubertería/ de acero inoxidable
stainless steel /cutlery/
acertijo puzzle
aclarado rinse (n) (clothes)
aclarar clarify
acompañante escort (n)
acompañar escort (vb)
acondicionador (m) conditioner (for
hair)
un frasco de acondicionador a bottle
of hair conditioner
aconsejar un descanso advise a rest
acordarse remember
me acuerdo /del nombre/
I remember /the name/
no me acuerdo I don't remember
acortar shorten
actor (m) actor
actriz (f) actrices (pl) actress -es
acuarela watercolour
acuerdo (convenio) agreement
estar de acuerdo agree
estoy de acuerdo I agree
no estar de acuerdo con disagree
with
no estoy de acuerdo con /usted/ I
disagree with /you/
acuerdo (disposición) arrangement
adaptador (m) adaptor plug
adelantado
por adelantado in advance
reserva por adelantado advance
booking
adelantar overtake
adelanto advance (advance of money)
adiós goodbye
adivinar guess (vb)
adjuntar enclose
adjunto
le mandamos adjunto please find
enclosed
administrativo office worker

adolescente (m&f) teenager
adorno ornament
aduana (s) Customs (pl)
  impreso de declaración de aduana
  customs declaration form
  pasar mercancías por la aduana
  clear goods through Customs
adulto adult
  sólo adultos adults only
advertencia warning
advertir warn
aéreo
  carta aérea air letter
  correo aéreo airmail
  línea aérea airline
aeromodelo model aeroplane
aeropuerto airport
  autobús (m) **servicio aeropuerto**
  airport bus -es
aerosol (m) aerosol
afeitado shave (n)
afeitar
  cuchilla de afeitar razor blade
  máquina de afeitar eléctrica electric
  razor
  maquinilla de afeitar razor
  un paquete de cuchillas de afeitar a
  packet of razor blades
afeitar shave (vb)
  brocha de afeitar shaving brush -es
  crema de afeitar shaving cream
  un tubo de crema de afeitar a tube
  of shaving cream
  jabón (m) **de afeitar** shaving soap
  una barra de jabón de afeitar a stick
  of shaving soap
afición (f) hobby -ies
aficionado fan (n) (sports)
afilado sharp (of things)
afilar sharpen
afortunado lucky
  ser afortunado be lucky
  es afortunado he's lucky
  afortunadamente fortunately
agencia agency -ies
  agencia de apuestas betting shop
agente (m) agent

agente (m) **de la propriedad** estate
agent
agitar shake (vb)
agosto August
agotado sold out
agradable nice, pleasant
**agradecerle / / ** thank you for / /(vb)
  le agradezco su hospitalidad thank
  you for your hospitality
agradecido grateful
agrietado cracked
  está agrietado it's cracked
agua water
  agua caliente hot water
  agua corriente running water
  agua destilada distilled water
  agua dulce fresh water (ie not salt)
  agua fría cold water
  agua potable drinking water
agua de colonia eau-de-Cologne, toilet
water
  una botella de agua de colonia a
  bottle of eau-de-Cologne
agua mineral mineral water
  agua mineral con gas fizzy mineral
  water
  agua mineral sin gas still mineral
  water
  una botella de agua mineral a bottle
  of mineral water
  un vaso de agua mineral a glass of
  mineral water
aguacate (m) avocado
aguarrás (m) turpentine
aguja needle
  agujas (fpl) **de punto** knitting needles
aguja stylus
  diamante diamond
  zafiro sapphire
agujero hole
ahora now
ahorrar save (money)
ahumado smoked (of fish & meat etc)
  /jamón/ ahumado smoked /ham/
ahuyentador (m) **de moscas** fly spray
aire (m) air
  aire (m) **acondicionado** air
  conditioning

aire fresco some fresh air
presión (f) **de aire** air pressure
piscina al aire libre open-air swimming pool
restaurante (m) **al aire libre** open-air restaurant
ajedrez (m) chess (s)
  jugar a ajedrez play chess
  una partida de ajedrez a game of chess
ajo garlic
ajustar adjust
ala wing (bird or plane)
alambre (m) wire
  un trozo de alambre a piece of wire
alargar lengthen
alarma (f) **de incendios** fire alarm
albaricoque (m) apricot
albergue (m) hostel (= youth hostel)
  albergue (m) **de juventud** youth hostel
alcachofa artichoke
alcanzar reach (= attain) (vb)
alcohol (m) alcohol
  alcohol (m) **metilado** methylated spirit
  una botella de alcohol metilado a bottle of methylated spirits
alcohólico alcoholic (adj)
alérgico allergic
  soy alérgico /a la penicilina/ I'm allergic /to penicillin/
aleta (coche) wing (car)
aletas (fpl) (natación) flippers (pl)
  un par de aletas a pair of flippers
alfabeto alphabet
alfarería pottery (substance)
alfiler (m) pin
alfombra carpet
alfombrilla mat, rug
  alfombrilla de baño bath mat
  alfombrilla de puerta door mat
algo something
  algo de beber something to drink
  algo de comer something to eat
  algo (negación, pregunta) anything
  ¿algo más? anything else?
algodón (m) cotton

un ovillo de algodón a reel of cotton
algodón (m) **hidrófilo** cotton wool
alguien someone, somebody
alheña henna
alicates (mpl) pliers (pl)
  unos alicates a pair of pliers
aliento breath
  sin aliento out of breath
aliño dressing (salad dressing)
alistarse enroll
allá
  más allá (de) beyond (prep)
  más allá /de la estación/ beyond /the station/
allí there
  allí over there
  por allí that way
almidón (m) starch -es (n)
almidonar starch (vb)
almohada pillow
  funda de almohada pillow case
almorzar have lunch
almuerzo lunch -es
  almuerzo para llevar packed lunch
alojamiento accommodation
alquilar hire (vb), rent
  alquilar /un chalet/ rent /a villa/
alquiler (m) rent (n) (payment)
alrededor around
  alrededor /de la mesa/ around /the table/
alrededor de (aproximadamente) about (= approximately)
alternativa alternative (n)
alto (cosas) high
  marea alta high water
  sillita alta high chair
alto (persona) tall
altura height
alud (m) avalanche
alumno pupil
  alumno de auto-escuela learner (driver)
ama de casa housewife -ves
amabilidad (f) kindness -es
amable kind (adj) (= friendly)
  es muy amable de su parte it's very

kind of you
amanecer (m) *dawn* (n), *sunrise*
amar *love* (vb)
amargo (ácido) *bitter* (adj)
amargo (agrio) *sour*
amarillo *yellow*
ambos/los dos *both*
ambulancia *ambulance*
amiga (también novia) *girlfriend*
amigdalitis (f) *tonsillitis*
amigo (también novio) *boyfriend*
amigo (también **amiga** (f) (en general) *friend*
  amigo por correspondencia *pen friend*
amistoso *friendly*
  poco amistoso *unfriendly*
amor (m) *love* (n)
  hacer el amor *make love*
amoratado *bruised*
amortiguador (m) *shock absorber* (car)
ampliar *enlarge*
ampolla *blister*
amueblado *furnished*
  /piso/ amueblado *furnished /flat/*
amueblar *furnish*
añadir *add*
analgésico *painkiller*
ancho *wide*
anchura *width*
ancla *anchor*
andando *walking*
  ir andando *do some walking*
andar *walk* (vb)
andén (m) **/ocho/** *platform /eight/*
anémico *anaemic*
  estoy anémico *I'm anaemic*
anestésico *anaesthetic* (n)
anfitrión (m) *host*
anfitriona *hostess -es*
anillo de matrimonio *wedding ring*
animal (m) *animal*
  animal (m) **doméstico** *pet*
aniversario *anniversary -ies*
  aniversario de boda *wedding anniversary*
año *year*
  el año pasado *last year*

el año próximo *next year*
este año *this year*
tiene /seis/ años de edad *he is /six/ years old*
anoche *last night*
anochecer (m) *dusk, sunset*
anorak (m) *anorak*
ante (m) *suede* (n)
  /chaqueta/ de ante *suede /jacket/*
antena *aerial*
antes de *before* (prep)
  antes de /salir/ *before /leaving/*
  antes del /desayuno/ *before /breakfast/*
anti-adherente *nonstick*
  /sartén/ (m) **anti-adherente** *nonstick /frying-pan/*
antibiótico *antibiotic*
antichoque *shockproof* (eg of watch)
anticonceptivos (mpl) *contraceptives* (pl)
  la Píldora *the Pill*
  un paquete de preservativos *a packet of sheaths* (=Durex)
anticongelante (m) *antifreeze*
  un bidón de anticongelante *a can of antifreeze*
anticuado *old-fashioned*
antigüedad (f) *antique* (n)
  tienda de antigüedades *antique shop*
antiséptico *antiseptic*
  pomada antiséptica *antiseptic cream*
  un tubo de pomada antiséptica *a tube of antiseptic (cream)*
anual *annual*
anualmente *yearly*
anunciar *advertise*
anuncio *advertisement, notice*
  tablón (m) **de anuncios** *notice board*
apagado (of light etc)
apagar *switch off, turn off*
aparato *gadget*
  aparato para sordos *hearing aid*
aparcamiento *car park*
  zona de aparcamiento *lay-by*
aparcar *park* (vb)
  prohibido aparcar *no parking*

apellido *surname*
  apellido de soltera *née*
apendicitis (f) *appendicitis*
aperitivo *aperitif*
apio *celery*
  una cabeza de apio *a head of celery*
apostar *bet (vb)*
aprender /inglés/ *learn /English/*
apretado *tight*
apretar *press (vb) (eg button)*
apropiado *suitable*
aproximadamente *roughly
  (=approximately)*
apuesta *bet (n)*
aquí *here*
  por aquí *this way*
araña *spider*
arañar *scratch (vb)*
arañazo *scratch -es (n)*
árbitro *umpire*
árbol (m) *tree*
arena *sand*
arenoso *sandy*
arenque (m) *herring*
arma de fuego *gun*
armario *cupboard*
armario (ropa) *wardrobe*
arpón (m) *harpoon gun*
arquitecto *architect*
arrancar *start (vb) (eg a car)*
  no arranca *it won't start*
arreglar *fix (vb), mend*
arriba (posición) *up*
arriba (piso) *upstairs*
arroz (m) *rice*
arrugar *crease (vb)*
  ¿se arruga? *does it crease?*
artículos (mpl) de papelería *stationery*
artículos (mpl) libres de impuestos
  duty-free goods (pl)
artificial *artificial*
  respiración (f) artificial *artificial
  respiration*
artista (m&f) *artist*
asa *handle (eg of a case)*
asar *roast (vb)*
  asar a la parrilla *grill (vb)*

pollo asado *roast chicken*
ascensor (m) *lift (n) (=elevator)*
asegurar *insure*
  asegurar /mi vida/ *insure /my life/*
  ¿está asegurado (m)
  asegurada (f)? *are you insured?*
asesinato *murder (vb)*
asesinato *murder (n)*
así que *so (=therefore)*
asiento *seat*
  al final *at the back*
  al lado de la ventanilla *by the
  window*
  delante *at the front*
  en el centro *in the middle*
  en el teatro *at the theatre*
  en el tren *on a train*
  en la sección de fumadores *in the
  smoking section (aeroplane)*
  en la sección de no fumadores *in
  the non-smoking section (aeroplane)*
  en un autocar *on a coach*
  en un departamento de fumadores
  in a smoker (train)
  en un departamento de no
  fumadores *in a non-smoker (train)*
  junto a la salida *by the exit*
asistir *attend*
  asistir a una ceremonia /católica/
  attend a /Catholic/ service
asma (m) *asthma*
áspero (de una persona) *coarse (of
  person)*
áspero (no suave) *rough (=not smooth)*
aspirador (m) *vacuum cleaner*
aspiradora *hoover (tdmk)*
aspirina *aspirin*
  una botella de aspirinas *a bottle of
  aspirins*
  una caja de aspirinas *a packet of
  aspirins*
asqueroso *disgusting*
ataque (m) *attack (n)*
  un ataque de / / *an attack of / /*
atar *tie (vb)*
ataúd (m) *coffin*
aterrizado *landed (of a plane)*

atlas (m) *atlas -es*

atractivo *attractive*

atrapar / / *trap (vb)*

atrás
 hacia atrás *backwards*

atropellar / / *run over / /*

au pair (f) *au pair*

auriculares (mpl) *headphones (pl)*
 un par de auriculares *a pair of headphones*

ausente *away (absent)*

auténtico *genuine*

autobús (m) *bus -es*
 el autobús para / / *the bus for / /*
 en autobús *by bus*
 estación (f) **de autobús** *bus station*
 parada (f) **de autobús** *bus stop*

autocar (m) *coach -es*
 en autocar *by coach*

autolavado *car wash*

automático *automatic*

automovilista (m&f) *motorist*

autopista *motorway*

autor (m) *author*

autoridades (fpl) *authorities (pl)*

autostop
 hacer autostop *hitchhike*

avergonzarse
 estar avergonzado (de / /) *be ashamed (of / /)*
 estoy avergonzado de /él/ *I'm ashamed of /him/*

avería *breakdown (car)*

aves (fpl) *poultry*
 pato *duck*
 pavo *turkey*
 pollo *chicken*

avión (m) *aeroplane, plane*
 por avión *by air*
 en avión *by plane*

avispa *wasp*
 picadura de avispa *wasp sting*

ayer *yesterday*

ayuda *help (n)*
 ayuda doméstica *domestic help*

ayudar *help (vb)*

ayuntamiento *town hall*

azafata *stewardess -es (plane or boat)*

azúcar (m) *sugar*
 una cucharada de azúcar *a spoonful of sugar*
 terrón (m) **de azúcar** *sugar lump*

azul *blue*

B

babero *bib*

baca *roof rack*

bacalao *cod*

bacina *bedpan*

bacón (m) *bacon*

badminton (m) *badminton*
 jugar a badminton *play badminton*
 un partido de badminton *a game of badminton*

bahía *bay (=part of sea)*

bailar *dance (vb)*
 ir a bailar *go dancing*

bailarín (m) **bailarina** (f) *dancer*

baile (m) *ball, dance*
 sala de baile *dance hall*
 salón (m) **de baile** *ballroom*

bajar en / / *get off at / /*

bajo *low (=not high)*
 marea baja *low water*

bajo (no fuerte) *low (=not loud)*

bajo (grados) *minus*

bajo (estatura) *short (people)*

balanza (s) *scales (pl) (=weighing machine)*

balcón (m) *balcony -ies*

ballet (m) *ballet*
 bailarín (m) **bailarina** (f) *ballet dancer*

balón *football (=ball)*

baloncesto *basketball (=game)*
 jugar al baloncesto *play basketball*
 un partido de baloncesto *a game of basketball*

balsa *raft*
 balsa salvavidas *life raft*

banco *bank*

bandeja *tray*

bandera *flag*

banqueta *stool*

bañador (m) bathing trunks (pl)
bañar bathe (eyes etc)
bañarse have a swim, bathe
  ir a bañarse go swimming
baño (eg de mar) swim (n)
baño (en bañera) bath
  alfombra de baño bath mat
  baño turco Turkish bath
  gorro de baño swimming cap
  tomar un baño have a bath
bar (m) bar (= for drinks)
bar (m) (para comidas) canteen (eating place)
barato cheap
barbacoa barbecue
barbilla chin
barco boat
barco de remo rowing boat
  barco de vela sailing dinghy
  en barco by boat
barniz (m) varnish -es(n)
barnizar varnish (vb) (eg boat)
barra loaf -ves (of bread)
  una barra grande a large loaf
  una barra pequeña a small loaf
barrer sweep (vb)
barrera barrier
barril (m) barrel
  un barril de / / a barrel of / /
barrio periférico suburb
barro mud
bastante enough
  bastante dinero enough money
  bastante rápido fast enough
bastante quite
bastón (m) walking stick
basura litter, rubbish
basurero dustman/dustmen (pl)
batería battery -ies (car)
  tengo la batería descargada I've got a flat battery
batidora mixer (of food)
batín (m) dressing gown
baúl (m) trunk (for luggage)
bebé (m) baby -ies
beber drink (vb)
bebida drink (n)

bebida alcohólica spirits (pl) (= alcohol)
bebida no alcohólica soft drink
beca grant (for studies)
beige beige
berenjena aubergine
besar kiss (vb)
beso kiss -es (n)
betún (m) shoe polish
biberón (m) feeding bottle
Biblia Bible
biblioteca library -ies
bicicleta/bici (infml) bicycle/bike (infml)
  farol (m) **de bicicleta** bicycle lamp
bien (adv) well (= all right)
  ¡bien hecho! well done! (congratulation)
bien (adj) fine (adj) (= OK)
  ¡bien gracias! fine thanks!
bienvenida welcome (n)
  dar la bienvenida welcome (vb)
  bienvenido a / / welcome to / /
bigote (m) moustache
bikini (m) bikini
billar (ms) billiards
  jugar al billar play billiards
  una partida de billar a game of billiards
billete (m) (precio) fare
  billete de autobús bus fare
  billete de avión air fare
  billete de ida single fare
  billete de ida y vuelta return fare
  billete de tren train fare
  billete entero full fare
  medio billete half fare
billete (m) (dinero) note (= money)
  billete de /cinco/ libras /five/ pound note
billete (m) (eg de avión) ticket
  billete de grupo group ticket
  billete de ida single
  billete de ida y vuelta return ticket
  billete de niño child's ticket
  billete de primera clase first class ticket
  billete de segunda clase second

class ticket
billete de temporada *season ticket*
biombo *screen (=movable partition)*
bistec (m) *steak*
  muy hecho *well-done*
  no muy hecho *medium*
  poco hecho *rare*
blanco (piel) *fair (adj) (skin)*
blanco *white*
blando *soft (=not hard)*
bloc (m) **de dibujo** *sketchpad*
blusa *blouse*
boca *mouth*
bocadillo *sandwich*
boceto *sketch -es (n)*
boda *wedding*
bodega *cellar*
boina *beret*
bolera *bowling alley*
bolígrafo *ballpoint pen, biro (tdmk)*
bollo *bun (bread)*
bolos (mpl) *bowling (= ten pin bowling)*
bolsa *bag*
  bolsa de compras *carrier bag*
  bolsa de cuerda *string bag*
  bolsa de papel *paper bag*
  bolsa de plástico *plastic bag*
  bolsa de agua caliente *hot-water bottle*
bolsillo *pocket*
  edición (f) **de bolsillo** *paperback*
bolso de compras *shopping bag*
bolso de mano *handbag*
bomba (explosivo) *bomb*
bomba (a presión) *pump*
  bomba de agua *water pump*
bombero *fireman /firemen (pl)*
bomberos
  coche (m) **de bomberos** *fire engine*
  servicio de bomberos *fire brigade*
bombilla *bulb (= light bulb)*
  40/60/100/200 watios
  40/60/100/200 watt
bombilla *light bulb*
  bombilla del faro *headlamp bulb*
  /cuarenta/ watios */forty/ watt*
bombín (m) **de bicicleta** *bicycle pump*
bombones (mpl) *chocolates*

una caja de bombones *a box of chocolates*
bonito *pretty*
bordado *embroidery*
borracho *drunk (adj) (=not sober)*
borrador (m) *eraser*
bosque (m) (selva) *forest*
bosque (m) (grupo de árboles) *wood (group of trees)*
botas (fpl) *boots (pl)*
  botas de agua *rubber boots, Wellingtons*
  botas de esquí *ski-boots*
  un par de botas *a pair of boots*
bote (m) *dinghy -ies*
  bote de goma *rubber dinghy*
  bote salvavidas *lifeboat*
botella *bottle*
  una botella de / / *a bottle of / /*
botiquín (m) *first aid kit*
botón (m) *button*
boxeador (m) *boxer*
boxeo *boxing*
  pelea de boxeo *boxing match*
boya *buoy*
bragas (fpl) *pants (pl)*
  unas bragas *a pair of pants*
brazo *arm*
brécoles (mpl) *broccoli*
brida *bridle*
bridge (m) *bridge (=card game)*
  una partida de bridge *a game of bridge*
brillante *shiny*
brillantina *hair oil*
  un frasco de brillantina *a bottle of hair oil*
brocha *paintbrush -es*
  brocha de afeitar *shaving brush*
broche (m) *brooch -es*
  broche de plata *silver brooch*
bronceado (n) *suntan*
bronceado (adj) *suntanned*
brújula *compass -es*
bucear *diving*
  bucear con botellas de oxígeno *go scuba-diving*

bucear con equipo *go skin-diving*
botella de oxígeno para bucear *aqualung*
ir a bucear *go diving*
buceo (n) *skin diving*
Budista (m&f) *Buddhist*
bueno (tiempo) *fine (adj) (of weather)*
hace buen tiempo *it's fine*
bueno (personas, cosas) *good*
bufanda *scarf -ves*
bufanda de /seda/ */silk/ scarf*
bujía *sparking plug (car)*
bulto (en el cuerpo) *lump (body)*
bultos (mpl) **de mano** *hand luggage*
bungalow (m) *bungalow*
burro *donkey*
buscar *look for*
buscar /mi pasaporte/ *look for /my passport/*
búsqueda *search -es (n)*
butano *butane, calor gas*
buzón (m) *letter box -es, postbox -es*

C

caballo *horse*
caballo de carreras *racehorse*
carreras (fpl) **de caballos** *horse racing*
cabaña *hut*
cabeza *head (part of body)*
dolor (m) **de cabeza** *headache*
cabina telefónica *call box -es*
cable (m) *cable (n)*
cabo *cape (eg Cape of Good Hope)*
cabra *goat*
cacahuete (m) *peanut*
un paquete de cacahuetes *a packet of peanuts*
cacao *cocoa*
una taza de cacao *a cup of cocoa*
cacerola *saucepan*
cachemir (m) *cashmere*
suéter (m) **de cachemir** *cashmere sweater*

cada (inv) *every, each*
cada día *every day*
cada uno /de los niños/ *each /of the children/*
cadena *chain*
cadera *hip*
caducar *expire (= run out)*
/mi visado/ está caducado */my visa/ has expired*
caer *fall (vb)*
me caí por las escaleras *I fell downstairs*
café (m) *café*
café (m) (bebida) *coffee*
café con leche *white coffee*
café descafeinado *decaffeinated coffee*
café (m) **exprés** *espresso coffee*
café hecho en cafetera *percolated coffee*
café instantáneo *instant coffee*
café molido *ground coffee*
café sólo *black coffee*
una cafetera llena *a pot of coffee*
una taza de café *a cup of coffee*
cafeína *caffeine*
cafetera *coffeepot*
cafetera exprés *percolator*
caída *fall (n)*
caja *box -es*
una caja de / / *a box of / /*
caja (para pagar) *cash desk*
caja fuerte *safe (n)*
cajero *cashier*
cajón (m) *drawer*
calambre (m) (en la pierna etc) *cramp (n)*
calambre (m) (descarga eléctrica) *electric shock*
calcetines (mpl) *socks (pl)*
calcetines cortos *short socks, ankle socks*
calcetines de /lana/ */woollen/ socks*
calcetines largos *long socks*
un par de calcetines *a pair of socks*
calculadora *calculator*
calculadora de bolsillo *pocket*

calculator
calcular *calculate*
  calcular /el coste/ *calculate /the cost/*
calefacción (f) *heating*
  calefacción (f) **central** *central heating*
calendario *calendar*
calentador (m) *heater*
calentar *warm* (vb)
calidad (f) *quality -ies*
  de mala calidad *poor (poor quality)*
caliente (alta temperatura) *hot*
  está caliente *it's hot (of things/food)*
caliente (templado) *warm (adj)*
calmante (m) *sedative*
calor (m) *heat (n)*
  hace calor *it's hot (of the weather)*
  ola de calor *heat wave*
  tengo calor *I'm hot*
calorías (fpl) *calories (pl)*
calvo *bald*
  es calvo *he's bald*
calzoncillos (mpl) *underpants (pl) (for men)*
  unos calzoncillos *a pair of underpants*
callado *quiet*
calle (f) *street*
  calle principal *main street*
callista (m&f) *chiropodist*
callo *corn (eg on a toe)*
cama *bed*
  cama doble *double bed*
  cama sencilla *single bed*
  en la cama *in bed*
  hacer la cama *make the bed*
  irse a la cama *go to bed*
cama plegable *camp bed*
camafeo *cameo (brooch)*
cámara de aire *inner tube (tyre)*
cámara fotográfica *camera*
  cámara de cine *cine camera*
  cámara de 35mm *35 mm camera*
camarera (hotel) *chambermaid*
camarera (restaurante) *waitress -es*
camarero (avión, barco) *steward (plane or boat)*

camarero (restaurante) *waiter*
camarote (m) *cabin*
  camarote de /cuatro/ literas */four/ berth cabin*
  lancha con camarotes *cabin cruiser*
cambiar *change (vb), exchange*
  cambiar /este suéter/ *exchange /this sweater/*
  cambiar /la rueda/ *change /the tyre/*
  quiero cambiar /unos cheques de viajero/ *I'd like to change /some traveller's cheques/*
cambiarse (de ropa) *change (vb) (clothes)*
cambio (reforma) *change (n) (= alteration)*
cambio (dinero) *change (n) (=money)*
camilla *stretcher*
camino *way (n) (to a place)*
  camino de acceso *drive (n) (=entrance)*
camión (m) *lorry -ies*
camionero (m) *lorry driver*
camisa *shirt*
  camisa de /algodón/ */cotton/ shirt*
  camisa de diario *casual shirt*
  camisa de manga corta *short-sleeved shirt*
  camisa de vestir *formal shirt*
  una camisa que no necesita plancha *a drip-dry shirt*
camiseta (ropa sport) *T-shirt*
camiseta (ropa interior) *vest*
  camiseta de algodón *cotton vest*
  camiseta de lana *woollen vest*
camisón (m) *nightdress -es*
campamento *camp (n)*
  campamento de vacaciones *holiday camp*
camping (m) *camping*
  ir de camping *go camping*
camping (m) (lugar) *campsite, caravan site*
campo (el campo) *country (=countryside)*
campo (un campo) *field (n)*
canal (m) *canal*

canal (m) **de televisión** television channel

cancelación (f) cancellation

cancelado cancelled

cancelar /mi vuelo/ cancel /my flight/

canción (f) song

canción folklórica folk song

canción pop pop song

candado padlock (n)

cangrejo crab

canoa canoe (n)

canoso (pelo) grey (=grey-haired)

cansado (persona) tired

cansado (que causa) tiring

cantante (m&f) singer

cantar sing

caña de pescar rod (=fishing rod)

caoba mahogany

capa cape (=cloak)

capitán (m) captain

capucha hood (of a garment)

caqui khaki (colour)

cara face

caramelo sweet (n) (=confectionery)

caravana caravan

aparcamiento de caravana caravan site

caravana de /cuatro/ camas /four/-berth caravan

carbón (m) coal

carbón (m) **de leña** charcoal

cárcel (f) gaol, prison

en la cárcel in gaol

carey

de carey tortoiseshell (adj)

cargar load (vb)

carnaval (m) carnival

carne (f) meat

carne de vaca beef

carnero mutton

cerdo pork

cordero lamb

fiambre (m) cold meat

carnet (m) **de conducir** driving licence

carnet internacional de conducir international driving licence

carnet (m) **de identidad** identity card

carnicería butcher's

caro expensive

servicio urgente express service

carrera (competición) race (n) (=contest)

caballo de carreras racehorse

carrera de caballos horse race

carrera de coches motor race

circuito de carreras racecourse

hacer una carrera race (vb)

carrete (m) (fotos) cartridge (=film cartridge)

carrete (m) (de hilo) reel (of cotton)

carretera road

carretera de circunvalación ring road

carretera de dos carriles dual carriageway

carretera principal main road

carretera secundaria side road

carril (m) (tráfico) lane (=traffic lane)

carrito trolley (=luggage trolley)

carta (mapa) chart (=sea map)

carta (correspondencia) letter (correspondence)

carta certificada registered letter

carta por correo aéreo air-letter

carta urgente express letter

carta de vinos wine list

cartas (fpl) cards (pl)

una baraja a pack of cards

una partida de cartas a game of cards

carta verde 'green card' (car insurance)

cartel (m) poster

cartera wallet

cartilla de propiedad logbook (car)

cartón (m) **de /cigarrillos/** carton of /cigarettes/ (=200)

cartucho cartridge (for gun)

casa (hogar) home

en casa (en el hogar) at home

ir a casa go home

casa (edificio) house

en casa (dentro de casa) indoors

casa de labranza farmhouse

casado married

cascanueces (m) **cascanueces** (mpl)
nutcrackers (pl)
casco *crash helmet*
casi *almost*
casillero *locker*
  casillero de consigna *left-luggage*
  locker
casino *casino*
casita de campo *cottage*
caso *case*
  en caso de /incendio/ *in case of*
  /fire/
caspa (s) *dandruff (s)*
cassette (f) *cassette*
  cassette grabada *pre-recorded*
  cassette
cassette (f) (aparato) *cassette player,*
  cassette recorder
castaña *chestnut*
castaño *maroon (colour)*
castigar *punish*
castigo *punishment*
castillo *castle*
catálogo *catalogue*
catedral (f) *cathedral*
católico *Catholic (adj)*
causa (origen) *cause (n)*
  a causa /del tiempo/ *because of*
  /the weather/
cavar *dig (vb)*
caza (animales) *game (animals)*
  codorniz (f) **codornices** (fpl) *quail*
  faisán (m) *pheasant*
  jabalí (m) *wild boar*
  liebre (f) *hare*
  ortega (m) *grouse*
  perdiz (f) *partridge*
  pichón (m) *pigeon*
caza (deporte) *hunting*
  ir de caza *go hunting*
cazuela *casserole (container)*
cebolla *onion*
cebolleta *spring onion*
CEE *EEC*
ceja *eyebrow*
celoso *jealous*
  está celoso de /mi/ *he's jealous of*

/me/
cementerio *cemetery*
cemento *cement (n)*
cena *dinner (=evening meal), supper*
cenar *have dinner, have supper*
cenicero *ashtray*
centígrados *Centigrade*
centímetro *centimetre*
centralita *switchboard (company)*
centro *centre*
  centro ciudad *town centre*
  centro commercial *shopping centre*
  en el centro *in the centre*
cepillo *brush -es*
  cepillo de ropa *clothes brush*
  cepillo de dientes *toothbrush*
  cepillo de pelo *hairbrush*
  cepillo de uñas *nailbrush*
  cepillo de zapatos *shoebrush*
cera *wax*
cerámico *ceramic*
cerca (de) *near*
  cerca / de la estación/ *near /the*
  station/
cerdo (animal) *pig*
cerdo (carne) *pork*
cereal (m) *cereal (=breakfast cereal)*
ceremonia *ceremony -ies*
cereza *cherry*
cerilla *match -es*
  una caja de cerillas *a box of*
  matches
cero *zero*
  bajo cero *below zero*
  sobre cero *above zero*
cerrado *closed (adj), shut (adj)*
  cerrado con llave *locked (adj)*
  no cerrado con llave *unlocked (adj)*
cerrar *close (vb), shut (vb)*
  cerrar con llave *lock (vb)*
cerrojo *lock (n)*
certificado (n) *certificate*
  certificado médico *health certificate*
certificado (adj) *registered (mail)*
cerveza *beer*
  una botella de cerveza *a bottle of*
  beer

una cerveza *a beer*
una lata de cerveza *a can of beer*
un tercio de cerveza *a pint of beer*
cesta *basket*
una cesta de / / *a basket of / /*
cesta de compras *shopping basket*
cicatriz (f) **cicatrices** (pl) *scar*
ciclismo *cycling*
hacer ciclismo *go cycling*
ciego *blind (adj)*
cielo *sky -ies*
cien (m) **cientos** (mpl) *hundred*
cientos de / / *hundreds of / /*
ciencia *science*
cigarrillo *cigarette*
cigarrillo rubio *cigarette (American type)*
cigarrillos con filtro *filter-tipped cigarettes*
un cartón de cigarrillos *a carton of cigarettes (=200)*
un paquete de cigarrillos *a packet of cigarettes*
fumar un cigarrillo *smoke a cigarette*
cine (m) *cinema*
cinta (de tela) *ribbon*
cinta (de tela) *ribbon*
cinta para máquina de escribir *typewriter ribbon*
un trozo de cinta *a piece of ribbon*
cinta (grabada) *tape (n)*
cinta cassette *cassette*
cinta métrica *tape measure*
cintura *waist*
cinturón (m) *belt*
cinturón (m) **de seguridad** *safety belt*
circo *circus -es*
circunvalación (f) *bypass (n) -es*
ciruela *plum*
ciruela pasa *prune*
cita *appointment*
hacer una cita *make an appointment*
tengo una cita *I've got an appointment*
ciudad (f) (grande) *city -ies*
la parte nueva de la ciudad *the new part of the city*
la parte vieja de la ciudad *the old*

part of the city
ciudad (f) *town*
centro ciudad *town centre*
ciudadano (n) *citizen*
civilización (f) *civilisation*
claro (obvio) *clear (=obvious)*
claro (no oscuro) *light (adj) (=not dark)*
clase (f) (en transportes) *class -es*
clase de camarote *cabin class*
clase turista *tourist class*
/primera/ clase */first/ class*
clase (f) (=tipo) *kind (n) (=type)*
una clase de /cerveza/ *a kind of /beer/*
clásico *classical (eg music)*
música clásica *classical music*
clavel (m) *carnation*
clavícula *collar bone*
clavo *nail (metal)*
clima (m) *climate*
clínica *clinic*
clínica privada *private clinic*
clip (m) *paper clip*
club (m) *club*
club de golf *golf club (institution)*
club de juego *gambling club*
club nocturno *nightclub*
cobrar (reintegro) *cash (vb)*
cobrar /un cheque de viajero/ *cash /a traveller's cheque/*
cobrar (hacer pagar) *charge (vb) (=payment)*
cobre (m) *copper*
cocer (al horno) *bake*
cocer al vapor *steam (vb)*
coche (m) *car*
alquiler (m) **de coches** *car hire*
coche (m) **de karting** *go-kart*
coche (m) **deportivo** *sports car*
en coche *by car*
coche (m) (de un tren) *carriage (in a train)*
coche cama *sleeper (on a train), sleeping car*
coche (m) **restaurante** *buffet car*
cochecito de niño *pram*

cocina *cooker*
  cocina de gas *gas cooker*
  cocina eléctrica *electric cooker*
cocina (española etc) *cooking*
cocina (lugar) *kitchen*
cocinado *cooked*
cocinar *cook (vb)*
coco *coconut*
cocodrilo
  de cocodrilo *crocodile (leather)*
cóctel (m) *cocktail*
codeína *codeine*
código *code*
codo *elbow*
codorniz (f) **codornices** (fpl) *quail*
  (= bird)
coger (flores etc) *pick (= gather flowers
  etc)*
coger (una enfermedad) *catch (illness)*
coger /una enfermedad/ *catch /an
  illness/*
cojín (m) *cushion*
col (f) *cabbage*
col (f) **de Bruselas** *sprout (= Brussels
  s.)*
cola *queue (n)*
  hacer cola *queue (vb)*
colchón (m) *mattress -es*
colección (f) *collection (of objects)*
colecta *collection (in a church)*
colega (m&f) *colleague*
colgar *hang*
coliflor (f) *cauliflower*
colina *hill*
collar (m) *necklace, string of beads*
  collar (m) **de perro** *dog collar*
colocar *fit (vb) (eg exhaust)*
colonia *cologne, toilet water*
color (m) *colour*
  ¿de qué color es? *what colour is it?*
columna vertebral *spine (part of body)*
columpio *swing (n) (children's swing)*
combinación (f) (ropa) *petticoat*
comedor (m) *dining room*
comenzar *start (vb)*
  comenzar /el viaje/ *start /the
  journey/*
comer *eat*

comercio *commerce*
comestibles (mpl) *groceries (pl)*
cometa *kite*
comida (alimento) *food*
  comida de régimen *health food*
  ¿dónde puedo comer? *where can I
  buy some food?*
comida (de cada día) *meal*
  comida ligera *light meal*
comienzo *start (n)*
comisaría de policía *police station*
comisión (f) *commission (= payment)*
¿cómo? *how?*
  ¿cómo está? *how are you?*
  ¿cómo? (¿qué?) *sorry? (= pardon?)*
  ¿cómo es? *what's it like?*
como *like*
cómoda (n) *chest of drawers*
comodidades (fpl) *amenities (pl)*
cómodo *comfortable*
compartir *share (vb)*
competición (f) *competition*
completo (entero) *complete (adj)*
completo (= lleno) *full*
comprar *buy*
  comprar /un paraguas/ *buy /an
  umbrella/*
  **¿dónde puedo comprar /un
  paraguas/?** *where can I buy /an
  umbrella/?*
compras (fpl) *shopping*
  ir de compras *go shopping*
compresas (fpl) *sanitary towels (pl)*
comprobar *check (vb)*
  **¿podría comprobar /el aceite y el
  agua/ por favor?** *could you check
  /the oil and water/ please?*
comprobar (poner en duda) *query (vb)*
  quiero comprobar /la cuenta/ *I
  would like to query /the bill/*
computador (m) *computer*
comunica *engaged (telephone)*
comunicación (f) *announcement*
  hacer una comunicación *make an
  announcement*
con *with*
coñac (m) *brandy -ies*

una botella de coñac *a bottle of brandy*
un coñac *a brandy*
concertar *arrange*
  concertar/una reunión/ *arrange /a meeting/*
concierto *concert*
concurrido *crowded*
concha *shell (sea-shell)*
condición (f) *(estado) condition*
  en buenas condiciones (fpl) *in good condition*
  en malas condiciones (fpl) *in bad condition*
condiciones (fpl) *(términos) terms (pl)*
condimento *seasoning*
conducir *(barco) steer (vb) (boat)*
conducir *(coche) drive (vb)*
conducta *behaviour*
conductor (m) **conductora** (f) *driver*
conductor (m) *(autobús) bus driver*
  conductor (m) **de taxi** *taxi driver*
conectar *connect*
conejo *rabbit*
conferencia *long distance call*
  poner una conferencia *make a long distance call*
confianza
  digno de confianza *reliable*
confiar *trust (vb)*
  confío en ella *I trust /her/*
confirmar /mi vuelo/ *confirm /my flight/*
confitura *jam*
confuso *confused*
  estoy confuso *I'm confused*
congelado *frozen (=deep frozen)*
  alimentos (mpl) **congelados** *frozen food*
congelador (m) *deep freeze (=machine)*
congelar *freeze*
congreso *conference*
conocer *know (a person)*
  le conozco *I know him*
consejo *advice*
  quiero consejo *I'd like some advice*

consentir en / / *agree to / /*
conserje (m) *porter (hotel)*
consigna *left-luggage office*
constipado (n) *cold (n)*
  estoy constipado *I've got a cold*
constructor (m) *builder*
cónsul (m) *consul*
consulado *consulate*
  el consulado / español / *the /Spanish/ Consulate*
consulta *surgery -ies (=place)*
  consulta del médico *doctor's surgery*
contable (m) *accountant*
contador (m) *meter*
  contador de gas *gas meter*
  contador de luz *electricity meter*
contagioso *contagious, infectious*
contar *(números) count (vb)*
contar *(decir)*
  contarme *(algo)* **de / /** *tell me (something) about / /*
  /me/ lo contó *he told /me/ about it*
contenido (s) *contents (pl) (eg of a parcel)*
contento *(feliz) glad*
  está contento *he's glad*
contento *(=satisfecho) pleased*
  contento con / / *pleased with / /*
contestación (f) *answer (n)*
contestar *answer (vb)*
continental *continental*
continuar /un viaje/ *continue /a journey/*
continuo *continual*
contra *against*
contrato *contract (n)*
conveniente *convenient (of time and distance)*
copia *copy (n) -ies*
copiar *make a copy, copy*
coral (m) *coral*
corazón (m) *heart*
  ataque (m) **de corazón** *heart attack*
  enfermedad (f) **de corazón** *heart trouble*
corbata *tie (n)*
  alfiler (m) **de corbata** *tiepin*

corcho *cork*
cordero *lamb*
  chuleta de cordero *lamb chop*
  una pierna de cordero *a leg of lamb*
cordillera *range (=mountain range)*
cordón (m) *string*
  un ovillo de cordón *a ball of string*
  un trozo de cordón *a piece of string*
cordones (mpl) **de zapatos** *shoelaces (pl)*
  unos cordones de zapatos *a pair of shoelaces*
coro *choir*
corona de flores *wreath -es (funeral wreath)*
correa *strap*
  correa de reloj *watch-strap*
corrección (f) *correction*
correcto *correct (adj), right*
corredor (m) **de apuestas** *bookmaker*
corregir *correct (vb)*
correo *mail*
  correo aéreo *by air-mail*
  correo ordinario *surface mail*
  correo urgente *express mail*
correos (ms) *post office*
correr *run (vb)*
corriente (adj) *ordinary, common*
  poco corriente *unusual*
corriente (f) (n) *current (=electric current)*
  corriente alterna *A.C. (alternating current)*
  corriente directa *D.C. (direct current)*
  ciento veinte/doscientos cuarenta voltios *one hundred and twenty/ two hundred and forty volt*
corriente (f) (n) **(de agua)** *current (of water)*
  corriente fuerte *strong current*
corriente (m) (n) **(de aire)** *draught (of air)*
cortada *slice (n)*
  una cortada de / */ a slice of / /*
  cortada de bacon *rasher of bacon*
cortar *cut (vb)*
  cortar a rebanadas *slice (vb)*

cortar (se) (teléfono) *cut off (eg of telephone)*
  se ha cortado la comunicación *I've been cut off*
corte (m) *cut (n)*
  un corte y secado a mano *a cut and blow dry*
cortina *curtain*
corto *short*
  corto circuito *short circuit*
cosa *thing*
cosecha *harvest*
coser *sew*
costa *coast (n)*
costar *cost (vb)*
coste (m) (honorario) *charge (n) (=payment)*
coste (m) (precio total) *cost (n)*
costilla *rib (part of body)*
costumbre (f) *custom*
costura *sewing*
  hacer costura *do some sewing*
crecer *grow (of person)*
crédito *credit*
  a crédito *on credit*
  condiciones (fpl) **de crédito** *credit terms*
creer *believe*
  creer/me/ *believe /me/*
  no lo creo *I don't believe it*
crema *cream (=lotion)*
  crema de afeitar *shaving cream*
  crema de manos *handcream*
  crema limpiadora *cleansing cream*
cremallera *zip (n)*
cricket (m) *cricket*
  jugar al cricket *play cricket*
  un partido de cricket *a game of cricket*
crimen (m) *crime*
criminal (m&f) *criminal*
crisis nerviosa (f) **crisis nerviosas** (fpl) *nervous breakdown*
cristal (m) *glass (=substance)*
cristalería *glassware shop*
cristiano *Christian*
Cristo *Christ*

cruce (m) (de calles) *crossroads /crossroads (pl)*
cruce (m) (carreteras) *junction*
cruce (m) **giratorio** *roundabout (n)*
crucero *cruise*
  hacer un crucero *go on a cruise*
crucigrama (m) *crossword puzzle*
crudo *raw*
cruzar /la calle/ *cross /the road/*
cuaderno de notas *notebook*
cuadrado *square (shape)*
cuadro *picture (drawing or painting)*
¿cuál? (m&f) **¿cuáles?** (pl) *which one?/which ones?*
  ¿cuál es /su dirección/? *what's /your address/?*
¿cuándo? *when?*
  ¿cuándo abren /las tiendas/? *when do /the shops/ open?*
¿cuánto? (m) **¿cuánta?** (f) *how much?*
  ¿cuántos? (mpl) **¿cuántas?** (fpl) *how many?*
  ¿cuánto tiempo? *how long? (time)*
cuarto *quarter*
  un cuarto de /hora/ *a quarter of /an hour/*
cuarto de baño *bathroom*
cubierta (n) *deck*
  cubierta inferior *lower deck*
  cubierta superior *upper deck*
cubierto (adj)
  /piscina/ cubierta *indoor /swimming pool/*
cubiertos (mpl) *cutlery*
cubo *bucket*
  un cubo y pala *a bucket and spade*
cubo *cube*
  cubo flash *flash cube*
  cubo de basura *dustbin*
cucaracha *cockroach -es*
cuchara *spoon*
cucharada *spoonful*
  una cucharada de / / *a spoonful of / /*
cucharadita *teaspoon*
  una cucharadita de / / *a teaspoonful.of / /*

cuchillo *knife -ves*
  cuchillo de bolsillo *pocketknife -ves*
  cuchillo de cortar carne *carving knife*
cuello (ropa) *collar*
cuello (cuerpo) *neck*
cuenta (de hotel etc) *bill (for food, hotel, etc), account*
  cuenta bancaria *bank account*
  cuenta corriente *current account*
cuentas (fpl) (=collar) *beads (pl)*
cuerda (cordel) *cord*
cuerda (gruesa) *rope*
  cuerda de remolque *tow rope*
  cuerda de tender *clothes line*
cuero *leather*
  tienda de artículos de cuero *leather goods shop*
cuerpo *body -ies*
cuesta *slope*
cueva *cave*
¡cuidado! *look out!*
cuidadoso *careful*
cuidar *look after, mind*
  cuidar /al niño/ *look after /the baby/*
  ¿podría cuidarme /el bolso/ por favor? *could you mind /my bag/ please?*
cuidar niños *baby-sit*
  persona que cuida niños *baby-sitter*
culpa *fault*
  es culpa mía *it's my fault*
culpable *guilty*
cultivar *grow (=cultivate)*
cumpleaños (m) **cumpleaños** (mpl) *birthday*
cuna *cot*
  cuna portátil *carrycot*
cuñada *sister-in-law/sisters-in-law (pl)*
cuñado *brother-in-law /brothers-in-law (pl)*
cupón (m) *coupon*
  cupón de /gasolina/ */petrol/ coupon*
curar (salud) *cure (yb) (health)*
curry (m) *curry -ies*
  polvos (mpl) **de curry** *curry powder*
curva *bend (in a road)*

CH

chal (m) *shawl*
chaleco *waistcoat*
  chaleco salvavidas *life jacket*
chalet (m) *chalet, villa* (=*holiday villa*)
champán (m) *champagne*
  una botella de champán *a bottle of champagne*
champiñón (m) *mushroom*
  /crema/ de champiñón *mushroom /soup/*
champú (m) *shampoo* (n)
  dar un champú *shampoo* (vb)
  una bolsita de champú *a sachet of shampoo*
  un frasco de champú *a bottle of shampoo*
chaqueta *jacket*
  chaqueta de /tweed/ */tweed/ jacket*
charla *talk* (n) (*discussion, chat*)
cheque (m) *cheque*
  cheque de viajero *traveller's cheque*
  cheque cruzado *crossed cheque*
  pagar con cheque *pay by cheque*
chequeo *check up* (n) (=*of health*)
  chequeo médico *medical examination*
chica *girl*
  chica de servicio *maid*
chicle (m) *chewing gum*
chico *boy*
chillido *scream* (n)
chimenea *chimney -ies*
chincheta *drawing pin*
si, por favor *yes please* (acceptance of offer)
chiste (m) *joke*
chocar (con) *crash* (into)
chocolate (m) *chocolate*
  una barra de chocolate *a bar of chocolate*
chófer (m) *chauffeur*
choque (m) *crash* (car crash) -*es*
christmas (m) **christmas** (mpl) *Christmas card*

chubasquero *showerproof coat*
chuleta (con hueso) *chop* (n)
  chuleta de cerdo *pork chop*
  chuleta de cordero *lamb chop*
chuleta (sin hueso) *cutlet*
  chuleta de cordero *lamb cutlet*
  chuleta de ternera *veal cutlet*
chupete (m) *dummy* (baby's dummy)

D

dados (mpl) *dice/dice* (pl)
damas (fpl) *draughts* (pl)(game)
  una partida de damas *a game of draughts*
dañado *damaged*
daño *damage* (n) (s)
  hacerse daño en *hurt* (vb) (inflict pain)
  me he hecho daño en /la pierna/ *I've hurt /my leg/*
dar *give*
  dé/me/lo por favor *give it to /me/ please*
dar la hora *strike* (vb) (of clock)
dardos (mpl) *darts* (pl)
  jugar a dardos *play darts*
  una partida de dardos *a game of darts*
  tablón (m) **de dardos** *dartboard*
dátil (m) *date* (=*fruit*)
de (posesión) *of*
de (origen)
  de /ocho/ a /diez/ *from /eight/ to /ten/*
  soy de / / *I come from / /*
debajo *under*
  debajo /de la silla/ */ under /the chair/*
deber *owe*
  ¿cuánto le debo? *how much do I owe you?*
  me debe / / *you owe me / /*
deber llegar *be due*
  /el tren/ debe llegar /a las dos de la tarde/ */the train/'s due /at two o'clock/*
deber (m)(n) (obligación) *duty* (=*obligation*) -*ies*

débil weak (physically)
decidir (se) decide
  decidir de /hacer algo/ decide to
  /do something/
  decidirse por /un plan/ decide on /a
  plan/
decir say (something)
declarar /este reloj/ declare /this
  watch/
dedo finger
  dedo del pie toe
  uña del dedo del pie toenail
defecto
  con defecto imperfect (goods)
defectuoso faulty
definitivamente definitely
definitivo definite
dejar leave
  dejar /mi equipaje/ leave /my
  luggage/
  déjeme en paz leave me alone
  he dejado /mi maleta/ I've left /my
  suitcase/ behind
dejar (=permitir) let (=allow)
  déje/me/ probar let /me/ try
dejar (dinero) deposit (vb) (money)
delante ahead
delante de in front of
  delante de /mí/ in front of /me/
deletrear spell
delgado thin (of person)
delicado delicate (health)
demasiado (adv) too (=more than can
  be endured)
  demasiado /grande/ too /big/
demasiado (adj) too much
  demasiados (mpl) **demasiadas** (fpl)
  too many
demostrar prove
dentadura postiza dentures (pl), false
  teeth (pl)
dentista (m&f) dentist
  tengo que ir al dentista I must go to
  the dentist's
dentro inside (adv)
dentro de into
  dentro de /la casa/ into /the house/

denunciar report (vb)
  denunciar /una pérdida/ report /a
  loss/
departamento (tren) compartment (in
  train)
  departamento de fumadores
  smoking compartment
  departamento de no fumadores
  non-smoking compartment
departamento (de tienda, sociedad)
  department
  departamento de caballeros men's
  department
  departamento de cuentas accounts
  department
  departamento de niños children's
  department
  departamento de señoras women's
  department
departamento department (of company)
depender depend
  depende it depends
  depende /del tiempo/ it depends on
  /the weather/
dependiente (m) assistant
  dependiente de una tienda shop
  assistant
deporte (m) sport
depósito (objetos) deposit (n)
  dejar en depósito /algo de dinero/
  deposit /some money/
  **dejar en depósito /estos artículos
  de valor/** deposit /these valuables/
depósito (líquidos) tank
  depósito de agua water tank
derecha right (=not left)
  a la derecha right (direction)
  que usa la mano derecha
  right-handed
derecho
  **tener el derecho a /cupones de
  gasolina/** be entitled to /petrol
  coupons/
derramado spilt
desabrochar unfasten
desafilado blunt (eg knife)

desafortunado
 ser desafortunado *be unlucky*
 es desafortunado *he's unlucky*
desagraciadamente *unfortunately*
desagradable *unpleasant*
desagüe (m) *drains (pl) (= sanitary system)*
 el desagüe está embozado *the drain's blocked*
desatar *untie*
desayunar *have breakfast*
desayuno *breakfast (continental breakfast)*
 desayuno al estilo inglés *English breakfast*
 desayuno en mi habitación *breakfast in my room*
 desayuno para /dos/ *breakfast for /two/*
 habitación (f) **y desayuno** *bed and breakfast*
 servir el desayuno *serve breakfast*
descafeinado *decaffeinated*
descansar *rest (vb)*
descanso (espectáculos) *interval (= break)*
descanso *rest (n)*
 tomar un descanso *have a rest*
descolorido *faded (colour)*
desconectar *disconnect*
descongelante (m) *deicer*
descontar *deduct*
 descontar /quinientas pesetas/ de la cuenta *deduct /five hundred pesetas/ from the bill*
describir *describe*
descripción (f) *description*
descuento (m) *discount (n)*
descuidado *careless*
desde
 desde /Barcelona/ a /Londres/ *from /Barcelona/ to /London/*
 desde luego *certainly*
desembarcar *disembark*
desfile (m) **de modelos** *fashion show*
deshacer las maletas *unpack*
deshonesto *dishonest*

desilusionado *disappointed*
desinfectante (m) *disinfectant*
 una botella de desinfectante *a bottle of disinfectant*
desmayarse *faint (vb)*
 me siento desmayado *I feel faint*
desnudo *bare*
desodorante (m) *deodorant*
desorden (m) *mess -es*
despacho *office*
despacio *slow*
 más despacio *slower*
despertador (m) *alarm clock*
despertar/me/ *wake /me/ up*
despierto *awake*
 está despierto *he's awake*
después (de) (prep) *after*
después (adv) *afterwards*
desteñir *run (vb) (colour)*
 ¿destiñe? *does it run?*
destino *destination*
destornillador (m) *screwdriver*
desviación (f) (rodeo) *detour*
desviación (f) (obligatoria) *diversion*
desviarse *make a detour*
detallado *elaborate (adj)*
detalle (m) *detail*
detergente (m) *detergent, washing powder*
detrás (de) *behind (prep)*
 detrás /de la casa/ *behind /the house/*
devolución (f) (=reembolso) *refund (n)*
devolver (=reembolsar) *refund (vb)*
devolver (pagar) *repay*
 devolver el dinero *repay the money*
 devolver /me/ *repay /me/*
devolver (algo prestado) *return (= give back)*
 devolver/este suéter/ *return /this sweater/*
día (m) *day*
 buenos días *good morning*
 cada día *every day*
diabetes (f) *diabetes*
diabético *diabetic*
diamante (m) *diamond*

diapositivas (fpl) *slides (pl)*
  diapositivas en color *colour slides*
  visor (m) **de diapositivas** *slide viewer*
diario (adj) *daily*
diario (n) *(personal) diary -ies*
diarrea *diarrhoea*
dibujar *draw (a picture)*
diccionario *dictionary -ies*
  diccionario de bolsillo *pocket dictionary*
  diccionario de inglés/español *English/Spanish dictionary*
  diccionario de español/inglés *Spanish/English dictionary*
diciembre (m) *December*
diente (m) *tooth/teeth (pl)*
  cepillo de dientes *toothbrush -es*
  pasta de dientes *toothpaste*
  un tubo de pasta de dientes *a tube of toothpaste*
diferente *different*
  diferente de / / *different from / /*
difícil *difficult, hard*
dificultad (f) *difficulty -ies*
¡diga!/¡dígame! *hello (on telephone)*
dinero *money*
  dinero de bolsillo *pocket money*
  hacer dinero *make money*
Dios/dios (m) *God/god*
diplomático *diplomat*
dirección (f) *(domicilio) address -es*
  dirección eventual *temporary address*
dirección (f) *(tráfico) direction*
  dirección (=única) *one-way street*
dirección (f) *(coche) steering (n) (car)*
directo *direct (adj)*
  línea directa *direct line*
  ruta directa *direct route*
director (m) *director, manager*
disco *record (n)*
  disco de treinta y tres r.p.m. *thirty-three r.p.m. record*
  disco de cuarenta y cinco r.p.m. *forty-five r.p.m. record/single*
  disco de jazz *jazz record*
  disco de música clásica *classical record*
  disco de música ligera *light music record*
  disco de música pop *pop record*
  tienda de discos *record shop*
discoteca *disco*
disculpa *apology -ies*
disculpar
  disculparse *apologise*
  me disculpo *I apologise*
discusión (f) *argument*
discutir *argue*
disentería *dysentry*
diseñar *design (vb)*
diseño *design (n)*
disfraz (m) **disfraces** (mpl) *fancy dress (s)*
dislocación (f) *sprain (n)*
dislocado *sprained*
disparo *shot (n)*
disponible *available*
distancia *distance*
  ¿a qué distancia está /Brighton/? *how far is it to /Brighton?/*
distribuidor (m) **de encendido** *distributor (car)*
distrito postal *postcode*
diversión (f) *fun*
divertido *amusing, enjoyable*
divertirse *have fun*
dividir *divide (vb)*
divorciado *divorced*
doblado *bent (adj)*
doblar *(una curva) bend (vb)*
doblar (=plegar) *fold (vb)*
doble *double*
  habitación doble *double room*
  pagar el doble *pay double*
  un whisky doble *a double whisky*
docena *dozen*
  media docena *half a dozen*
  una docena de /huevos/ *a dozen /eggs/*
documentos (mpl) *documents (pl)*
  documentos del coche *car documents*
  documentos de viaje *travel*

documents
dólar (m) *dollar*
doler *hurt (vb) (feel pain)*
  me duele /el pie/ *my /foot/ hurts*
dolor (m) *ache, pain*
  dolor de garganta *sore throat*
  dolor de muelas *toothache (s)*
  tengo dolor de espalda *I've got
  backache*
  tengo dolor de estómago *I've got
  stomachache*
  tengo dolor de oído *I've got earache*
dolorido *sore (adj)*
doloroso *painful*
domado *tame (adj)*
domingo *Sunday*
  el domingo *on Sunday*
  los domingos *on Sundays*
dominó (s) *dominoes (pl)*
  jugar al dominó *play dominoes*
  una partida de dominó *a game of
  dominoes*
¿dónde? *where?*
  ¿de dónde es? *where are you from?*
  ¿por dónde? *which way?*
dormir *sleep (vb)*
  duerme *he's asleep*
dormitorio *bedroom*
dos *two*
  los dos *both*
dosis de /medicamento/ (f) **dosis
  de /medicamento/** (fpl) *dose
  of /medicine/*
droga *drug*
ducha *shower (= shower bath)*
  gorro de ducha *shower cap*
duda *doubt*
  poner en duda *query (vb)*
dudar *doubt (vb)*
  lo dudo *I doubt it*
duerme *he's asleep*
dulce *sweet (= not savoury) (adj)*
durante /la noche/ *during /the night/*
duro (no blando) *hard (= not soft)*
duro (no fresco) *stale (bread, cheese
  etc)*
duro (carne) *tough (meat etc)*

E

edad (f) *age*
  de mediana edad *middle-aged*
edificio *building*
  edificio público *public building*
  edificio de apartamentos *block of
  flats*
educación (f) *education*
educado *polite*
educativo *educational*
efectivo
  dinero en efectivo *cash (n)*
  pagar en efectivo *pay cash*
  pago en efectivo *cash payment*
efervescente *fizzy*
eficiente *efficient*
ejemplo *example*
  por ejemplo *for example*
ejército *army*
él *he*
  para él *for him*
el (m) **la** (f) **los** (mpl) **las** (fpl) *the*
  el /seis de julio/ *on /July 6th/*
elástico *elastic (n)*
elección (f) (preferencia) *choice*
  elección entre / / y / / *choice
  between / / and / /*
elección (f) (política) *election (s)*
electricidad (f) *electricity*
electricista (m) *electrician*
eléctrico *electric*
elegante *smart (appearance)*
elegir *choose*
  elegir entre / / y / / *choose
  between / / and / /*
ella *she*
  para ella *for her*
ellos (mpl)/**ellas** (fpl) *they*
  para ellos (mpl)/**para ellas** (fpl) *for
  them*
embajada *embassy -ies*
  la embajada /española/ *the
  /Spanish/ Embassy*
embajador (m) *ambassador*
embalaje (m) *packing materials (to
  prevent breakages)*

embarazada *pregnant*
embarcar (avión) *board (vb) (eg a plane)*
embarcar (barco) *embark*
embarque (m) *embarkation*
 tarjeta de embarque *boarding card*
embotellamiento *traffic jam*
embozado *blocked (eg drain)*
embrague (m) *clutch (n) (car)*
emergencia *emergency -ies*
 salida de emergencia *emergency exit*
emisión (f) *broadcast (n)*
emitir *broadcast (vb)*
emocionante *exciting*
emotivo *emotional*
 es muy emotiva *she's very emotional*
empacar *pack (vb)*
empastar *fill (tooth)*
empaste (m) *filling (tooth)*
empezar *begin*
 ¿cuándo empieza? *when does it
 begin?*
empinado *steep*
empleado (n) *attendant*
empleado por / / *employed by / /*
empresa *company -ies, firm (n)*
empujar *push (vb)*
en
 en /autobús/ *by /bus/*
 en /el hotel/ *at /the hotel/*
 en /el parque/ *in /the park/*
 en /julio/ *in /July/*
 en /la universidad/ *at /the university/*
 en paro *unemployed (adj)*
 en /verano/ *in /summer/*
en calma *calm (of sea)*
encaje (m) *lace (= material)*
encantado (m) **encantada** (f) *how do
 you do?*
encantador *charming*
encendedor (m) *cigarette lighter*
 encendedor de gas *gas lighter*
 encendedor no recargable
 disposable lighter
 gas (m) **para encendedor** *lighter fuel*
encender (luz) *switch on, turn on*
encender (fuego) *light a (fire)*
encendido *on (of light etc)*

enchufar *plug in*
enchufe (m) (en aparato) *plug (electric)*
enchufe (m) (de pared) *socket*
 enchufe de luz *light socket*
 enchufe para máquina de afeitar
 electric razor socket
encía *gum (of mouth)*
encima *above (adv)*
 encima de /mi cabeza/ *above /my
 head/*
 volar por encima de /las montañas/
 fly over /the mountains/
encontrar *find (vb)*
 encontrar /esta dirección/ *find /this
 address/*
encontrarse *meet (= get to know)*
 encontrarse con /su familia/ *meet
 /your family/*
endosar (documentos) *endorse*
 endosar mi billete para / / *I endorse
 my ticket to / /*
 endosar mi pasaporte/ *endorse
 /my passport/*
enero *January*
enfadado *angry*
 estoy enfadado con /él/ *I'm angry
 with/ him/*
enfermedad (f) *disease*
 enfermedad (f) **venérea** *venereal
 disease (VD)*
enfermera *nurse*
enfermo *ill (not well)*
 está enfermo *he's ill*
enfrente *opposite (adv)*
 enfrente /de la estación/ *opposite
 /the station/*
enfriar (muy frío) *chill (vb)*
enfriar (= refrescar) *cool (vb)*
enfundar *cap (vb) (tooth)*
engordar
 que engorda *fattening*
engrasar *grease (vb)*
enhorabuena *congratulations (pl)*
enjuagar *rinse (vb)*
enjuague (m) **bucal** *mouthwash -es*
 un frasco de enjuague bucal *a bottle
 of mouthwash*

enmarcar *frame (vb)*
enmohecido *mouldy*
ensalada *salad*
 aliño para ensalada *salad dressing*
 ensalada de lechuga *green salad*
 ensalada mixta *mixed salad*
enseñar (=mostrar) *show (vb)*
 enseñarme/lo/ *show /it/ to me*
enseñar (enseñanza) *teach*
 enseñar (me) **/español/** *teach (me) /Spanish/*
 (me) **enseña /inglés/** *he teaches (me) /English/*
entender *understand*
 no entiendo *I don't understand*
entero *whole*
 /el mes/ entero *the whole /month/*
 /un mes/ entero *a whole /month/*
enterrar *bury*
entierro *funeral*
entonces *then*
entrada *entrance*
 entrada lateral *side entrance*
 entrada principal *main entrance*
 precio de entrada *entrance fee*
entrar *enter*
 entrar en /un país/ *enter /a country/*
entre (varios) *among*
 entre /mis amigos/ *among /my friends/*
entre /Madrid/ y /Londres/ *between /Madrid/ and /London/*
entregar *a deliver to*
entremés (m) *starter, hors d'oeuvre*
entrenarse *practise* (=train)
entretenido *entertaining*
entrevista *interview (n)*
 tengo una entrevista *I've got an interview*
entrevistar *interview (vb)*
envenenamiento *poisoning*
 envenenamiento por ingestión de alimentos *food poisoning*
enviar *send*
 enviar /un recado/ *send /a message/*
 enviarme /   / *send /   / to me*

enviarlo por correo /   / *send it by /   / mail*
enviar a *forward to*
enviar (por correo) *post (vb)*
 como papel impreso *as printed matter*
 certificado *registered*
 enviar esto por correo aéreo *post this airmail*
 por correo normal *surface mail*
 como paquete postal *parcel post*
 urgente *express*
envío *delivery (goods)*
envolver *wrap (vb)*
 envolver para regalo *gift-wrap (vb)*
epidemia *epidemic (n)*
epiléptico *epileptic (adj)*
equipaje (m) *luggage*
 equipaje de cabina *cabin luggage*
 equipaje de mano *hand luggage*
 estante (m) **de equipaje** *luggage rack (in train)*
 furgón (m) **de equipaje** *luggage van (in train)*
 vagón (m) **de equipaje** *luggage van (on train)*
equipar *equip*
equipo (material) *equipment*
 equipo de oficina *office equipment*
 equipo fotográfico *photographic equipment*
equipo (para deporte) *gear*
 equipo de bucear *diving gear*
 equipo de escalar *climbing gear*
equipo (conjunto) *side, team*
equitación (f) *riding* (=horse riding)
equivocación (f) *mistake (n)*
 por equivocación *by mistake*
equivocado *wrong*
 número equivocado *wrong number*
 no estar equivocado *be wrong*
 no estoy equivocado *I'm wrong*
error (m) *mistake (n)*
erupción (f) *rash -es*
escala *scale (on a map)*
 a gran escala *large scale*
 a pequeña escala *small scale*
escalar *climb (vb)* (=c. mountains)

escalera *staircase*
  escalera de mano *ladder*
  escaleras (fpl) *stairs (pl)*
escalfar *poach*
escalón (m) *step (n) (part of staircase)*
escapar de / / *escape from / /*
escaparate (m) *shop window*
escarcha *frost*
escarchado *frosty*
escenario *stage (in a theatre)*
escocés (tejido)
  falda escocesa *tartan skirt*
escolar (m) *schoolboy*
escolar (f) *schoolgirl*
escribir *write*
  escribir a máquina *type (vb)*
escuchar /música/ *listen to /some music/*
escuela *school*
  escuela de idiomas *language school*
escultura *sculpture*
escupir *spit (vb)*
ése (m) **ésa** (f) *that one*
esfera *face (of watch)*
esguince
  un esguince vertebral *a slipped disc*
esmalte (m) **de uñas** *nail varnish*
esmoquin (m) *dinner jacket*
esos (mpl) **esas** (fpl) *those*
  ésos (mpl) **ésas** (fpl) *those ones*
espalda *back*
  dolor de espalda *backache*
espantoso *dreadful*
esparadrapo *Elastoplast (tdmk), sticking plaster*
espárrago *asparagus*
  puntas (fpl) **de espárrago** *asparagus tips*
especia *spice*
  con especias *spicy*
especial *special*
espectáculo *show (n)*
  espectáculo de strip-tease *strip show*
  espectáculo de variedades *variety show*
  espectáculo (cabaret) *floor show*

espejo *mirror*
  espejo de mano *hand-mirror*
esperar *hope (vb)*
  espero que no *I hope not*
  espero que sí *I hope so*
esperar/me/ *wait /for me/*
  espére/me/, por favor *please wait /for me/*
espeso *thick*
espinacas (fpl) *spinach (s)*
espléndido *splendid*
esponja *sponge (bath sponge)*
esposa *wife/wives (pl)*
esquí (m) *skiing*
  esquí acuático *water-skiing*
  hacer esquí acuático *go water skiing*
esquiar
  ir a esquiar *go skiing*
esquina *corner*
esquís (mpl) *skis (pl)*
  esquís acuáticos *water skis*
  un par de esquís *a pair of skis*
esta noche *tonight*
establo (m) *stable (for horses)*
estación (f) (del año) *season*
estación (f) *station*
  estación de autobuses *bus station*
  estación de autocares *coach station*
  estación de ferrocarril *railway station*
  estación de metro *underground station*
  estación de servicio *petrol station*
  estación terminal *terminus*
estadio *stadium*
estado *state (n)*
  estado de shock *state of shock*
estanque (m) *pond*
estante (m) *shelf -ves*
estantería *bookshelf*
estar *be*
  estar /elegante/ *look /smart/*
  estar en casa *be in (adv)*
estátua *statue*
este (m) (punto cardinal) *east*
éste (m) **ésta** (f) (pron) *this one*
estéreo *stereo*
  equipo estéreo *stereo equipment*

estilo style
estirar pull
estómago stomach
  tengo dolor de estómago I've got a stomach ache
  tengo un trastorno estomacal I've got a stomach upset
estornudar sneeze (vb)
estos (mpl) **estas** (fpl) (adj) these
  estos (mpl) **estas** (fpl) (pron) these ones
estrechar la mano shake hands
estrecho narrow
estrella star
  estrella de cine film star
estreñido constipated
estropear spoil (vb)
estudiante (m&f) student
estudiar study
  estudiar en / / study at / /
  estudiar /inglés/ study /English/
estudio (TV, arte) studio
estudio de mercado market research
estupendo! great!
etiqueta label (=luggage label)
  etiqueta adhesiva stick-on label
evitar avoid
exactamente exactly
exacto exact
examen (m) examination (=school etc.)
examinar examine (medically)
excedente (m) surplus -es
excelente excellent
excepto except
exceso excess
  exceso de equipaje excess baggage
excursión (f) excursion
  ir de excursión go on an excursion
excursión (f) **con guía** conducted tour
  en una excursión con guía go on a conducted tour
excusa excuse (n)
  dar una excusa make an excuse
expedición (f) expedition
experiencia experience
  con experiencia experienced

experto (adj) expert (adj)
experto (n) expert (n)
explicación (f) explanation
explicar explain
exportación (f) export (n)
exportar export (vb)
exposición (f) exhibition
expreso fast train
exprimir squeeze (vb)
extensión /siete/ / / (f) (de teléfono) extension /seven/ (telephone)
extinctor (m) **de incendios** fire extinguisher
extra extra
extranjero
  al extranjero abroad
  él está en el extranjero he's abroad
extranjero (adj) foreign
extranjero (n) foreigner
extraño (n) stranger (n)
extras (mpl) extras (pl)

F

fabrica factory -ies
fabricado en / / made in / /
facial (m) (masaje) facial (= face massage)
fácil easy
facilmente easily
factura invoice (n)
facturar check in (vb) (= of hotel/plane)
fahrenheit Fahrenheit
faisán (m) pheasant
faja corset
faja-pantalón (f) panty-girdle
falda skirt
  falda corta short skirt
  falda larga long skirt
falso false
familia family -ies
familiar (m) **más cercano** next of kin
famoso famous
fangoso muddy
farmacia chemist's
favor (m) favour
  hacerme un favor do me a favour

¿podría hacerme un favor? *could you do me a favour?*
  por favor *please (request)*
favorito *favourite (adj)*
febrero *February*
fecha *date (calendar)*
  fecha de nacimiento *date of birth*
felicitar a /usted/ por / / *congratulate /you/ on / /*
feliz (s) **felices** (pl) *happy*
femenino *feminine*
feo *ugly*
feria *fair (=entertainment)*
ferretería *ironmonger's*
ferrocarril (m) *railway*
  estación (f) **de ferrocarril** *railway station*
ferry (m) *ferry -ies*
  en ferry *by ferry*
festival (m) *festival*
fichero *file (n) (for papers)*
fiebre (f) *fever*
  tengo fiebre *I've got a temperature*
  fiebre (f) **de heno** *hay fever*
  fiebre (f) **tifoidea** *typhoid*
fieltro *felt (material)*
fiesta (=reunión) *party -ies*
  fiesta de cumpleaños *birthday party*
  fiesta oficial (=vacación) *public holiday*
fila *row (of seats)*
  la /primera/ fila *the /first/ row*
filete (m) *fillet (n)*
final (m) (n) *end (n)*
firma *signature*
firmar /un cheque/ *sign /a cheque/*
  firme aquí *sign here*
flash (m) **flashes** (pl) *flash -es*
  lámpara de flash *flash bulb*
flecha *arrow*
flequillo (pelo) *fringe (hair)*
flor (f) *flower*
  un ramo de flores *a bunch of flowers*
florero *vase (=flower vase)*
floristería *florist's*
flotar *float (vb)*
folklore (m) *folklore*

folklórico *folk (adj)*
  arte (m) **folklórico** *folk art*
  baile (m) **folklórico** *folk dancing*
  música folklórica *folk music*
folleto *brochure, leaflet*
fondo
  fondo de / / *bottom of / /*
fontanero *plumber*
forma *shape (n)*
  en forma *fit (adj) (health)*
  está en forma *he's fit*
formación (f) *training (of personnel)*
forro *lining*
  forro de /pieles/ */fur/ lining*
  forros (mpl) **de freno** (coche) *brake linings/pads (pl) (car)*
foto (f) *print (n) (photographic)*
fotocopia *photocopy (n) -ies*
fotocopiadora *photocopier*
fotocopiar *photocopy (vb)*
fotografía
  tienda de artículos de fotografía *camera shop*
fotografía/foto (f) *photograph (photo)*
  fotografía en blanco y negro *black and white photograph*
  fotografía en color *colour photograph*
  hacer una fotografía *take a photograph*
fotográfico *photographic*
fotógrafo *photographer*
  estudio de fotografía *photographer's studio*
fotómetro *exposure meter*
frágil *fragile*
frambuesa *raspberry -ies*
  una cesta de frambuesas *a punnet of raspberries*
franela *flannel (=cloth)*
franqueo *postage*
frase (f) *phrase*
frecuente *frequent (adj)*
fregar (los platos) *wash up*
fregona *mop (n)*
freír *fry*
frenos (mpl) *brakes/braking system*
frente (f) (cara) *forehead*

fresa strawberry -ies
  una cesta de fresas a punnet of
  strawberries
fresco fresh
  comida fresca fresh food (not stale,
  not tinned)
frío cold (adj)
  está frío it's cold (of things)
  hace frío it's cold (of weather)
  hace mucho frío it's freezing
  tengo frío I'm cold
frontera border, frontier
frotar rub
fruta fruit
  fruta en lata tinned fruit
  fruta fresca fresh fruit
  zumo de fruta fruit juice
  una botella de zumo de fruta a
  bottle of fruit juice
  un vaso de zumo de fruta a glass of
  fruit juice
fuego
  ¿tiene fuego? have you got a light?
  fuego de campamento campfire
fuegos (mpl) artificiales fireworks (pl)
  exhibición (f) de fuegos artificiales
  firework display
fuente (f) fountain
fuera (de la ciudad) away
  está fuera he's away
fuera (adv) out
  está fuera (de casa) he's out
fuera (=parte de fuera) outside (adv)
fuera de (=en la parte de fuera)
  outside (prep)
  fuera de /la casa/ outside /the
  house/
fuerte (ruido) loud
fuerte (físicamente) strong (physically)
  /café/ fuerte strong /coffee/
fumador (m) smoker
  no fumador non-smoker
fumar /un cigarrillo/ smoke /a
  cigarette/
funcionar work (vb) (of machines)
  no funciona it doesn't work
funcionario official (n)

funcionario del Estado civil servant
funda cap (n) (for tooth)
fundirse fuse (vb)
  se han fundido las luces the lights
  have fused
funicular (m) funicular
furgoneta van
fusible (m) fuse (n)
  fusible de /tres/ amperios /three/
  amp fuse
  hilo de fusible fuse wire
fútbol (m) football (=game)
  jugar al fútbol play football
  un partido de fútbol a game of
  football
futuro (adj) future (adj)
futuro (n) future (n)

G

gabardina gabardine coat, raincoat
gafas (fpl) (óptica) glasses (pl)
  unas gafas a pair of glasses
gafas (fpl) (para el deporte) goggles (pl)
  gafas de bucear underwater goggles
gafas (fpl) **de sol** sunglasses (pl)
  gafas de sol polaroid polaroid
  sunglasses
  unas gafas de sol a pair of
  sunglasses
galería gallery -ies
  galería de arte art gallery
galleta biscuit
galón gallon
galopar gallop (vb)
gamba (grande) prawn
gamba (pequeña) shrimp
ganar (en juego) win (vb)
ganar (dinero) earn
gancho hook
ganga bargain (n)
  es una ganga it's a bargain
ganso goose/geese (pl)
  gansos (mpl) **salvajes** wild geese
garaje (m) garage
garantía guarantee (n)
garantizar guarantee (vb)

garganta *throat*
  dolor de garganta *sore throat*
  pastilla para la garganta *throat pastille*
gas (m) *gas*
gasolina *petrol*
  bidón (m) **de gasolina** *petrol can*
gasolinera *filling station*
gastado *worn-out*
gastar *spend (money)*
gato (animal) *cat*
gato (coche) *jack (car)*
gemelo *twin*
  dos camas sencillas *twin beds*
gemelos (mpl) (camisa) *cuff links (pl)*
  un par de gemelos *a pair of cuff links*
generador (m) *generator*
general (adj) *general (adj)*
generalmente *usually*
generoso *generous*
gente (fs) *people (pl)*
gimnasio *gymnasium*
ginebra *gin*
  una botella de ginebra *a bottle of gin*
  una ginebra *a gin*
  un gin-tonic *a gin and tonic*
gira *tour*
  gira con guía *conducted tour*
giro postal *postal order*
glaciar (m) *glacier*
globo *balloon*
gobierno *government*
gol (m) *goal*
golf (m) *golf*
  campo de golf *golf course*
  club (m) **de golf** *golf club (=institution)*
  palo de golf *golf club (=object)*
  pelota de golf *golf ball*
  una vuelta de golf *a round of golf*
golpear *hit (vb)*
goma *rubber (substance)*
  goma de borrar *rubber (=eraser)*
  goma de pegar *glue*
  goma elástica *elastic band, rubber band*
gordo (en general) *fat (adj)*

gordo (para personas) *overweight (people)*
  ser/estar gordo *be overweight*
  es/está gordo *he's overweight*
gorro *cap (=hat)*
  gorro de baño *swimming cap*
  gorro de ducha *shower cap*
gota /de agua/ *drop /of water/*
gotear *leak (vb)*
  está goteando *it's leaking*
gotera *leak (n)*
grabadora *cassette recorder*
grabar (arte) *engrave*
grabar (disco) *record (vb)*
gracias *thank you*
  no gracias *no thank you*
gracioso *funny (=amusing)*
grado (=nivel) *grade (=level)*
grados (mpl) (temperatura) *degrees (pl)*
gramática *grammar*
gramos (mpl) *grams (pl)*
grande *big, large*
grandes almacenes (mpl) *department store*
granja *farm*
grano (en cara etc) *spot (=blemish)*
grapadora *stapler*
grapas (fpl) *staples (n) (pl)*
grasiento (pelo) *greasy (of hair)*
graso *greasy (of food)*
grasoso (comida) *fatty (of food)*
gratis *free (=without payment)*
grieta *crack (n)*
grifo *tap*
  grifo de agua caliente *hot tap*
  grifo de agua fría *cold tap*
gripe (f) *flu*
gris (tiempo) *dull (of the weather)*
gris (color) *grey*
gritar *shout (vb)*
grito *shout (n)*
grosella *blackcurrant*
grupo *group*
  billete (m) **de grupo** *group ticket*
  grupo de juegos *playgroup*
guantes (mpl) *gloves (pl)*
  un par de guantes *a pair of gloves*

guapo *good-looking*
  un hombre guapo *a good-looking man*
  una mujer guapa *a good-looking woman*
guardacostas (m) **guardacostas** (mpl) *coastguard*
guardar *keep*
guardarropa (m) *cloakroom*
guardería infantil *nursery -ies (=day nursery for children)*
guardián (m) *guardian*
guerra *war*
guía (m) (persona) *guide (=person)*
guía (m) (libro) *guide book*
  guía de teléfonos *telephone directory*
guiar *guide (vb)*
guisante (m) *pea*
guitarra *guitar*
gustar *like (vb)*
  ¿le gusta /la natación/? *do you like /swimming/?*
  ¿le gustaría /tomar una copa/? *would you like /a drink/?*
  me gusta *I like it*
  me gustaría /ir a bañarme/ *I'd like to /go swimming/*
gusto *taste (n)*
  buen/mal gusto *good/bad taste*

H

haba *broad bean*
habitación (f) *room*
  con /ducha/ *with /shower/*
  habitación con vistas *room with a view*
  habitación de dos camas *twin-bedded room*
  habitación doble *double room*
  habitación sencilla *single room*
  habitación tranquila *quiet room*
  habitación y desayuno *bed and breakfast*
  sin /baño/ *without /bath/*
hablar (=conversar) *talk (vb)*

  hablarme de / */ talk to me about / /*
hablar (=dirigir la palabra) *speak*
  hablar /con el gerente/ *speak /to the manager/*
  ¿puedo hablar /con el gerente/ por favor? *may I speak /to the manager/ please? (on phone)*
  hablar /español/ *speak /Spanish/*
  ¿habla /español/? *do you speak /Spanish/?*
  no hablo /inglés/ *I don't speak /English/*
hace *ago*
  hace /tres años/ */three years/ ago*
hacer *do, make*
  hacer /dinero/ *make /money/*
  hacer /unas compras/ *do /some shopping/*
  hacer /una queja/ *make /a complaint/*
hamaca *deckchair*
hambre
  tener hambre *be hungry*
  tengo hambre *I'm hungry*
harina *flour*
harto
  estar harto *be fed up*
  estoy harto *I'm fed up*
hasta *until, till*
  hasta /el viernes/ *until /Friday/*
¡hasta la vista! *see you!*
hay *there is (s) there are (pl)*
  hay /cerveza/ *there's /some beer/*
  ¿hay /restaurantes/ por aquí? *are there /any restaurants/ near here?*
  no hay /hoteles/ por aquí *there aren't /any hotels/ near here*
  ¿qué hay de /Carmen/? *what about /Carmen/?*
hebilla *buckle*
hecho (n) *fact*
  hecho a mano *handmade*
  hecho en casa *homemade*
helado *ice cream*
helado (adj) *icy*
helicóptero *helicopter*

hembra *female (adj)*
hemorragia
  hemorragia nasal *nosebleed*
  detener la hemorragia *stop the bleeding*
hemorroides (fpl) *piles (illness)*
herida (n) *injury -ies, wound*
herido (adj) *hurt (adj)*
hermana *sister*
hermano *brother*
hermoso *beautiful*
héroe (m) *hero*
heroína *heroine*
herramienta *tool*
hervidora de agua *kettle*
hervir *boil (vb)*
hidrofoil (m) *hydrofoil*
  en hidrofoil *by hydrofoil*
hielo *ice*
  con hielo *iced (drink/water)*
hierba (campo) *grass*
hierba (médica) *herb*
hígado *liver*
higo *fig*
hija *daughter*
hijo *son*
hilo *thread*
  una bobina de hilo *a reel of thread*
hinchable *inflatable*
hinchado *swollen*
hinchador (m) de pie *foot pump*
hinchar *inflate*
hinchazón (f) *swelling*
hipoteca *mortgage (n)*
historia (universal etc) *history -ies*
historia (cuento) *story -ies*
hockey (m) *hockey*
  jugar al hockey *play hockey*
  un partido de hockey *a game of hockey*
hockey (m) sobre hielo *ice hockey*
  jugar a hockey sobre hielo *play ice-hockey*
  un partido de hockey sobre hielo *a game of ice hockey*
hoja *sheet (of paper)*
hola *hello*

¡hola! *hi!*
hombre (m) *man/men (pl)*
  hombre joven *young man*
hombre (m) de negocios *businessman /businessmen (pl)*
hombro *shoulder*
honrado *honest*
hora *hour*
  hora punta *rush hour*
  horas (fpl) de apertura *opening times (pl)*
  la hora *the time (clock)*
  ¿qué hora es? *what time is it?*
horario *timetable*
  horario de autobuses *bus timetable*
  horario de autocaros *coach timetable*
  horario de trenes *train timetable*
hormiga *ant*
horno *oven*
horrendo *horrific*
horrible *awful (of things)*
hospedarse *stay (somewhere)*
  ¿dónde se hospeda? *where are you staying?*
hospital (m) *hospital*
hospitalidad (f) *hospitality*
hotel (m) *hotel*
  hotel de precio medio *medium-priced hotel*
  hotel de primera clase *first class hotel*
  hotel económico *cheap hotel*
hovercraft (m) *hovercraft*
  en hovercraft *by hovercraft*
hoy *today*
hueco *hollow (adj)*
huelga *strike (n)*
  estar en huelga *be on strike*
hueso (del cuerpo) *bone*
hueso (frutas) *stone (of fruit)*
huevo *egg*
  huevo duro *hardboiled egg*
  huevo escalfado *poached egg*
  huevo frito *fried egg*
  huevo pasado por agua *boiled egg*
  huevos revueltos *scrambled eggs*
húmedo (ropas) *damp (adj)*

húmedo (clima) *humid*
humo *smoke (n)*
humor (m) (ironía) *humour*
  sentido del humor *sense of humour*
humor (m) (estado de ánimo) *mood*
  de buen/mal humor *in a good/bad mood*
hundir *sink (vb)*

I

idea *idea*
ideal *ideal (adj)*
identificación (f) *identification*
identificar *identify*
idioma (m) *language*
iglesia *church -es*
  una iglesia /protestante/ *a /Protestant/ church*
igual *equal*
ilegal *illegal*
ilusionado *excited*
ilustración *illustration*
impaciente *impatient*
imperdible (m) *safety pin*
impermeable (m) (n) *raincoat*
impermeable (adj) *waterproof (adj)*
importación (f) *import (n)*
importante *important*
importar (mercancías) *import (vb)*
importar (conceder importancia)
  no importa *it doesn't matter*
imposible *impossible*
impreso *form (= document)*
impresor (m) *printer*
imprimir *print (vb)*
impuesto (aduana) *duty (= tax) -ies*
impuesto (en general) *tax -es*
  impuesto de aeropuerto *airport tax*
  impuesto sobre la renta *income tax*
  libre de impuesto *tax free*
incendiado
  se ha incendiado *it's on fire*
incendio *fire (n)*
incluir *include*
  ¿está incluido /el servicio/? *is /service/ included?*

incluyendo *including*
incómodo *uncomfortable*
inconsciente *unconscious*
increíble *incredible*
indemnización (f) *compensation*
independiente *independent*
indesmallable *run-resistant (tights etc)*
indicación (f) *sign (n)*
indigestión (f) *indigestion*
  pastilla para la indigestión *indigestion tablet*
individual *individual (adj)*
industria *industry -ies*
ineficaz (s) **ineficaces** (pl) *inefficient*
inexperto *inexperienced*
infectado *infected*
Información (f) (teléfono) *Directory Enquiries*
información (f) *information (s)*
  mostrador (m) **de información** *information desk*
  oficina de información *information office*
  pedir información sobre / / *make an inquiry about / /*
  quiero información sobre /hoteles/ por favor *I'd like some information about /hotels/ please*
informal *informal*
informar *inform*
  informar /a la policía/ de / / *inform /the police/ of / /*
informe (m) *report (n)*
infracción (f) *offence*
  infracción de tráfico *parking offence*
ingeniero *engineer*
  ingeniero topógrafo *surveyor*
iniciales (fpl) *initials (pl)*
inmediatamente *immediately*
inmediato *immediate*
inmigración (f) *immigration*
  control (m) **de inmigración** *immigration control*
inmune *immune*
inmunidad (f) *immunity*
  inmunidad diplomática *diplomatic immunity*

inmunizar *immunise*
inocente *innocent (= not guilty)*
inoculación (f) *inoculation*
inocular *inoculate*
inscribirse *register (at) (eg a club)*
insecticida *insecticide*
  un frasco de insecticida *a bottle of insecticide*
insecto *insect*
  ahuyentador (m) **de insectos** *insect repellent*
  picadura de insecto *insect bite*
insolación (f) *sunstroke*
insomnio *insomnia*
instrucciones (fpl) *instructions (pl)*
instrumento *instrument*
  instrumento musical *musical instrument*
insulina *insulin*
inteligente *intelligent*
intensivo *intensive*
intercontinental *intercontinental (flight)*
interesado en / / *interested in / /*
interesante *interesting*
intermedio *interval (in theatre)*
internacional *international*
interno *internal*
interpretar *interpret*
intérprete (m&f) *interpreter*
interruptor (m) **de luz** *light switch -es*
inundación (f) *flood (n)*
inundado *flooded*
inválido *invalid (n)*
inversión *investment*
investigación (f) *research (n)*
invierno *winter*
  en invierno *in winter*
invitación (f) *invitation*
invitado (m) **invitada** (f) *guest*
invitar *invite*
inyección (f) *injection*
  quiero una inyección contra /el tétanos/ *I'd like a /tetanus/ injection*
ir *go*
  ¿cómo se va allí? *how do I get there?*
  ir /a casa/ *go /home/*
  ir a /un congreso/ *go to /a*

conference/
  ir /de compras/ *go /shopping/*
  ir /de picnic/ *go /on a picnic/*
  vamos *let's go*
  ¡vámonos! *let's go!*
  vamos a /tomar una copa/ *let's /have a drink/*
irregular *irregular*
irritación (f) *irritation (medical)*
isla *island*
IVA (m) *VAT*
izquierda *left (= not right)*
  a la izquierda *left (direction)*

J

jabón (m) *soap*
  escamas (fpl) **de jabón** *soap flakes*
  jabón de afeitar *shaving soap*
  una pastilla de jabón *a bar of soap*
jabonoso *soapy*
jalea *jelly*
jamón (m) *ham*
  /bocadillo/ de jamón *ham /sandwich/*
  /seis/ cortadas de jamón */six/ slices of ham*
jaqueca *migraine*
jardín (m) *garden*
  jardín (m) **de infancia** *nursery -ies (= school)*
jarra *carafe*
  una jarra de /vino/ *a carafe of /wine/*
jarra *jug*
  una jarra de / / *a jug of / /*
jarrita *mug*
jazz (m) *jazz*
jefe (m) **jefa** (f) *boss (n)*
jefe (m) **de ventas** *sales manager*
jengibre (m) *ginger (flavour)*
jerez (m) *sherry*
  una botella de jerez *a bottle of sherry*
  un jerez *a sherry*
jockey (m) *jockey*
joven *young*

hombre (m) **joven/ hombres jóvenes**
(mpl) *young man/young men* (pl)
mujer (f) **joven/ mujeres jóvenes**
(fpl) *young woman/young women*
joyas (fpl) *jewellery*
joyería *jeweller's*
jubilado *retired (adj)*
  estoy jubilado *I'm retired*
judía *bean*
  judía verde *French bean*
judío *Jew*
judo *judo*
  hacer judo *do judo*
juego (piezas) *set (n)*
  juego de té *tea service*
  juego de azar *gambling*
jueves (m) *Thursday*
  el jueves *on Thursday*
  los jueves *on Thursdays*
jugar *play (vb)*
  jugar al /tenis/ *play /tennis/*
  jugar una partida de / / *play a game of / /*
  jugar por dinero *gamble (vb)*
jugoso *juicy*
juguete (m) *toy*
  tienda de juguetes *toy shop*
julio *July*
junio *June*
junto a / / *next to / /*
juntos *together*
justo *fair (adj) (=just)*
  no es justo *that's not fair*

K

kilogramo/kilo *kilogramme/kilo*
kilómetro *kilometre*
kiosco de periódicos *newsstand*
Kosher (comida judía) *Kosher*

L

labio *lip*
  labio inferior *lower lip*
  labio superior *upper lip*
lápiz (m) **de labios** *lipstick*

labrador (m) *farmer*
lado (situación)
  al lado *next door*
  al lado /de la estación/ *next door /to the station/*
  la casa de al lado *the house next door*
lado (de objeto) *side (n) (of object)*
lago *lake*
lámpara *lamp*
lana *wool*
  de lana *woollen*
lancha motora *motor-boat*
lancha rápida *speedboat*
langosta *lobster*
lápiz (m) **lápices** (mpl) *pencil*
  lápiz de color (m) **lápices de color** (mpl) *crayon*
largo (m) *length*
  largo hasta los pies *full length*
  largo hasta la rodilla *knee length*
largo (adj) *long*
lata (para bebidas) *can (n)*
  una lata de /cerveza/ *a can of /beer/*
lata *tin*
  una lata de / / *a tin of / /*
lavabo *washbasin*
lavado *wash -es (n)*
  lavado y brushing *shampoo and blow dry*
  lavado y marcado *shampoo and set (n)*
lavadora *washing machine*
lavandería *launderette, laundry (place) -ies*
lavaplatos (m) **lavaplatos** (mpl) *dishwasher*
lavar *wash (vb)*
lavarse *have a wash*
laxante (m) *laxative*
  laxante fuerte *strong laxative*
  laxante suave *mild laxative*
lección (f) *lesson*
  lección de conducir *driving lesson*
  lección de /inglés/ */English/ lesson*
leche (f) *milk*

café (m) **con leche** white coffee
batido de leche milk shake (see under flavour)
leche condensada tinned milk
leche en polvo powdered milk
una botella de leche a bottle of milk
un vaso de leche a glass of milk
lechuga lettuce
leer read
leer /una revista/ read /a magazine/
legal legal
lejía bleach (n)
poner en lejía bleach (vb) (laundry)
lejos far
¿está lejos? is it far?
más lejos further
no lejos de / / not far from / /
lencería lingerie
departamento de lencería lingerie department
lengua tongue
lenguado sole (=fish)
lentamente slowly
lente (f) lens -es (of camera)
lente amplio espectro wide-angle lens
lente zoom zoom lens
lentes (fpl) **de contacto** contact lenses (pl)
tapa protectora de lente lens cap
lento slow
leotardos (mpl) tights (pl)
unos leotardos a pair of tights
letra letter (=of the alphabet)
levantado
estar levantado be up (=out of bed)
levantar lift (vb)
ley (f) law
libra pound
libre (=no obrigado) free (=unconstrained)
libre (=desocupado) vacant
librería bookshop
libro book
libro de bolsillo paperback
libro de frases phrase book
libro de texto textbook

licenciado por / / graduate of / /
licenciatura degree (=university degree)
licor (m) liqueur
liebre (f) hare
ligero (=no pesado) light (adj) (=not heavy)
ligero (abrigo etc) thin (coat etc)
liguero suspender belt
lima lime
zumo de lima lime juice
límite (m) limit (n)
límite de altura height limit
límite de peso weight limit
límite de velocidad speed limit
limón (m) lemon
una rodaja de limón a slice of lemon
zumo de limón lemon juice
limonada lemonade
una botella de limonada a bottle of lemonade
una lata de limonada a can of lemonade
un vaso de limonada a glass of lemonade
limpiador (m) **de pipa** pipe cleaner
limpiar (en general) clean (vb)
limpiar (pescado) fillet (vb)
limpiar (=secar) wipe (vb)
limpio clean (adj)
línea (de pesca) fishing line
línea line
línea exterior outside line
línea telefónica telephone line
línea de la costa coastline
linterna torch -es
líquido liquid
líquido de frenos (coche) brake fluid
liso even (surface)
lista list
lista de compras shopping list
listín (m) directory -ies
listo (de una persona) clever (of people)
listo (a punto) ready
¿está listo? (m) **¿está lista?** (f)**¿están listos?** (mpl) **¿están listas?** (fpl) are you ready?

¿cuándo estará listo? *when will it be ready?*
litera *berth*
  camarote (m) **de/cuatro/literas** */four/-berth cabin*
  litera de abajo *lower berth*
  litera de arriba *upper berth*
litera (tren) *couchette*
litro *litre*
local *local (adj)*
  artesanía local *local crafts*
loción (f) **para después del afeitado** *aftershave lotion*
loco *mad*
lona *canvas (=material)*
  bolsa de lona *canvas bag*
LP (m) *LP (=long playing record)*
lucha *fight (n)*
luchar *fight (vb)*
lugar (m) *place (exact location)*
  lugar de nacimiento *place of birth*
  lugar de trabajo *place of work*
lujo *luxury -ies*
luna *moon*
  luna de miel *honeymoon*
lunes (m) *Monday*
  el lunes *on Monday*
  los lunes *on Mondays*
lupa *magnifying glass -es*
luz (f) **luces** (fpl)**(eléctrica)** *light (n) (electric light)*

LL

llama *flame (n)*
llamada *call (n) (telephone call)*
  llamada de alarma *alarm call*
  llamada de cobro revertido *transferred charge call*
  llamada personal *personal call*
  llamada internacional *international call*
  llamada local *local call*
  hacer una llamada *make a call*

llamar (por teléfono) *call (vb) (=telephone)*
  llamar /la policía/ *call /the police/*
  llamar más tarde *call again later*
llamarse *be called (a name)*
  me llamo /Juan Gómez/ *my name's /Juan Gómez/*
  ¿como se llama por favor? *what's your name please?*
llave (f) *key*
  cerrar con llave *lock (vb)*
  llave (f) **inglesa** *spanner*
  llave inglesa ajustable *adjustable spanner*
llavero *key ring*
llegada *arrival*
  hora de llegada *time of arrival*
llegar *arrive (at), get to*
  ¿cuándo llega /el tren/ a /Brighton/? *when does /the train/ get to /Brighton/?*
  llegar a /las cuatro y media/ *arrive at /four-thirty/ p.m.*
  llegar el /lunes/ *arrive on /Monday/*
  llegar en /julio/ *arrive in /July/*
  llegar a /Cuenca/ *arrive in /Cuenca/*
llenar *fill (vessel)*
  ¡llénelo, por favor! *fill it up please! (petrol)*
llevar (en la mano) *carry*
llevar (en coche)
  ¿podría llevarme a / /? *could you give me a lift to / /?*
llevar (a otro lugar) *take away (vb)*
  comida para llevar *take-away meal*
  me lo llevo *I'll take it (in shop)*
llevar (ropa) *wear (vb) (clothes)*
llorar *cry (vb)*
  el niño está llorando *the baby's crying*
llover *rain (vb)*
  llueve *it's raining*
lluvia *rain (n)*
lluvioso
  el tiempo está lluvioso *it's wet (weather)*

M

maceta *flower pot*
madera *wood (substance)*
  de madera *wooden*
madre (f) *mother*
madrina *godmother*
maduro *ripe*
magnetófono *tape recorder*
maître (m) *headwaiter*
maíz (m) *corn*
  maíz dulce *sweet corn*
mal (adj) *bad*
mal (adv) *badly*
¡maldita sea! *damn!*
maleducado *rude*
maleta *suitcase, case*
  hacer /mi maleta/ *pack /my suitcase/*
malgastar *waste (vb)*
malherido *badly hurt*
malva *mauve*
mancha *stain*
manchado *stained*
mandíbula *jaw*
manga de riego *hose (=tube)*
mangas (fpl) *sleeves (pl)*
  mangas cortas *short sleeves*
  mangas largas *long sleeves*
  sin mangas *sleeveless*
manicura *manicure*
  juego de manicura *manicure set*
mano (f) *hand*
manta *blanket*
mantel (m) *tablecloth*
mantelería *linen (table)*
mantequilla *butter*
manzana *apple*
  zumo de manzana *apple juice* -es
mañana *tomorrow*
mañana (hora)
  de la mañana *a.m.*
  /las cuatro/ de la mañana */four/ a.m.*
mañana (tiempo) *morning*
  ayer por la mañana *yesterday morning*

  esta mañana *this morning*
  mañana por la mañana *tomorrow morning*
mapa (m) *map*
  mapa a gran escala *large-scale map*
  mapa de carreteras *road map*
  mapa de /Inglaterra/ *map of /England/*
maquillaje (m) *make-up (=face make-up)*
  maquillaje de ojos *eye make-up*
máquina *machine*
  máquina de escribir *typewriter*
  máquina tragaperras *slot machine*
maquinista (m) *train driver*
mar (m) *sea*
  por mar *by sea*
maravilloso *wonderful*
marca *brand (n) make (n) (eg of a car)*
  nombre (m) **de la marca** *brand name*
marcar (un número de telefono) *dial*
marcar (pelo) *set (vb)(hair)*
marcar /un gol/ *score /a goal/*
marchas (fpl) *gears (pl) (car)*
  primera marcha *first gear*
  segunda marcha *second gear*
  tercera marcha *third gear*
  cuarta marcha *fourth gear*
  quinta marcha *fifth gear*
  marcha atrás *reverse*
  hacer marcha atrás *reverse (vb)*
marco (marco de un cuadro) *frame (n) (=picture frame)*
marea *tide*
  marea alta *high tide*
  marea baja *low tide*
mareado (sentir vértigo) *dizzy*
  estoy mareado *I feel dizzy*
marearse (querer devolver) *be seasick*
  estoy mareado *I feel seasick*
margarina *margarine*
marido *husband*
marina *navy -ies*
marinero *sailor*
mariposa *butterfly -ies*
mariscos (mpl) *shellfish (s)/shellfish (pl)*
mármol (m) *marble (material)*

marrón brown
martes (m) Tuesday
  el martes on Tuesday
  los martes on Tuesdays
martillo hammer
marzo March
más (cantidad) more
  más /pastel/, por favor more /cake/
  please
más (además de) plus
masaje (m) massage (n)
máscara mask
  máscara de bucear con
  tubo de respiración snorkel mask
masculino masculine
mástil (m) mast
matar kill (vb)
máximo maximum (adj)
mayo May
mayonesa mayonnaise
mayor parte
  la mayor parte most
  la mayor parte /de la gente/ most
  /people/
  la mayor parte /del dinero/ most
  /money/
mazo mallet
me (a mí) me
  para mí for me
mecánico mechanic
mecanismo mechanism
mecanógrafo (m) **mecanógrafa** (f)
  typist
mecha wick (lamp, lighter)
mechón (m) streak (n) (of hair)
  quiero que me hagan mechas I'd like
  my hair streaked
medianoche midnight
medias (fpl) stockings (pl)
  medias de /nylon/ /nylon/ stockings
  medias finas fifteen/thirty denier
  un par de medias a pair of stockings
medicamento medicine
  un frasco de medicamento a bottle
  of medicine
médico (n) doctor
  tengo que ir al médico I must go to
  the doctor's
médico (adj) medical
medio (=normal) average (n)
medio (mitad) half -ves
  media /cortada/ half a /slice/
  medio /litro/ half a /litre/
medio (tamaño) medium (size)
medio (=centro) middle
  en el medio de / / in the middle of
  / /
mediodía midday
medir measure (vb)
medusa jellyfish/jellyfish (pl)
mejilla cheek (of face)
mejillón (m) mussel
mejor (superlativo) best
  el mejor /hotel/ the best /hotel/
mejor (comparativo) better
  es mejor it's better (things)
  está mejor he's better (health)
mejorar improve
melocotón (m) peach -es
melón (m) melon
  medio melón half a melon
  una rodaja de melón a slice of melon
menos (más pocos) fewer
menos (cantidad) less
mensual monthly
menta peppermint (=flavour/drink)
  pastilla de menta peppermint (sweet)
mentir lie (vb) (=tell an untruth)
mentira lie (n) (=untruth)
menú (m) menu
  menú a la carta à la carte menu
  menú del día set menu
mercado market
  mercado de carnes meat market
  mercado de frutas y verduras fruit
  and vegetable market
  mercado de pescado fish market
  plaza del mercado market place
mercancías (fpl) goods
  (=merchandise) (pl)
  tren (m) **de mercancías** goods train
merendar have tea
merienda tea (meal)
mermelada de naranja marmalade

un tarro de mermelada de naranja *a jar of marmalade*
mes (m) *month*
  el mes pasado *last month*
  el mes que viene *next month*
  este mes *this month*
mesa *table*
  mesa de escritorio *desk*
metal (m) *metal*
método *method*
metro (medida) *metre (=length)*
metro (tren) *underground (u. railway train)*
  en metro *by underground*
mezcla *mixture*
mezclar *mix (vb)*
mezquita *mosque*
mi (m&f) **mis** (pl) *my*
  mi pasaporte (m) *my passport*
  mi hermana (f) *my sister*
  mis billetes (mpl) *my tickets*
  mis llaves (fpl) *my keys*
microbús (m) *minibus -es*
micrófono *microphone*
miedo
  tener miedo (de / /) (algo) *be afraid (of / /) (things)*
  tengo miedo a / / (alguien) *I'm afraid of / / (people)*
miel (f) *honey*
  un tarro de miel *a jar of honey*
miembro *member (of a group)*
miércoles (m) *Wednesday*
  el miércoles *on Wednesday*
  los miércoles *on Wednesdays*
mil (m) **mil** (mpl) *thousand*
  miles de / / *thousands of / /*
milla *mile*
millón (m) *million*
  millones de / / *millions of / /*
mina (n) *mine (n)*
  mina de carbón *coal mine*
minero *miner*
mínimo *minimum (adj)*
minuto *minute (time)*
mío (pron)
  es mío (m) **es mía** (f) *it's mine*

mirar *look at, watch (vb)*
  mirar /esto/ *look at /this/*
  mirar /la tele/ *watch /T.V./*
  ¡mire! *look!*
  sólo estoy mirando *I'm just looking*
misa *mass (=Catholic service)*
mismo *same*
  el mismo que / / *the same as / /*
mobiliario *furniture*
mochila *rucksack*
moda
  de moda *fashionable*
modelo (objeto) *model (object)*
  el último modelo *the latest model*
modelo (persona) *model (profession)*
moderno *modern*
modista (f) *dressmaker*
modo (s) **de empleo** *instructions for use*
mojado *wet*
  /esta toalla/ está mojada */this towel/ is wet*
  estoy mojado *I'm wet*
molestar *bother (vb)*
  no se moleste *don't bother*
  siento molestarle *I'm sorry to bother you*
molesto (ser) *annoying*
molesto (estar) *upset (adj)*
momento *moment*
  ¡un momento! *just a minute!*
moneda (dinero) *coin*
  moneda fraccionaria *small change*
moneda (moneda corriente de un país) *currency -ies*
monedero *purse*
moño *bun (hair)*
  en un moño *in a bun*
mono *mono (adj)*
montaña *mountain*
montañero *mountaineer*
montañismo *climbing*
  hacer montañismo *go climbing*
montañoso (colinas) *hilly*
montañoso (montañas) *mountainous*
montar *ride (vb)*
  ir a montar a caballo *go riding*

montar a caballo *ride a horse*
  montar en bicicleta *ride a bicycle*
montar en pony *pony trekking*
  ir a montar en pony *go pony trekking*
monumento *monument*
  monumentos (mpl) (de una ciudad)
  sights (pl)(*of a town*)
moqueta (f) *fitted carpet*
mora *blackberry -ies*
morado *purple*
moradura *bruise* (n)
moreno *dark*
morir *die* (vb)
mosca *fly* (=insect)
mosquitera *mosquito net*
mosquito *mosquito*
mostaza *mustard*
motel (m) *motel*
moto (f) *motor scooter*
  moto (f) **de pequeña velocidad**
  moped
motocicleta *motorbike*
motor (m) (coche) *engine* (eg for a car)
motor (m) *motor*
  motor (m) **de arranque** (coche)
  starter motor (car)
  motor fuera bordo *outboard motor*
mover *move* (vb)
movido (no en calma) *rough* (=not
  calm)
movimiento *movement*
mozo de estación *porter* (railway)
mucho *a lot of, much*
  mucho /dinero/ *a lot of /money/*
  no mucho *not much*
muchos *a lot of, many*
  no muchos *not many*
muebles
  tienda de muebles *furniture shop*
muela del juicio *wisdom tooth*
  dolor (m) **de muelas** *toothache*
muelle (m) (colchón) *spring* (=wire coil)
  muelles (mpl) (=puerto) *docks* (pl)
muerto *dead*
mujer (f) *woman/women* (pl)
multa *fine* (n) (=sum of money)
  pagar una multa *pay a fine*

multitud (f) *crowd*
mundo *world (the world)*
muñeca (juguete) *doll*
muñeca (brazo) *wrist*
músculo *muscle*
museo *museum*
música *music*
  música clásica *classical music*
  música folklórica *folk music*
  música ligera *light music*
  música pop *pop music*
musical (m) *musical* (=an
  entertainment)
músico *musician*
muslo *thigh*
musulmán (m) *Muslim*
muy *very*

N

nabo *turnip*
nacimiento *birth*
  certificado de nacimiento *birth
  certificate*
  fecha de nacimiento *date of birth*
  lugar (m) **de nacimiento** *place of birth*
nación (f) *nation*
nacional *national*
nacionalidad (f) *nationality -ies*
nada *nothing*
  de nada (respuesta a 'gracias') *not at
  all, you're welcome* (in reply to 'thank
  you')
  nada de /dinero/ *no /money/*
nadar *swim* (vb)
nadie *no one*
naranja *orange*
  naranja gaseosa *orangeade*
  zumo de naranja *orange juice*
  una botella de zumo de naranja *a
  bottle of orange juice*
  un vaso de zumo de naranja *a glass
  of orange juice*
nariz (f) **narices** (fpl) *nose*
nata *cream (from milk)*
natación (f) *swimming*
natural *natural*

naturaleza *nature*
naufragio *wreck (n)*
náusea *nausea*
navaja *penknife -ves*
navegación (f) **a vela** *sailing*
  hacer navegación a vela *go sailing*
navegar *sail (vb), navigate*
Navidad (f) *Christmas*
  día (m) **de Navidad** *Christmas Day*
neblina *mist*
nebuloso *foggy*
necesario *necessary*
necesidad (f) *necessity -ies*
necesitar *need (vb)*
  necesito /más dinero/ *I need /more money/*
negativo *negative* (= *film n.*)
negro *black*
nervioso *nervous* (= *apprehensive*)
neumático *tyre*
  (neumático) **sin cámara** *tubeless (tyre)*
nevar *snow (vb)*
  nieva *it's snowing*
nevera *fridge*
niebla *fog*
  hay niebla *it's foggy*
nieto/nieta (m&f)
  grandchild/grandchildren (pl)
  nieta *granddaughter*
  nieto *grandson*
nieve (f) *snow (n)*
ningún
  en ninguna parte *nowhere*
niño (m) **niña** (f) *child /children (pl)*
nivel (m) *level (n)* (= *grade*)
nivelado *level (adj)*
no (con verbos etc) *not*
  no funciona *out of order*
no (opuesto a 'si') *no (opposite of 'yes')*
noche (f) *night*
  buenas noches *good night*
  esta noche *tonight*
  mañana por la noche *tomorrow night*
nogal (m) *walnut (wood)*
nombre (m) (completo) *name*
  en nombre de / / *on behalf of / /*
  nombre de pila *first name*

noreste (m) *northeast*
normal (= corriente) *normal*
noroeste (m) *northwest*
norte (m) *north*
nosotros (acusativo) *us*
  para nosotros *for us*
nosotros (sujeto) *we*
nota (= apunte) *note (written)*
nota (para recordar algo) *memo*
noticias (fpl) *news (s)*
novia (día de boda) *bride*
novia *fiancée*
noviembre (m) *November*
novio (día de boda) *bridegroom*
novio *fiancé*
nube (f) *cloud*
nublado *cloudy*
nuera *daughter-in-law/daughters-in-law (pl)*
nuestro *our*
  nuestro pasaporte (m) *our passport*
  nuestra hermana (f) *our sister*
  nuestros billetes (mpl) *our tickets*
  nuestras llaves (fpl) *our keys*
  es nuestro (m) **es nuestra** (f) *it's ours*
nuevo *new (of things)*
nuez (f) **nueces** (fpl) *nut*
  almendra *almond*
  cacahuete *peanut*
número *number*
  número de teléfono *telephone number*
  número equivocado *wrong number*
  número /siete/ *number /seven/*
número (zapatos) *size (shoes)*
nunca *never*
nylon (m) *nylon*
  un par de medias de nylon *a pair of nylons (stockings)*

O

o *or*
objetivo *viewfinder*
obligatorio *compulsory*
obra de teatro *play (n) (at theatre)*
obrero *factory worker*

octubre (m) *October*
oculista (m) *optician*
ocupado *busy*
ocupado (servicios) *engaged (toilet)*
odiar *hate (vb)*
oeste (m) *west*
oferta *offer (n)*
  hacer una oferta *make an offer*
oficial *official (adj)*
oficina de objetos perdidos *lost*
  property office
oído *ear*
  dolor (m) **de oído** *earache*
oír *hear*
ojo *eye*
ola *wave (sea)*
óleo *oil painting*
oler *smell (vb)*
  huele /bien/ *it smells /good/*
olla a presión *pressure cooker*
olor (m) *smell (n)*
olvidar *forget*
onda *wave (radio)*
  onda corta *short wave*
  onda media *medium wave*
  onda larga *long wave*
  UHF *VHF*
ONU *UN*
OPEP *OPEC*
ópera *opera*
  teatro de la ópera *opera house*
operación (f) (médica) *operation*
  (surgical)
operar *operate (surgically)*
orden
  orden (m) **del día** *agenda*
  poner en orden *tidy (vb)*
ordenado *tidy (adj)*
oreja (external) **/oído/** (internal) *ear*
organización (f) *organisation*
organizar *organise*
original *original*
orina *urine*
orinar *urinate*
oro *gold (n)*
  de oro *gold (adj)*
orquesta *band, orchestra*

oscuro *dark*
  está oscuro *it's dark*
  /verde/ oscuro *dark /green/*
ostra *oyster*
  una docena de ostras *a dozen*
  oysters
otoño *autumn*
  en otoño *in autumn*
otro *another*
  otro /vaso de vino/ *another /glass of*
  wine/
otra vez *again*
otro (adj) *other*
  el otro /tren/ *the other /train/*
oveja *sheep/sheep (pl)*
ovillo
  un ovillo de /cordón/ *a ball of*
  /string/
oxígeno *oxygen*

P

paciente (adj) *patient*
paciente (m&f) (n) *patient*
  paciente externo *outpatient*
padecer *suffer*
  padecer de /dolores de cabeza/
  suffer from /headaches/
padre (m) *father*
padre (m) (ó madre) *parent*
padrino *godfather*
pagar *pay*
  al contado *in cash*
  con /tarjeta de crédito/ *by /credit*
  card/
  en /libras esterlinas/ *in /pounds/*
  la cuenta *the bill*
  por adelantado *in advance*
página *page (of a book)*
país (m) *country (=nation) -ies*
paisaje (m) (campo) *countryside*
paisaje (m) (decorado) *scenery*
pajarita *bow tie*
pájaro *bird*
pajita *straw (=drinking s.)*
pala (playa) *spade*
palabra *word*

palacio palace
pálido pale (of people & things)
palillo toothpick
  palillos (mpl) (para comer) chopsticks (pl)
palo (cricket) bat (cricket)
palo stick (n)
  palo de golf golf club (object)
paloma pigeon
palomitas (fpl) **de maíz** popcorn
pan (m) bread
  bollo de pan bread roll
  pan blanco white bread
  pan con mantequilla bread and butter
  pan de molde sliced bread
  pan integral brown bread
  una barra de pan a loaf of bread
  una rebanada de pan a slice of bread
pana corduroy
panadería baker's
panecillo roll (=bread r.)
pantalones (mpl) trousers (pl)
  un par de pantalones a pair of trousers
  pantalones (mpl) **cortos** shorts (pl)
  unos pantalones cortos a pair of shorts
pantalla (de luz) lampshade
pantalla (cine etc) screen (=film screen)
pañal (m) nappy -ies
  pañales (mpl) **de usar y tirar** disposable nappies
paño cloth
  paño de secar dishcloth
  paño estilo tejano denim (=material)
pañuelo (de nariz) handkerchief -ves
pañuelo (complemento) square (=scarf)
  un pañuelo de /seda/ a /silk/ square
pañuelos (mpl) **de celulosa** /Kleenex** tissues (pl) /Kleenex (tdmk)
  una caja de pañuelos de celulosa a box of tissues
papel (m) paper
  papel carbón carbon paper
  papel de avión airmail paper

papel de celo sticky tape (eg Sellotape (tdmk))
papel de dibujo drawing paper
papel de envolver wrapping paper
papel de escribir writing paper
papel de fumar cigarette paper
papel de máquina typing paper
papel higiénico toilet paper
  un rollo de papel higiénico a roll of toilet paper
papel liso unlined paper
papel rayado lined paper
papel secante blotting paper
  una hoja de papel a sheet of paper
papelera wastepaper basket
paperas (fpl) mumps
paquete (m) (=cajetilla) packet
  un paquete de /cigarrillos/ a packet of /cigarettes/(=20)
paquete (m) (envuelto) parcel
  paquete postal by parcel post
par (m) pair
  un par de / / a pair of / /
para (prep) for (prep)
  para /mí/ for /me/
  ¿para qué es? what's it for?
para (tiempo) by (time)
  para /las tres/ by /three o'clock/
parada stop (n)
  parada de autobús bus stop
  parada de tranvía tram stop
paraguas (m) paraguas (mpl) umbrella
parar stop (vb)
  pararse en / / stop at / /
parches (mpl) **de callos** corn pads (pl)
pared (f) wall (=inside w.)
pareja couple (married c.)
pariente (m) relative, relation
parlamento parliament
paro unemployment
párpado eyelid
parque (m) park (n)
parquímetro parking meter
parte (f) part
  en alguna parte somewhere
  en otra parte elsewhere
  una parte de / / a part of / /

parte superior top
la parte superior de / / the top of
/ /
partido/partida game, match -es
un partido de /tenis/ a game of
/tennis/
pasa raisin
pasa de corinto currant
pasado last (= previous)
/el martes/ pasado last /Tuesday/
pasado de moda (ropa)
unfashionable, out of date (clothes)
pasaje (m) passage (on a boat)
pasajero passenger
pasajero en tránsito transit
passenger
pasaporte (m) passport
pasar go past
pasar por delante /de la estación/
go past /the station/
pasar (tiempo) spend (time)
pasarlo bien enjoy oneself
¡que lo pase bien! enjoy yourself!
pasar (=entrar) come in
¡pase! come in! (command)
pasar (=suceder) happen
¿qué le pasa? what's the matter?
Pascua Easter
pase (m) (para entrar en algún sitio)
pass -es (n) (=p. to enter building)
paseo (en coche)
dar un paseo en coche go for a drive
paseo (andar) walk (n)
dar un paseo go for a walk
pasillo corridor
paso (movimiento) step (n) (movement)
paso a nivel level crossing
paso subterráneo subway
pasta de dientes toothpaste
un tubo de pasta de dientes a tube
of toothpaste
pastel (m) cake
un trozo de pastel a piece of cake
pastelería cake shop
pastilla (=píldora) pill
pastilla de garganta throat pastille
pastillas para dormir sleeping pills

un frasco de pastillas a bottle of pills
la Píldora (pastilla) the Pill
pastor (m) vicar
patata potato -es
patatas (fritas en paquete) crisps
(=potato c.)
patatas fritas (fpl) chips (pl) (potato)
paté (m) pâté
paté de hígado liver pâté
patinaje (m) skating
hacer patinaje go skating
patinaje sobre hielo ice-skating
hacer patinaje sobre hielo go
ice-skating
patinaje sobre ruedas roller-skating
ir a patinar go roller skating
patinar (coche) skid (vb) (car)
patinazo skid (n)
patinete (m) scooter (=child's s.)
pato duck/duckling
patrón (m) pattern
patrón de punto knitting pattern
patrón de vestido dress pattern
patrona landlady -ies
pavo turkey
peatón (m) pedestrian
paso de peatones p. crossing
pecho (mujer) breast
dar el pecho breast-feed
pecho chest (part of body)
pedir (un favor) ask (a favour)
pedir /un bistec/ order /a steak/
pedir (=reclamar) claim (vb)
pedir /indemnización/ claim
/damages/
**pedir indemnización a /la compañía
de seguros/** claim on /the insurance/
pedir prestado borrow
pedir prestada una pluma borrow /a
pen/
¿me puede prestar /su pluma/? may
I borrow /your pen/?
pegajoso sticky
peine (m) comb (n)
pelador (m) **de patatas** potato peeler
pelar (=pelar) peel (vb)
pelea quarrel (n)

pelicula (para cámara) film (for camera)
  ASA (marca) ASA (tdmk)
  carrete (m) **de pelicula** cartridge film
  carrete (m) **polaroid** Polaroid film (tdmk)
  DIN (marca) DIN (tdmk)
  pelicula en blanco y negro black and white film
  pelicula de color colour film
  16mm 16mm
  35mm 20/36 fotos 35mm 20/36 exposures
  120/127/620 120/127/620
  Super 8 Super 8
pelicula (cine, TV) film (=entertainment)
  pelicula de miedo thriller
  pelicula de terror horror film
  pelicula del oeste Western
  pelicula pornográfica pornographic film
peligro danger
peligroso dangerous
pelo hair
  cepillo de pelo hairbrush
  corte (m) **de pelo** haircut
  horquilla de pelo hairgrip
  pelo castaño brown hair
pelota ball
  pelota de fútbol football
  pelota de golf golf ball
  pelota de ping-pong table tennis ball
  pelota de playa beach ball
  pelota de squash squash ball
  pelota de tenis tennis ball
peluca wig
peluquero hairdresser
pendientes (mpl) earrings (pl)
  pendientes de agujero earrings for pierced ears
  pendientes de clip clip-on earrings
penicilina penicillin
  soy alérgico a la penicilina I'm allergic to penicillin
pensar en /algo/ think about /something/
pensión (f) **alimenticia** board (n) (=cost of meals)

media pensión half board
pensión completa full board
peor worse
  peor que / / worse than / /
  es peor it's worse
  está peor he's worse
  el peor worst
  el peor /hotel/ the worst /hotel/
  la peor /habitación/ the worst /room/
pepino cucumber
pequeño little , small
  el más pequeño smallest
  más pequeño smaller
  un niño pequeño a little boy
pera pear
percha coat hanger
perder lose, miss
  he perdido /mi cartera/ I've lost /my wallet/
  perder /el tren/ miss /the train/
perdido lost
  me he perdido I'm lost
perdiz (f) partridge
perdonar excuse (vb), forgive
  ¡perdón! sorry! (apology)
  ¡perdone! excuse me!
perezoso lazy
perfecto perfect (adj)
perfume (m) perfume
  un frasco de perfume a bottle of perfume
periódico newspaper
  periódico de la tarde evening paper
  periódico /inglés/ /English/ newspaper
  periódico local local newspaper
  periódico matutino morning paper
periodo period
perla pearl
permanente (f) (n) perm (=permanent wave)
permanente (adj) permanent
permiso (documento) licence, permit (n)
permiso (comentimiento) permission
  permiso para /entrar/ permission to /enter/

permitir *allow, permit*
 permitir /fumar/ *allow /smoking/*
 permitido *allowed*
pero *but*
perro *dog*
 collar (m) **de perro** *dog collar*
persianas (fpl) *blinds, shutters (pl)*
persona *person*
personal *personal*
pesado *heavy*
pesar *weigh*
 pesar demasiado *be overweight (things)*
pesca *fishing*
 ir de pesca *go fishing*
pescadería *fishmonger's*
pescado *fish*
pescar
 caña de pescar *fishing rod*
peso *weight*
 límite (m) **de peso** *weight limit*
 peso neto *net weight*
petición (f) *request (n)*
 hacer una petición *make a request*
piano *piano*
picadura *sting (n), bite*
 picadura de /abeja/ */bee/ sting*
picar *mince (vb)*
 carne (f) **picada** *minced meat*
picar *(insectos) sting (vb)*
picazón (m) *itch*
picnic (m) *picnic*
 ir de picnic *go on a picnic*
pie (m) *foot /feet/ (pl) (=part of body)*
 a pie *on foot*
 estar de pie *stand (vb)*
piedra *stone (substance)*
 piedra preciosa *precious stone*
piel (f) *skin*
 piel (f) **de carnero** *sheepskin*
 /alfombra/ de piel de carnero *sheepskin /rug/*
 muy hecho *well-done (eg of steak)*
 poco hecho *undercooked*
pieles (fpl) *fur*
 abrigo de pieles *fur coat*
 forrado de pieles *lined with fur*

pierna *leg*
pieza (=pedazo) *patch (n)*
pieza (coche) *part (car)*
 piezas (fpl) **de recambio** *spare parts*
pijama (ms) *pyjamas (pl)*
 un pijama *a pair of pyjamas*
pila (radio) *battery -ies (radio)*
pila (cocina) *sink (n)*
Píldora (anticonceptiva) *the Pill*
 tomar la Píldora *be on the Pill*
piloto *pilot*
pimienta *pepper (condiment)*
pimiento *pepper (=vegetable)*
 pimiento rojo *red pepper*
 pimiento verde *green pepper*
pincel (m) *paintbrush*
pinchazo *puncture*
pino *pine (wood)*
pinta *pint*
pintura (paredes) *paint*
 caja de pinturas *box of paints*
 un bote de pintura *a tin of paint*
pintura (cuadro) *painting (n)*
 pintura al óleo *oil painting*
pinza (de la ropa) *peg (=clothes p.)*
pinzas (fpl) **de depilar** *tweezers (pl)*
 unas pinzas de depilar *a pair of tweezers*
piña *pineapple*
 una cortada de piña *a slice of pineapple*
 zumo de piña *pineapple juice*
pipa *pipe (smoker's)*
 limpiador (m) **de pipa** *pipe cleaner*
piragüismo *canoeing*
 hacer piragüismo *go canoeing*
piscina *swimming pool*
 piscina al aire libre *open air swimming pool*
 piscina caliente *heated swimming pool*
 piscina cubierta *indoor swimming pool*
 piscina pública *public swimming pool*
piso (vivienda) *flat (n)*
 piso amueblado *furnished flat*
 piso sin amueblar *unfurnished flat*

piso (suelo) *floor (of building)*
  planta baja (B) *ground floor* (G)
  /primer/ piso */first/ floor*
  sótano (S) *basement* (B)
  último piso *top floor*
pista *track*
  pista de carreras *race track*
  pista de tenis *tennis court*
pitillera *cigarette case*
placa de la dentadura postiza *plate*
  (= dental plate)
plan (m) *plan (n)*
plancha *iron (n) (object)*
  no necesita plancha *drip-dry*
  plancha de viaje *travelling iron*
planchar *iron (vb)*
planear *plan (vb)*
plano (adj) *flat (adj)*
plano (n) *map*
  plano de la ciudad *street map*
planta *plant (n)*
plantar *plant (vb)*
plantilla *staff (= employees)*
plástico *plastic (adj)*
plata *silver (n)*
  de plata *silver (adj)*
plátano *banana*
platija *plaice/plaice (pl)*
platino *platinum*
platito *saucer*
  una taza y platito *a cup and saucer*
plato (menú) *course (of food)*
  plato principal *main course*
  primer plato *first course*
  último plato *last course*
plato (cocinado) *dish (food) -es*
plato (para servir) *dish (container for food) -es*
plato (para comer) *plate (= dinner plate)*
plato (tocadiscos) *turntable (on record player)*
plato hondo *bowl*
playa *beach -es*
  caseta de playa *beach hut*
plaza (en ciudad) *square (place)*
  plaza principal *main square*
  plaza libre *vacancy -ies (room)*

plegable *folding*
  /cama/ plegable *folding /bed/*
  /silla/ plegable *folding /chair/*
pluma (de animal) *feather*
pluma (de escribir) *pen*
  pluma estilográfica *fountain pen*
población (f) *population*
pobre *poor (= not rich)*
poco
  poca /gente/ *few /people/*
  poco a poco *gradually*
  pocos (mpl) *few*
  unos pocos *a few*
  un poco *little (n)*
  un poco de dinero *a little money*
poder (vb) *can (vb)*
  puedo /hacerlo/ *I can /do it/*
  no se puede /aparcar/ /aquí/ *you mustn't /park/ /here/*
  no puedo /hacerlo/ *I can't /do it/*
  ¿podría /cambiar/ /la rueda/ por favor? *could you /change/ /the tyre/ please?*
podrido *rotten*
póker (m) *poker (= game)*
  jugar al poker *play poker*
  una partida de póker *a game of poker*
policía (cuerpo de policía) *police (pl)*
policía (miembro) *policeman/policemen (pl)*
política (s) *politics (pl)*
político (adj) *political*
político (n) *politician*
pollo *chicken*
polvo (limpieza) *dust*
polvos *powder*
  polvos (mpl) **de talco** *talcum powder*
  polvos de talco para niños *baby powder*
  polvos (mpl) **de tocador** *powder (face powder)*
  polvos (mpl) **para las pulgas** *flea powder*
pomada *ointment*
  un tarro de pomada *a jar of ointment*
  un tubo de pomada *a tube of*

ointment

pomelo *grapefruit (fresh)*
  pomelo en lata *tinned grapefruit*
pomo *knob (door)*
poner *put*
  poner /mi abrigo/ *put on /my coat/*
  poner una corona *crown (vb) (tooth)*
pony (m) *pony -ies*
popa *stern (of boat)*
popular *popular*
por
  por año *per annum*
  por avión *by air*
  por avión *(carta) by airmail*
  por ciento *per cent*
  por encima de *over (=above)*
  por fin *at last*
  por la mañana *in the morning*
  por /las calles/ *through /the streets/*
  ¿por qué? *why?*
  por todas partes *everywhere*
porcelana *china*
pornográfico *pornographic*
porque *because*
portafolios (m) **portafolios** (mpl)
  briefcase
portátil *portable*
portero *caretaker*
portero *(edificio) doorman /doormen*
  (pl)
portero *(=guardameta) goalkeeper*
posesiones (fpl) *belongings (pl)*
posible *possible*
posición (f) *position*
poste (m) **indicador** *signpost*
postre (m) *dessert, sweet*
pozo *well (n)*
práctica *practice (=training)*
practicar *practise*
precio *price (n)*
  lista de precios *price list*
  precio al contado *cash price*
  precio de entrada *admission (=cost)*
precioso *precious*
  piedra preciosa *precious stone*
preferir *prefer*
prefijo *dialling code*

pregunta *question (n)*
preguntar *ask*
  por favor pregunte cuánto es *please*
  ask how much it is
premio *prize*
prendas de punto *knitwear*
preocupado *worried*
preparar *prepare*
presentación (f) *introduction*
  carta de presentación *letter of*
  introduction
presentar *introduce*
presente (adj) *present*
presente (m) (n) *present (time)*
preservativo *sheath (=Durex)*
  un paquete de preservativos *a*
  packet of sheaths
presidente (m) *chairman /chairmen*
  (pl), president (of company)
presión (f) *pressure*
  presión (f) **de los neumáticos** *tyre*
  pressure
prestar *lend*
  ¿podría prestarme /dinero/? *could*
  you lend me some /money/?
presupuesto *estimate (n)*
primavera *spring (=season)*
  en primavera *in spring*
primero *first*
  de primera clase *first class (adj)*
  en primer lugar *first of all*
  primera clase *first class (n)*
primeros auxilios (mpl) *first aid*
  equipo de primeros auxilios *first aid*
  kit
primo (m) **prima** (f) *cousin*
princesa *princess -es*
principal *main*
  carretera principal *main road*
príncipe (m) *prince*
principio (comienzo)
  al principio *at first*
prisa *hurry (n)*
  darse prisa *hurry (vb)*
  ¡por favor dése prisa! *please hurry !*
  tengo prisa *I'm in a hurry*
prismáticos (mpl) *binoculars (pl)*

unos prismáticos *a pair of binoculars*
privado *private*
/baño/ privado *private /bath/*
proa (s) *bows (pl) (of ship)*
probable *likely, probable*
probador (m) *fitting room (in shop)*
probar (sabor) *taste (vb) (perceive with tongue)*
probar (=comprobar) *test (vb)*
probar *try (vb)*
  probar /este helado/ *try /this ice-cream/*
  probarse /este suéter/ *try on /this sweater/*
problema (m) *problem*
  tengo problemas *I'm in trouble*
procesión (f) *procession*
producir *produce (vb)*
producto (n) *product*
profesor (m) **profesora** (f) *teacher*
profundidad (f) *depth*
profundo *deep*
programa (m) *programme (of events)*
programa (m) **de televisión** *television programme*
promesa *promise (n)*
prometer *promise (vb)*
prometido *engaged (to be married)*
promoción (f) *promotion*
pronto *soon*
  ¡hasta pronto! *see you soon!*
pronunciar *pronounce*
propiedad (f) *property -ies*
propietario (de piso en alquiler) *landlord*
propietario (de algo) *owner*
propina (n) *tip (money)*
  dar una propina *tip (vb) (money)*
  dar una propina /al camarero/ *tip /the waiter/*
prospecto *prospectus -es*
prostituta *prostitute*
protección (f) *protection*
protector (adj) *protective*
proteger *protect*
  protegerme de / / *protect me from / /*

protegido *sheltered*
protestante *Protestant (adj)*
  iglesia (f) **protestante** *Protestant church*
proveer *supply (vb)*
provisiones (fpl) *provisions (pl), supply -ies (n)*
proyectado *planned (=already decided)*
prueba (=confirmación) *proof*
prueba (=comprobación) *test (n)*
público (teatro, etc) *audience*
público *public*
  edificios (mpl) **públicos** *public buildings (pl)*
  /jardín/ (m) **público** *public /garden/*
  servicios (mpl) **públicos** *public convenience*
puchero *pot*
pueblecito *village*
puente (m) *bridge*
  puente de peaje *toll bridge*
puerta *door, gate*
  puerta delantera *front door*
  puerta trasera *back door*
puerto (de mar) *harbour*
  jefe (m) **de tráfico portuario** *harbour master*
puerto (de montaña) *mountain pass*
pulga *flea*
  picadura de pulga *fleabite*
pulgada *inch -es*
pulgar (m) *thumb*
pulimento *polish (n)*
pulir *polish (vb)*
pulmonía *pneumonia*
pulsera *bracelet*
  pulsera de plata *silver bracelet*
punta *point (n) (=a sharpened point)*
punta (de una pluma) *nib*
puntapié *kick (n)*
  dar un puntapié *kick (vb)*
puntiagudo *pointed*
punto *knitting*
  agujas (fpl) **de punto** *knitting needles*
  hacer punto *do some knitting, knit*
  prendas (fpl) **de punto** *knitwear*

punto (pinta) *spot* (= *dot*)
puro (n) *cigar*
  una caja de puros *a box of cigars*
  un habano *a Havana cigar*
puro (adj) *pure*
pus (m) *pus*

Q

¿que? *what?, which?*
  ¿qué /avión/? *which /plane/?*
  ¿qué hora? *at what time?*
quedar *meet (at a given time)*
  quedemos /a las nueve/ *let's meet /at nine/*
quedarse en / / *stay at / /*
  desde / / hasta / / *from / / till / /*
  hasta / / *till / /*
  una noche *for a night*
  /dos/ noches *for /two/ nights*
  una semana *for a week*
  /dos/ semanas *for /two/ weeks*
queja *complaint*
quejarse *complain*
  quejarse /al director/ *complain /to the manager/*
  quejarse /del ruido/ *complain /about the noise/*
quemado *burnt*
  quemado por el sol *sunburnt*
quemadura *burn (n)*
  quemadura del sol *sunburn*
quemar *burn (vb)*
querer *want*
  querer /comprar/ lo *want to /buy/ it*
  querer /una habitación/ *want /a room/*
queso *cheese*
  /tortilla/ de queso *cheese /omelette/*
¿quién? *who?*
  ¿de quién? *whose?*
  ¿de quién es? *whose is it?*
quilate (m) *carat*
  oro de /nueve/ quilates */nine/ carat gold*
quinina *quinine*

quitamanchas (m) **quitamanchas** (mpl) *stain remover*
quitar *remove*
  quitarse /un abrigo/ *take off /a coat/*
quizás *perhaps*

R

rábano *radish -es*
rabia *rabies*
rabino *rabbi*
ración (f) *portion*
  una ración de / / *a portion of / /*
radiador (m) *radiator (car)*
radio (f) *radio*
  radio del coche *car radio*
  radio portátil *portable radio*
  radio transistor *transistor radio*
rallye (m) *rally -ies*
  rallye de coches *motor rally*
ramo *bunch -es*
  un ramo de /flores/ *a bunch of /flowers/*
rapidamente *quickly*
rápido *quick, fast*
  ¡rápido! *quick!*
raqueta *racquet*
  raqueta de squash *squash racquet*
  raqueta de tenis *tennis racquet*
raro *rare* (= *unusual*)
raso *satin (n)*
rastro *flea market*
ratón (m) *mouse/mice (pl)*
ratonera *mousetrap*
ratto *rat*
rayado *striped*
rayo x *x-ray*
razón (f) *reason (n)*
razonable *reasonable*
real *real*
realmente *really*
rebaja (= *descuento*) *reduction*
rebaja (saldo) *sale*
rebajar (sonido) *lower (vb)*
rebajar (precio) *reduce (price)*
  rebajar el precio *reduce the price*
rebeca *cardigan*

recado *message*
  ¿puedo dejar un recado por favor?
  can I leave a message please?
  ¿quiere dejar algun recado? *can I
  take a message?*
recalentado *overheated (of engine)*
recambio *(boligrafo etc) refill*
recambio
  de recambio *spare (adj)*
  piezas (fpl) **de recambio** *spare parts
  (pl)*
recargar *recharge (battery)*
Recepción (f) *Reception (eg in a hotel)*
receta *(médica) prescription*
receta *(cocina) recipe*
recetar *prescribe*
recibir *receive*
recibo *receipt*
reciente *recent*
recoger *(de) collect (from)*
  recoger /mi equipaje/ *collect /my
  luggage/*
recogida
  última recogida *last collection (of
  post)*
recomendar *recommend*
recompensa *reward (n)*
recompensar *reward (vb)*
reconocer *recognise*
recorder *(hacer memoria a otro) remind*
recortar *trim (vb)*
recorte (m) *trim (n)(haircut)*
rectangular *rectangular*
recto *straight*
recuerdo *memory -ies*
  recuerdos (mpl) **felices** *happy
  memories (pl)*
  un buen/mal recuerdo *a good/bad
  memory*
recuerdo *(objeto) souvenir*
  tienda de recuerdos *souvenir shop*
recuerdos (=saludos)
  **dele recuerdos a /Julie/ de mi
  parte** *give /Julie/ my regards*
red (f)*(de pescar) net (= fishing n.)*
redecilla de pelo *hair net*
redondo *round (adj)*

reembolsar *reimburse*
reformar *(ropa) alter (=clothes)*
refrigerador (m)/**nevera**
  refrigerator/fridge (infml)
regalo *gift, present*
  tienda de regalos *gift shop*
regatear *bargain (vb)*
  regatear con / / *bargain with / /*
régimen (m) *diet (=slimming d.)*
  estar a régimen *be on a diet*
región (f) *area (of country)*
registrar *search (vb)*
registro
  número de registro *registration
  number*
regla *period*
regla *(para medir) ruler (for measuring)*
reglamento (s) *regulations (pl)*
reglas (fpl) *(normas) rules (pl)*
regular *regular*
  /servicio/ regular *regular /service/*
reina *queen*
reir *laugh (vb)*
religión (f) *religion*
religioso *religious*
  servicio religioso *service (church)*
reloj (m) *(de pared, mesa) clock*
  reloj despertador *alarm clock*
reloj (m) *(de pulsera) watch -es (n)*
  correa de reloj *watch strap*
relojería *watchmaker's*
rellenar *fill in (form)*
  rellenar /un impreso/ *fill in /a form/*
relleno *stuffing*
remar *row (a boat)*
remedio *remedy -ies*
remendar *patch (vb)*
remo *oar, paddle*
remojar *soak (vb)*
remolacha *beetroot/beetroot (pl)*
remolcar *tow (vb)*
remolque (m) *trailer*
remontar *wind (vb) (clock)*
remover *stir (vb)*
renovar *renew*
reparación (f) *repair (n)*
  hacer reparaciones *do repairs*

reparaciónes de relojes watch repairs (=shop)

reparaciónes de zapatos shoe repairs (=shop)

reparar repair (vb)

repetir repeat

repiqueteo rattle (noise)

reponer replace

representación (f) performance

representante (m&f) sales representative

representar represent

reproducción (f) reproduction (=painting)

resbaladizo slippery

reserva booking, reservation

reserva por anticipada advance booking

reservar make a reservation, reserve

reservado reserved

asiento reservado reserved seat

reses (fpl) cattle (pl)

respirar breathe

responsable responsible

responsable de / / responsible for / /

respuesta reply -ies (n)

respuesta pagada reply-paid

restaurante (m) restaurant

restaurante de auto-servicio self-service restaurant

restricciones (fpl) restrictions (pl)

resultado result

retrasado delayed

retraso (m) delay (n)

retrato portrait

reúma (m) rheumatism

reunión (f) meeting (business)

revelar develop

revelar y hacer copias develop and print (a film)

reventado burst (adj)

una tubería reventada a burst pipe

revertir el cobro reverse the charges

quiero revertir el cobro I'd like to reverse the charges

revés

al revés upside-down

revisar service (vb)(car)

revisión (f) service (n) (car)

revista magazine

rey (m) king

riachuelo stream (n)

rico rich

rígido stiff

rímel (m) mascara

rincón/esquina corner

riñones (mpl) kidneys (pl)

río river

rizar curl (vb)

robado stolen

robar steal

roble (m) oak (wood)

robo burglary -ies, theft

roca rock (n)

rodilla knee

rojo red

rollo de /papel higiénico/ roll of /toilet paper/

rompecabezas (m) rompecabezas (mpl) jigsaw puzzle

romper break (vb)

romper (tela) tear (vb) (material)

ron (m) rum

ropa (s) clothes (pl)

cepillo de ropa clothes brush

pinza de ropa clothes peg

ropa (s) **de cama** bed clothes (pl), bed linen

ropa interior underwear

ropa interior de caballeros men's underwear

ropa interior de niños children's underwear

ropa interior de señoras women's underwear

ropa sucia laundry (washing)

rosa (adj) pink

rosa (n) rose

un ramo de rosas a bunch of roses

rosbif (m) roast beef

roto (adj) broken

roto (n) (tela) tear (n) (= hole in material)

rotulador (m) felt-tip pen

rubeola *German measles*
rubio *blonde, fair*
rueda *wheel*
  rueda pinchada *flat tyre*
rugby (m) *rugby*
  jugar a rugby *play rugby*
  un partido de rugby *a game of rugby*
ruidosamente *loudly*
ruidoso *noisy*
rulos (mpl) *curlers (pl)*
ruta *route*

S

sábado *Saturday*
  el sábado *on Saturday*
  los sábados *on Saturdays*
sábana *sheet (bed linen)*
sabañón (m) *chilblain*
saber *know (a fact)*
  lo sé *I know*
  no sé *I don't know*
saber a *taste (vb) (=have a certain taste)*
sabor (m) *flavour, taste*
  a chocolate *chocolate*
  a fresa *strawberry*
  a grosella negra *blackcurrant*
  a plátano *banana*
  a vainilla *vanilla*
sabroso *tasty*
sacacorchos (m) **sacacorchos** (mpl) *corkscrew*
sacapuntas (m) **sacapuntas** (mpl) *pencil sharpener*
sacar *take out (tooth)*
sacarina *saccharine*
  tableta de sacarina *saccharine tablet*
sacerdote (m) *priest*
saco de dormir *sleeping bag*
sádana *duvet*
  sádana-cubre *duvet cover*
saeta *hand (of watch)*
sal (f) *salt (n)*
sala *hall*
  sala de conciertos *concert hall*
  sala de espera (aeropuerto) *departure lounge*
  sala de espera (=consulta) *waiting room*
  sala de hospital *ward (in hospital)*
  sala de juegos recreativos *amusement arcade*
  sala de televisión *TV lounge*
salado *salted, savoury*
salchicha *sausage*
sales (fpl) **de baño** *bath salts (pl)*
salida (horario)
  hora de salida *departure time*
  sala de salidas *departure lounge*
salida (puerta) *exit*
  salida (de aeropuerto) *gate (=airport exit)*
  salida de emergencia *emergency exit*
  salida de incendios *fire escape*
salir *leave, depart*
  salir a /las cuatro y media/ *leave /at four-thirty p.m./*
  salir con / / *go out with / /*
  salir el /lunes/ *leave on /Monday/*
  salir en /julio/ *leave in /July/*
salmón (m) *salmon/salmon (pl)*
  salmón ahumado *smoked salmon*
salón (m) *lounge (in hotel)*
  salón (m) **de belleza** *beauty salon*
salsa *sauce*
  salsa para carne *gravy*
saltar *jump (vb)*
salud (f) *health*
  ¡salud! *cheers! (toast)*
salvaje *wild (=not tame)*
  animal (m) **salvaje** *wild animal*
salvamanteles (m) **salvamanteles** (mpl) *tablemat*
salvar *save (=rescue)*
salvavidas (m) **salvavidas** (mpl) *lifebelt*
  bote (m) **salvavidas** *lifeboat*
  chaleco salvavidas *life jacket*
sandalias (fpl) *sandals (pl)*
  unas sandalias *a pair of sandals*
sandwich (m) *sandwich -es*
  un sandwich de /queso/ *a /cheese/ sandwich*
sangrar *bleed*

me sangra la nariz my nose is bleeding
sangre (f) blood
sanguíneo
  grupo sanguíneo blood group
  tensión (f) **sanguínea** blood pressure
sano healthy
santo saint
sarampión (m) measles
sardina sardine
sartén (f) frying pan
sastre (m) tailor
sastrería de caballero men's outfitter's
satisfactorio satisfactory
sauna sauna
secador (m) **de pelo** hair dryer
secar dry (vb)
seco dry (adj)
secretaria secretary -ies
secreto (adj/n) secret
secuestro (de avión) hijack (n)
sed
  tener sed be thirsty
  tengo sed I'm thirsty
seda silk (n)
  de seda silk (adj)
seguir follow
  se ruega hacer seguir please forward
segundo second (of time)
seguridad (f) security
  cinturón (m) **de seguridad** safety belt
  control (m) **de seguridad** security control, security check
seguro (adj) (=cierto) certain, sure
  estoy seguro I'm certain
seguro (adj) (=no peligroso) safe (adj)
seguro (n) insurance
  certificado de seguros insurance certificate
  póliza de seguros insurance policy -ies
sello stamp (n)
  un sello de /diez/ pesetas a /two/ franc stamp
semáforos (mpl) traffic lights (pl)
semana week
  esta semana this week

  fin (m) **de semana** weekend
  la semana pasada last week
  la semana próxima next week
semanal weekly (adj)
semi-dulce medium-sweet
semi-hecho medium-rare (eg of steak)
semi-seco medium-dry
sencillo plain, simple
sendero footpath, path
sentar bien suit (vb)
sentarse sit
  siéntese, por favor please sit down
sentir feel
  /me/ sienta mal it disagrees with /me/ (food)
  me siento enfermo I feel ill
  me siento mareado I feel sick
señal (f) signal (n)
señalar point (vb) (=indicate)
señas
  hacer señas signal (vb)
señor / / Mr / /
señora lady -ies
  señora / / Mrs / /
señorita / / Miss / /
separado separate (adj)
séptico septic
septiembre (m) September
ser be
  son las tres it's three o'clock
serpiente (f) snake
  mordedura de serpiente snakebite
servicio service
  servicio de habitación room service
  servicio de urgencias casualty department (hospital)
  servicio despertador early morning call
  servicio permanente twenty-four hour service
servicios (mpl) (wc) lavatory -ies
  servicios caballeros Gents'
  servicios señoras Ladies'
servilleta napkin, serviette
  servilleta de papel paper napkin
servilletero napkin ring
servir serve

sexo *sex -es*
si (condicional) *if*
  si es posible *if possible*
  si puede *if you can*
sí (afirmación) *yes*
sidra *cider*
  una botella de sidra *a bottle of cider*
  una sidra *a cider*
siempre *always*
siglo *century -ies*
significar *mean (vb) (of a word)*
  ¿qué significa? *what does it mean?*
siguiente *next*
silbato *whistle (n)*
silencio *silence*
  ¡silencio, por favor! *quiet please!*
silencioso *silent*
silla *chair*
  silla de montar *saddle*
  silla de ruedas *wheelchair*
sillita alta *high chair*
sillita de niño *pushchair*
similar *similar*
sin *without*
  sin parar *nonstop*
sinagoga *synagogue*
sincero *sincere*
sintético *man-made, synthetic*
  fibra sintética *man-made fibre*
síntoma (m) *symptom*
sistema (m) **de encendido** *ignition system*
sistema (m) **de escape** *exhaust system (car)*
sistema (m) **eléctrico** *electrical system (car)*
sitio (=asiento) *place (eg on a plane)*
sitio (=espacio) *space (room)*
snack-bar (m) *snack-bar*
sobre (prep)
  sobre /la mesa/ *on /the table/*
sobre (m) (n) *envelope*
  sobre (m) **con la propia dirección** *self-addressed envelope*
  sobre de correo aéreo *airmail envelope*
  un paquete de sobres *a packet of envelopes*
sobrevivir *survive*
sobrina *niece*
sobrino *nephew*
sobrio *sober*
socio (negocios) *partner (business)*
soda *soda (water)*
  una botella de soda *a bottle of soda (water)*
  un vaso de soda *a glass of soda (water)*
sol (m) *sun*
  al sol *in the sun*
  tomar el sol *sunbathe*
solamente *only*
solar (m) *site*
soldado *soldier*
soleado *sunny*
solicitar *apply*
  solicitar /un trabajo/ *apply for /a job/*
  solicitar /un visado/ a / / *apply to / / for /a visa/*
solicitud
  impreso de solicitud *application form*
sólido *solid*
solitario *lonely*
solo (=no acompañado) *alone*
solo (bebidas) *neat (of a drink)*
soltero *single (= not married)*
sombra *shade*
  a la sombra *in the shade*
sombrero *hat*
sombrilla *beach umbrella, sunshade*
somnífero *sleeping pill*
sonajero *rattle (baby's rattle)*
sonido *sound (n)*
sopa *soup*
  sopa de /pollo/ */chicken/ soup*
sordo *deaf*
sorprendido *surprised*
  sorprendido /del resultado/ *surprised at /the result/*
sorpresa *surprise (n)*
sortija *ring*
  sortija de compromiso *engagement ring*

sortija de /diamantes/ /diamond/ ring
sospechar suspect (vb)
sótano basement
squash (m) squash
 jugar a squash play squash
 una partida de squash a game of squash
standard standard (adj)
stock (m) stock (n) (of things)
su (m&f) **sus** (pl) (de ella) her (adj)
 su pasaporte (m) her passport
 su hermana (f) her sister
 sus billetes (mpl) her tickets
 sus llaves (fpl) her keys
su (m&f) **sus** (pl) (de él) his
 su pasaporte (m) his passport
 su hermana (f) his sister
 sus billetes (mpl) his tickets
 sus llaves (fpl) his keys
su (m&f) **sus** (pl) (de ellos/ellas) their
 su pasaporte (m) their passport
 su hermana (f) their sister
 sus billetes (mpl) their tickets
 sus llaves (fpl) their keys
su (s) **sus** (pl) (de usted/ustedes) your (polite form)
 su pasaporte (m) your passport
 su hermana (f) your sister
 sus billetes (mpl) your tickets
 sus llaves (pl) your keys
suave (no fuerte) mild
suave (al tacto) smooth
subasta auction (n)
subastar auction (vb)
subir
 ¿sube usted? are you going up?
 subir en / / get on at / /
sucio dirty
sucursal (f) branch (of company) -es
sudar sweat (vb)
sudor (m) sweat (n)
suegra mother-in-law/mothers-in-law (pl)
suegro father-in-law/fathers-in-law (pl)
suela sole (of shoe)
sueldo salary -ies

suelo (de habitación) floor (of room)
suelo (tierra) ground (= the ground)
sueño sleep (n)
 tener sueño be sleepy
 tengo sueño I'm sleepy
suerte (f) luck
 buena suerte good luck
suéter (m) sweater
 suéter de /cachemir/ /cashmere/ sweater
 suéter de cuello alto polo neck sweater
 suéter de manga corta short-sleeved sweater
 suéter de manga larga long-sleeved sweater
 suéter de pico V -necked sweater
 suéter sin mangas sleeveless sweater
sugerir suggest
suite (f) suite (= hotel suite)
sujetador (m) bra
superficie (f) surface (n)
supermercado supermarket
suplemento excess fare
supositorio suppository -ies
supuesto
 ¡por supuesto! of course!
sur (m) south
sureste (m) southeast
surfing (m) surfing
 hacer surfing go surfing
suroeste (m) southwest
surtido range (= range of goods)
suscribirse a / / subscribe to / /
suscripción (f) subscription
suspensión (f) suspension (car)
sustancia substance
susto shock (n)
suyo (de él)
 es suyo (m) **es suya** (f) it's his
suyo (de ella)
 es suyo (m) **es suya** (f) it's hers
suyo (de ellos/ellas)
 es suyo (m) **es suya** (f) it's theirs
suyo (de vd)
 es suyo (m) **es suya** (f) it's yours (polite form)

T

tabacalera *tobacconist's*
tabaco *tobacco*
tabla de surf *surfboard*
tacaño *mean (=not generous)*
tacón (m) *heel (=part of shoe)*
  tacón alto *high heeled*
  tacón bajo *low heeled*
tacto
  ser / / al tacto *feel / /*
  es /áspero/ al tacto *it feels /rough/*
talón (m) (del pié) *heel (=part of body)*
talonario *cheque book*
tamaño *size*
  tamaño grande *large size*
  tamaño medio *medium size*
  tamaño pequeño *small size*
  ¿qué talla? *what size?*
también *also*
tampones (mpl) *tampons (pl)*
  una caja de tampones (eg Tampax
  (tdmk)) *a box of tampons (eg Tampax
  (tdmk))*
tapadera *lid (of pot)*
tapón (m) *plug (for sink)*
  tapones (mpl) (para los oidos)
  earplugs (pl)
taquilla *booking office, ticket office*
taquilla (teatro) *box office*
tardar *take (time)*
tarde (f) (n) (después de las 6) *evening*
  ayer por la tarde *yesterday evening*
  buenas tardes *good evening*
  esta tarde *this evening*
  mañana por la tarde *tomorrow
  evening*
tarde (adj) *late*
  es tarde *it's late (=time of day)*
  llega tarde *he's late*
  más tarde *later (=at a later time)*
tarde
  siento llegar tarde *I'm sorry I'm late*
tarde (f) (n) (hasta las 6) *afternoon*
  buenas tardes *good afternoon*
  ayer por la tarde *yesterday afternoon*
  esta tarde *this afternoon*

  mañana por la tarde *tomorrow
  afternoon*
  por la tarde *p.m.*
tarifa *rate (n)*
  tarifa de cambio *exchange rate*
  tarifa diaria *rate per day*
  tarifa económica *cheap rate (mail,
  telephone)*
  tarifa postal *postal rate*
  tarifa postal para /España/ *postal
  rate for /Spain/*
tarjeta *card (business card)*
  tarjeta de crédito *credit card*
  tarjeta de cumpleaños *birthday card*
  tarjeta postal *postcard*
tarro *jar*
  un tarro de /confitura/ *a jar of /jam/*
taxi (m) *taxi*
  en taxi *by taxi*
  parada de taxi *taxi rank*
taza *cup*
  una taza de / / *a cup of / /*
  taza de /plástico/ */plastic/ cup*
té (m) *tea*
  té chino *China tea*
  té indio *Indian tea*
  bolsa de té *teabag*
  una taza de té *a cup of tea*
  una tetera con té *a pot of tea*
teatro *theatre*
  programa (m) de teatro *theatre
  programme*
  teatro de la ópera *opera house*
tebeo *comic (=funny paper)*
techo (habitación) *ceiling*
techo (edificio) *roof*
tela *material (=cloth)*
  tela de cuadros *checked material*
  tela de rizo *towelling (material)*
  tela gruesa *heavy material*
  tela ligera *lightweight material*
  tela lisa *plain material*
teleférico *cable car*
telefonear *telephone (vb)*
  telefonear a este número *telephone
  this number*
  telefonear a la central *telephone the*

exchange
telefonear a la operadora *telephone the operator*
telefonear a Recepción *telephone Reception*
teléfono *telephone/phone (n)*
  al teléfono *on the phone*
  cabina de teléfono *call box -es*
  guía (m) de teléfonos *telephone directory -ies*
  llamada telefónica *telephone call*
  ¿puedo usar su teléfono por favor? *may I use your phone please?*
  teléfono exterior *external phone*
  teléfono interior *internal phone*
  tener teléfono *be on the phone (have a phone)*
telegrama (m) *telegram*
  enviar un telegrama *send a telegram*
  impreso de telegrama *telegram form*
telesilla *ski lift*
televisión (f)/**tele** (f) *television/TV (infml)*
  antena de televisión *television aerial*
  aparato de televisión *television set*
  canal (m) **de televisión** *television channel*
  en la televisión/en la tele *on television/on TV*
  programa (m) **de televisión** *television programme*
  televisión portátil *portable television*
télex (m)
  poner un télex *telex (vb)*
temperatura *temperature (atmosphere, body)*
templado (temperatura) *cool (adj)*
templado (clima) *mild (of weather)*
templo *temple*
temporal (m) (n) *gale*
temporal (adj) *temporary*
temprano *early*
  marcharse temprano *leave early*
tenedor (m) *fork (cutlery)*
tener *have*
  no tengo /dinero/ *I haven't got /any*

money/
  tengo /una cita/ *I've got /an appointment/*
  ¿tiene /sellos/? *have you got /any stamps/?*
tener cariño a *be fond of*
  tengo cariño a /él/ *I'm fond of /him/*
tener que *must*
  tengo que /irme a casa/ ahora *I must /go home/ now*
  ¿tengo que /pagar al contado/? *must I /pay by cash/?*
tenis (m) *tennis*
  jugar a tenis *play tennis*
  un partido de tenis *a game of tennis*
tenis (m) **de mesa** *table tennis*
  jugar al tenis de mesa *play table tennis*
  una partida de tenis de mesa *a game of table tennis*
tensión (f) **sanguínea** *blood pressure*
teñir *dye (vb)*
  teñir /este suéter/ de /negro/ *dye /this sweater/ /black/*
terciopelo *velvet*
terminal (f) *terminal*
terminal (f) **aérea** *air terminal*
  autobús servicio terminal *air terminal bus*
terminar *finish (vb)*
  terminar /mi desayuno/ *finish /my breakfast/*
término *term (=expression)*
termo *vacuum flask*
termómetro *thermometer*
  termómetro clínico *clinical thermometer*
  termómetro en centígrados *Centigrade thermometer*
  termómetro en fahrenheit *Fahrenheit thermometer*
ternera *veal*
terraza *terrace*
terreno de juegos *playground*
terrestre
  por vía terrestre *overland*
terrible *terrible*

terrón
  un terrón de azúcar *a lump of sugar*
terso *satin (adj)*
testigo (m&f) *witness -es(n)*
teta *teat*
tetera *teapot*
  una tetera llena *a pot of tea*
tía *aunt*
tiempo (hora) *time*
  a tiempo *on time*
  con tiempo *in time*
  tiempo libre *spare time*
tiempo (clima) *weather*
  estado del tiempo *weather conditions*
  (pl)
  predicción (f) **del tiempo** *weather*
  forecast (s)
  ¿qué tiempo hace? *what's the*
  weather like?
tienda *shop*
  tienda de alimentos selectos
  delicatessen (= food shop)
  tienda de artículos libres de
  impuestos *duty-free shop*
  tienda de campaña *tent*
  tienda de electrodomésticos
  electrical appliance shop
  tienda de periódicos y revistas
  newsagent's
  tienda de trastos *junk shop*
  tienda de una cadena comercial
  chain store
  tienda de vestidos *dress shop*
  tienda de vinos *wine merchant's*
tierno *tender (eg of meat)*
tierra (nuestro planeta) *earth (= the*
  earth)
tierra (en general) *land*
tijeras (fpl) *scissors (pl)*
  unas tijeras *a pair of scissors*
timbre (m) *bell*
tímido *shy*
tinta *ink*
  un frasco de tinta *a bottle of ink*
tintar *tint (vb)*
tinte (m) *colour rinse, tint (hair)*

tintorería *dry cleaner's*
tío *uncle*
típico *typical*
tipo *figure*
tirantes (mpl) (pantalones) *braces (pl)*
  unos tirantes *a pair of braces*
tirantes (mpl)
  sin tirantes *strapless*
tirar
  de usar y tirar *disposable*
  pañales (mpl) **de usar y tirar**
  disposable nappies
titulado *qualified*
título (libro, etc) *title*
  títulos (mpl) (profesionales)
  qualifications (pl)
toalla *towel*
  toalla de secar platos *tea towel*
  toallita de la cara *facecloth*
tobillo *ankle*
tocadiscos (m) **tocadiscos** (mpl)
  record player
tocar (instrumento) *play (vb) (an*
  instrument)
tocar (tacto) *touch (vb)*
  tocar el timbre *ring (vb) at the door*
todavía no *not yet*
todo *all, everything*
  todo el mundo *everyone*
  todo /el tiempo/ *all /the time/*
  todos /los niños/ *all /the children/*
tomar *take*
tomar (autobús, tren etc) *catch, get*
  (transport)
  tomar /el tren/ *catch /the train/*
  tomar /un taxi/ *get /a taxi/*
  ¿dónde puedo tomar /un taxi/?
  where can I get /a taxi/?
tomate (m) *tomato -es*
  salsa de tomate *tomato sauce*
  zumo de tomate *tomato juice*
  una botella de zumo de tomate *a*
  bottle of tomato juice
  una lata de zumo de tomate *a can of*
  tomato juice
  un vaso de zumo de tomate *a glass*

of tomato juice
tonelada ton
tónica tonic (water)
tono shade (colour)
tontería nonsense
tonto (adj) foolish
tonto (n) fool
tormenta storm
tormentoso stormy
tornillo screw
torre (f) tower
tortilla omelette
tos (f) cough (n)
  jarabe (m) **de la tos** cough mixture
  una botella de jarabe de la tos a
  bottle of cough mixture
  pastillas (fpl) **de la tos** cough pastilles
  (pl)
  tengo tos I've got a cough
toser cough (vb)
tostada toast (n)
  una tostada a slice of toast
tostar toast (vb)
total (adj) total
total (m) (n) total
tóxico toxic
trabajar work (vb) (of people)
trabajo (empleo) job
  ¿cual es tu trabajo? what's your job?
trabajo (ocupación) work (n)
  hacer un poco de trabajo do some
  work
  trabajo de media jornada part-time
  work
tradicional traditional
traducción (f) translation
traducir translate
traer bring
tráfico traffic
tragar swallow (vb)
traje (m) **de baño** (para mujeres)
  swimming costume
traje (m) **de baño** (para hombres)
  swimming trunks (pl)
traje (m) **de chaqueta** suit (n)
traje (m) **de noche** evening dress -
  evening dresses (for women)

trampa trap (n)
  hacer trampa cheat (vb)
tranquilizante (m) tranquilliser
tranquilo/callado quiet (adj)
transatlántico liner
transbordador (m) car ferry
transferir transfer (vb)
transformador (m) transformer
transistor (m) transistor (transistor
  radio)
tránsito
  en tránsito in transit
  pasajero en tránsito transit
  passenger
transmisión (f) transmission (car)
transparente clear, transparent
transportar por barco ship (vb)
transporte (m) transport (n)
  transporte (m) **de coches por tren**
  motorail (ie car on a train)
  transporte público public transport
tranvía (m) tram
  el tranvía para / / the tram for / /
  en tranvía by tram
  final (m) **de trayecto de tranvía** tram
  terminus
  parada de tranvía tram stop
trapo rag (for cleaning)
trasbordo
  hacer trasbordo en / / change at
  / / (of train)
  tengo que hacer trasbordo? do I
  have to change?
trasero (infml) bottom (part of body)
trastornos de estómago
  tengo trastornos de estómago I've
  got a stomach upset
tratamiento treatment
tratar treat (medically)
través
  a través del campo through the
  countryside
travieso naughty
tren (m) train
  tren de enlace con puerto boat train
  tren de primera hora early train
  Talgo express train

tren lento slow train
tren rápido fast train
triangular triangular
tribunal (m) **de justicia** court (law)
trimestre (m) term (=period of time)
trípode (m) tripod
tripulación (f) crew
  tripulación aérea air crew
  tripulación de barco ship's crew
  tripulación de tierra ground crew
triste sad
tronco trunk (of tree)
tropical tropical
trotar trot (vb)
trozo piece
  un trozo de / / a piece of / /
trucha trout/trout (pl)
truenos (mpl) thunderstorm
tu (infml) (s) (pron) you (infml) (s)
  para tí for you
tu (infml) (s) **tus** (infml) (pl) your (infml)
tubo (natación) snorkel (n)
  respirar con tubo snorkel (vb)
  tubo de respiración snorkel tube
tubo (pieza cilíndrica) tube
  un tubo de / / a tube of / /
  tubo flexible hose (car)
tuerca nut (metal)
  una tuerca y un perno a nut and bolt
tulipán (m) tulip
  un ramo de tulipanes a bunch of
  tulips
tumbarse lie (vb) (=lie down)
túnel (m) tunnel (n)
turismo
  oficina de turismo tourist office
turista (m&f)
  clase (f) **turista** tourist class
tuyo (infml) (s)
  es tuyo (m) **es tuya** (f) it's yours
  (infml)
tweed (m) tweed

U

UHF VHF
úlcera ulcer

último last (=final)
último /coche/ (m) rear /coach/
ultramarinos (ms) grocer's
un (m) **una** (f) (artículo) a (an)
  es la una it's one o'clock
un (m) **una** (f) (número) one (adj)
  (number)
único unique
unidad
  por unidad each (on price-tag)
uniforme (m) uniform (n)
  de uniforme in uniform
universidad (f) (colegio universitario)
  college
universidad (f) (conjunto de facultades
  universitario) university -ies
uña nail (finger/toe)
  cepillo de uñas nailbrush -es
  esmalte (m) **de uñas** nail varnish
  lima de uñas nail file
  tijeras (fpl) **de uñas** nail scissors
urgente (adj) urgent
  carta urgente express letter
  correo urgente express mail
usado second-hand
  un /coche/ usado a second-hand
  /car/
usar use (vb)
  usar /su teléfono/ use /your phone/
usted (s) **ustedes** (pl) you (polite form)
  para usted (s) **para ustedes** (pl) for
  you
utensilio utensil
útil (que ayuda) helpful
útil (provechoso) useful
uva grape
  un racimo de uvas a bunch of grapes

V

vaca cow
vacaciones (fpl) holiday
  campamento de vacaciones holiday
  camp
  de vacaciones on holiday
  vacaciones en grupo package
  holiday

vacante (f) *vacancy -ies (job)*
vaciar *empty (vb)*
vacio *empty (adj)*
vacuna *vaccine*
vacunación (f) *vaccination*
vacunar *vaccinate*
vainilla *vanilla*
vajilla *dinner set*
vale (m) *voucher*
  vale para hotel *hotel voucher*
vale *OK*
valer *be worth*
  vale /cinco/ libras *it's worth /five/ pounds*
válido *valid*
  /pasaporte/ (m) **válido** *valid /passport/*
valioso *valuable*
valle (f) *valley -ies*
valor (m) *value (n)*
  objetos (mpl) **de valor** *valuables (pl)*
valorar *value (vb)*
variables *variety -ies*
varicela *chicken pox*
variedad (f) *variety -ies*
varilla del nivel de aceite *dipstick*
varios *several*
varón *male (adj)*
vaselina *vaseline*
  un tubo de vaselina *a tube of vaseline*
vaso *glass -es*
  un juego de vasos *a set of glasses*
  un vaso de /agua/ *a glass of /water/*
vegetariano *vegetarian*
vehículo *vehicle*
vela *candle*
vela (barco) *sail (n)*
velocidad (f) *speed*
vena *vein*
venado *venison*
venda *bandage (n)*
vendar *bandage (vb)*
vender *sell*
vendido *sold*
veneno *poison*

venenoso *poisonous*
venir (de) *come (from)*
venir bien (ajustar) *fit (vb)*
  no me viene bien *it doesn't fit me*
  viene bien *it's a good fit*
ventaja *advantage*
ventana *window*
  ventana francesa *French window*
ventanilla *window (car)*
ventas (fpl) *sales (of a company)*
ventilador (m) *fan (n) (electric), ventilator*
ver *see*
  veo *I see (= understand)*
  ver /al director/ *see /the manager/*
  ver /el menú/ *see /the menu/*
verano *summer*
  en verano *in summer*
verdad (f) *truth*
  decir la verdad *tell the truth*
verdadero *true*
verde (color) *green*
verde (=no maduro) *unripe*
verdulería *greengrocer's*
verduras (fpl) *vegetables (pl)*
  panaché de verduras *mixed vegetables*
  verduras frescas *fresh vegetables*
vereda *lane (= small road)*
vestíbulo *foyer (in hotels and theatres)*
vestido *dress (n) -es*
vestir/se/ *get dressed*
  vestir /al niño/ *dress /the baby/*
vestuario *changing room*
vez (en lugar de)
  en vez (de) *instead (of)*
  en vez de /café/ *instead of /coffee/*
vez (frecuencia) *time (frequency)*
  a veces *sometimes*
  dos veces *twice*
  dos veces por semana *twice weekly*
  /seis/ veces */six/ times*
  una vez *once (=one time)*
via *via*
  viajar vía /Roma/ *travel via /Rome/*
viajar *travel (vb)*

a / / to / /
a pie on foot
en autocar, en coche by coach, by car
en avión by air
en barco, en autobús by boat, by bus
en ferry on the ferry
en hovercraft by hovercraft
en tren, en tranvía, en metro by train, by tram, by underground
por mar by sea
por tierra overland
viaje (m) journey -ies, trip
agencia de viajes travel agent's
viaje en autocar coach trip
¡buen viaje! have a good trip!
viaje (m) (por mar) voyage (n)
viajero
cheque (m) **de viajero** traveller's cheque
vida nocturna night life
vieira scallop
viejo old (of people and things)
viento (m) wind (n)
de viento (=ventoso) windy
hace viento it's windy
viernes (m) Friday
el viernes on Friday
los viernes on Fridays
vigilante (m) lifeguard
vinagre (m) vinegar
aceite y vinagre oil and vinegar
una botella de vinagre a bottle of vinegar
vino (m) wine
media botella de vino a half bottle of wine
una botella de vino a bottle of wine
una jarra de vino a carafe of wine
un vaso de vino a glass of wine
vino blanco white wine
vino dulce sweet wine
vino espumoso sparkling wine
vino rosado rosé
vino seco dry wine
vino tinto red wine
viña vineyard

violín (m) violin
visado visa
visibilidad (f) visibility
visitante (m&f) visitor
visitar a / / call on / / (=visit)
visitar los monumentos go sightseeing
visita a monumentos sightseeing
visitar /un museo/ visit /a museum/
visón (m) mink
abrigo de visón mink coat
vista view (n)
vitaminas (fpl) vitamin pills (pl)
un frasco de vitaminas a bottle of vitamin pills
viuda widow
viudo widower
vivir live
¿dónde vive? where do you live?
vivo (con vida) alive
está vivo he's alive
vodka (m) vodka
una botella de vodka a bottle of vodka
un vodka a vodka
volante (m) flywheel
volar a / / fly to / /
voltaje (m) voltage
alto voltaje high voltage
bajo voltaje low voltage
voltio volt
/ciento diez/ voltios / a hundred and ten/ volts
volumen (m) volume
volver return (=go back)
volver a /las cuatro y media/ return at / four-thirty/
volver en /julio/ return in /July/
volver el /lunes/ return on /Monday/
vomitar vomit (vb)
vómito vomit (n)
vosotros (infml) (pl) you (infml) (pl)
para vosotros for you
voz (f) voice
vuelo (avión) flight
vuelo charter charter flight
vuelo de conexión connecting flight
vuelo de estudiantes student flight

vuelo programado *scheduled flight*
vuelo (deporte) *flying*
  hacer vuelo *go flying*
vuelo sin motor *gliding*
  hacer vuelo sin motor *go gliding*
vuelta (=retorno) *return*
  billete (m) **de ida y vuelta** *return (ticket)*
  billete (m) **de ida y vuelta en el día** *day return*
vuelta (dar una vuelta)
  dar una vuelta (en coche) *go for a drive*
  dar una vuelta (paseo) *go for a walk*
vuestro *your (infml) (pl)*
  es vuestro (m) **es vuestra** (f) *it's yours (infml) (pl)*

W

watio *watt*
  /cien/ watios */a hundred/ watts*
whisky (m) (escocés) *whisky -ies*
  una botella de whisky *a bottle of whisky*
  un whisky *a whisky*

Y

y *and*
ya *already*
yate (m) *yacht*
yerno *son-in-law /sons-in-law (pl)*
yeso *plaster (for walls)*
yo *I*
yodo *iodine*
  una botella de yodo *a bottle of iodine*
yogur (m) *yoghurt*
  un yogur *a carton of yoghurt*
  yogur de fruta *fruit yoghurt*
  yogur natural *plain yoghurt*

Z

zambullirse en / / *dive into / /*
  zambullirse en /el agua/ *dive into /the water/*
zanahoria *carrot*
zapatería *shoeshop*
zapatillas (fpl) *slippers (pl)*
  un par de zapatillas *a pair of slippers*
  zapatillas (fpl) **de tenis** *plimsolls (pl)*
  un par de zapatillas de tenis *a pair of plimsolls*
zapatos (mpl) *shoes (pl)*
  un par de zapatos *a pair of shoes*
  zapatos cómodos para andar *walking shoes*
  zapatos de caballero *men's shoes*
  zapatos de niña *girls' shoes*
  zapatos de niño *boys' shoes*
  zapatos de señora *ladies' shoes*
  zapatos de tacón alto *high-heeled shoes*
  zapatos de tacón bajo *flat-heeled shoes*
zona *area (of town)*
  zona comercial *shopping centre*
zoo (m) *zoo*
zuecos (mpl) *clogs (pl)*
  un par de zuecos *a pair of clogs*
zumo *juice*
  zumo de limón *lemon juice*
  zumo de naranja *orange juice*
  zumo de piña *pineapple juice*
  zumo de pomelo *grapefruit juice*
  zumo de tomate *tomato juice*
zurcir *darn (vb)*
zurdo *left-handed*

La comida española

Spanish foods

Métodos culinarios

Cooking methods

ahumado	smoked
a la crema	creamed
al ajillo	fried with chopped garlic
a la parrilla	grilled
a la plancha	griddled
aliñado	dressed
al vapor	steamed
asado	roast, roasted
cocido al horno	baked
cocido en cazuela tapada	jugged
condimentado con picantes	devilled
crudo	raw
empanado	rolled in breadcrumbs
en conserva	tinned/pickled
en puré	mashed

en salsa	in sauce
en vinagre/a la vinagreta	in vinegar/pickled
escabechado	pickled
escalfado	poached
fresco	fresh
frito	fried
fundido	melted
gratinado	au gratin
guisado	stewed
hervido	boiled
muy hecho	well done
natural	fresh
no muy hecho	medium
pasado por agua	boiled
poco hecho	rare
rebozado	in batter
relleno	stuffed
revuelto	scrambled
salteado	sauté
tostado	toasted

Comida y bebida

Food and drink

aceite (m) — oil
  aceite de girasol — sunflower oil
  aceite de maíz — corn oil
  aceite de oliva — olive oil
aceituna — olive
  aceitunas rellenas de anchoas/pimiento — olives stuffed with anchovies/pimento
  aceitunas negras — black olives
  aceitunas sin huesos — stoned olives
acelgas (pl) — a kind of spinach
agua — water
  agua de soda — soda water

agua tónica	tonic water
aguacate (m)	avocado pear
ajo	garlic
albaricoque (m)	apricot
albóndiga	meatball
alcachofa	artichoke
aliño	dressing
aliño de aceite, vinagre y sal	oil and vinegar dressing
alioli (m)	mayonnaise with garlic
almeja	clam
almendra	almond
almíbar (m)	treacle
almuerzo	lunch
alubias	French beans
alubias blancas	white beans
alubias con chorizo	beans with spiced pork sausage
alubias pintas	kidney beans
amargo	bitter
limón amargo	bitter lemon
americano	large black coffee
anchoas	anchovies
anguila	eel
anguila ahumada	smoked eel
anguila al ally pebre	eel in garlic and pepper sauce (Valencia)
anguila en gelatina	jellied eel
angulas	baby eels
angulas al ajillo	baby eels fried in oil with garlic and chili
aperitivo	aperitif
apio	celery
arenque (m)	herring
arroz (m)	rice
arroz abanda	rice baked in fish stock and served with fish

arroz al horno	rice baked in oven
arroz blanco	white rice
arroz con leche	rice pudding
arroz con menudillos	rice with giblets
arroz cubana	white rice, fried egg, tomato and banana
arroz en costra	rice topped with egg, banana and herbs and baked in oven
atún(m)	tuna
ave (f)	poultry
avellana	hazelnut
azúcar	sugar
bacalao	cod
bacalao a la vizcaína	cod baked with onion, tomato and red pepper sauce
bacalao al pil-pil	cod in parsley sauce (Valencia)
bacón (m)	bacon
barra	loaf of bread
batido de leche	milkshake
bebidas	drinks, beverages
berberechos	cockles
berenjena	aubergine
besugo	sea bream
besugo a la parrilla	grilled sea bream
besugo al horno	baked sea bream
bistec (m)	steak
bistec a la parrilla	grilled steak
bistec al minuto	minute steak
bizcocho	sponge cake
bocadillo	sandwich
bogavante (m)	a kind of large lobster
bollos	buns

bizcochos	sponge fingers
brioche (m)	brioche
croissant	croissant
ensaimada	light round coffee cake
madalenas	small round sponge cakes
palmera	flat light pastry
panecillos	bread rolls
suizos	danish pastry
valencianas	sponge cakes
bombón (m)	a chocolate, a sweet
bonito	type of tunny fish
boquerones fritos (mpl)	whitebait
boquerones en vinagre	whitebait in vinegar
brazo de gitano	swiss roll
brécoles (mpl)	broccoli
budín (m)	pudding
buñuelos	fritters
butifarra	veal sausage (Catalonia)
caballa	mackerel
cabrito	kid
café (m)	coffee
café americano	large black coffee
café con leche	white coffee
café con whisky escocés y nata	coffee with cream and whisky
café cortado	coffee with a dash of milk
café irlandés	Irish coffee
café solo	black coffee
carajillo	coffee with brandy
calabacín (m)	marrow
calamares (mpl)	squid
calamares a la romana	squid cut into small rings and fried in batter
calamares en su tinta	squid in their ink

calamares rellenos	stuffed squid
caldeirada	fish soup
caldereta	lamb stew
caldo	broth
caldo de cocido	clear soup of meat stock
caldo gallego	soup made with stock from ham bones with spring greens and potatoes
callos	tripe
callos a la madrileña	tripe in spicy sauce with garlic and red sausage
canelones (mpl)	cannelloni
canelones de atún y huevo duro	cannelloni stuffed with tuna and hard-boiled egg
canelones de foie-gras	cannelloni stuffed with paté
canelones rellenos de carne	cannelloni stuffed with minced meat (Valencia)
cangrejo	crab
cangrejo de río	crayfish
capón (m)	capon
caracoles (mpl)	snails
carajillo	coffee with brandy
carne (f)	meat
carne de vaca	beef
carne de venado	venison
carnero	mutton
carta	menu
carta de vinos	wine list
menú del día (m)	set menu
castaña	chestnut
catsup (m)	ketchup
caviar (m)	caviare
cebolla	onion
cebollinos	chives
cena	dinner

centollo	spider crab
cerdo	pork
chuleta de cerdo	pork chop
lomo de cerdo	loin of pork
manos de cerdo	hand of pork
solomillo de cerdo	pork fillet
cereales (mpl) .	cereals
cereza	cherry
cerveza	beer
cerveza amarga	bitter
cerveza de barril	draught ale
cerveza estilo Pilsen	lager
cerveza negra	brown ale
cerveza rubia	light ale
un quinto de cerveza	⅕ of a litre of beer
un tercio de cerveza	⅓ of a litre of beer
cigalas (mpl)	king prawns
ciruela	plum
ciruela pasa	prune
cocido madrileño	pot-au-feu made with cabbage, potatoes, chickpeas and meat stock
coco	coconut
cocochas	hake's gills (a Basque speciality)
cóctel (m)	cocktail
cochinillo	suckling pig
cochinillo asado	roast suckling pig
codorniz (f) codornices (pl)	quail
col (f)	cabbage
col roja	red cabbage
coles (fpl) de bruselas	Brussels sprouts
coliflor (f)	cauliflower
comida	meal, lunch
conejo	rabbit
cóngrio	conger eel

consommé (m)	thin soup
consommé al jerez	thin soup with sherry
coñac (m)	brandy
corazón (m)	heart
cordero	lamb
cordero al ajillo	lamb cooked in garlic
cordero caldereta/chilindrón	stewed lamb with onion, pepper and tomato
cordero lechal	suckling lamb
costilla de cordero	lamb cutlet
chuleta de cordero	lamb chop
estofado de cordero	lamb stew
pierna de cordero	leg of lamb
cortado	coffee with a dash of milk
costilla	cutlet, rib
costilla de cordero	lamb cutlet
costilla de vaca	rib of beef
crema	thick soup
crema de champiñones	mushroom soup
crema de espárragos	asparagus soup
crema de espinacas	spinach soup
crêpes soucete (mpl)	Crêpes Suzette
criadillas	sweetbreads
criadillas empanadas con arroz	sweetbreads fried and served with rice
croissant (m)	croissant
croqueta	croquette
croqueta de bacalao	cod croquette
croqueta de jamón	ham croquette
croqueta de pollo	chicken croquette
cuajada	curds
cubierto	price of set meal
changurro	meat of spider crab served in breadcrumb sauce
chanquetes (mpl)	tiny fish similar to whitebait (Andalucia)

chipirones (mpl)	baby squid
chirivía	parsnip
chocolate (m)	chocolate
chopitos	baby cuttlefish
chorizo	hard spicy red sausage
chuleta	chop
chuleta de cerdo	pork chop
chuleta de cordero	lamb chop
churrasco	rump steak
churros	fritters (long and thin)
dátiles (m)	dates
desayuno	breakfast
donut (m)	doughnut
embutidos	sausages
empanada	pie
empanada gallega	pie stuffed with tuna, red pepper and tomato
empanadilla	pastry
empanadilla de atún	pastry stuffed with tuna, red pepper and tomato
empanado	rolled in breadcrumbs and fried
emperador (m)	type of swordfish
endibia	chicory
ensaimada	light round coffee cake
ensaimada de Mallorca	large light round coffee cake stuffed with sweet thin vermicelli
ensalada	salad
ensalada de lechuga	green salad
ensalada de tomate	tomato slad
ensalada mixta	mixed salad
ensalada rusa	potato salad
entremeses (m)	hors d'oeuvres
escalope (m)	escalope

escalope de ternera	escalope of veal
escarola	endive lettuce
espaguettis (mpl)	spaghetti
espárragos	asparagus
puntas de espárragos	asparagus tips
tortilla de espárragos	asparagus omelette
espinacas	spinach
espinacas con bechamel	spinach in béchamel sauce
espinacas crema	creamed spinach
estofado	stew
estofado de cordero	stewed lamb
fabada asturiana	stew of white beans and pork sausage (Asturias)
faisán (m)	pheasant
fiambres (m)	cold meats
fideos	noodles
filete (m)	fillet
filete châteaubriand	Châteaubriand steak
filete de bacalao	cod fillet
filete de pescado	fillet of fish
filete de platija	fillet of plaice
flan (m)	caramel custard
flan de huevo	egg caramel custard
flan de vainilla	vanilla caramel custard
frambuesa	raspberry
fresa	strawberry
frijoles (mpl)	kidney beans
fritura	fried dish
fruta	fruit
pastel (m) de fruta	fruitcake
frutos secos	dried fruit
gajos de pomelo	grapefruit segments
galletas	biscuits
gallina	chicken

caldo de gallina	chicken consommé
gallina en petitoria	chicken cooked in dried fruit sauce
pechuga de gallina	chicken breast
gallo	white fish similar to sole
gamba	prawn
cóctel (m) de gambas	prawn cocktail
gambas al ajillo	prawns in garlic
gambas con gabardina	fried prawns
gamba grande	king prawn
ganso	goose
garbanzos	chick peas
gazpacho andaluz	cold soup made with tomatoes, green peppers, onions, garlic, cucumber, oil and vinegar
gazpachuelo	a dish of fish, potatoes and mayonnaise
ginebra	gin
granada	pomegranate
grosella	gooseberry
grosella roja	redcurrant
guisado	ragoût, stew
guisado de carne	meat stew
guisado de cordero	ragoût of lamb
guisado de ternera/pollo con salsa bechamel	veal/chicken stew with béchamel sauce
guisante (m)	pea
habas	broad beans
habas a la catalana	baby broad beans stewed with various types of sausage and meat
habas con jamón	broad beans with cured ham
habas estofadas	stewed broad beans
habas fritas	fried broad beans

halibut (m) halibuts (pl)	halibut
hamburguesa	hamburger
hamburguesa de ternera	beefburger
harina de maíz	cornflour
helado	ice cream
helado con macedonia de frutas	ice cream and fruit salad
helado con melocotón en almíbar	peach melba
helado con nueces y chocolate	ice cream with nuts and chocolate
hielo	ice
hierbas	herbs
hígado	liver
hígado de cerdo	pigs' liver
hígado de cordero	lambs' liver
hígado de ternera	calves' liver
hígado de vaca	ox liver
hígado encebollado	liver fried with onion
hojaldre (m)	puff pastry
huevo	egg
huevos al plato	baked eggs
huevos duros	hard-boiled eggs
huevos escalfados	poached eggs
huevos fritos	fried eggs
huevos revueltos	scrambled eggs
huevos revueltos con tomate	scrambled eggs with tomato
infusiones (fpl) de hierbas	herbal teas
jamón (m)	ham
jamón cocido	cooked ham
jamón de york	York ham
jamón serrano	uncooked, cured ham
jengibre (m)	ginger
jerez (m)	sherry

judías	beans
judías verdes	French beans
lacón (m)	shoulder of pork
lacón con grelos	boiled gammon with greens
lamprea	lamprey
langosta	lobster
langostinos	langoustines
lasaña	lasagna
leche (f)	milk
batido de leche	milkshake
leche frita	small milk cake made with flour, egg, butter and lemon
lechecillas	sweetbreads
lechuga	lettuce
lengua	tongue
lenguado	sole
filete de lenguado	fillet of sole
lenguado al horno	baked sole
lenguado meunière	sole meunière
lentejas	lentils
lentejas con chorizo	lentils with spicy pork sausage
lentejas guisadas	stewed lentils
licor (m)	spirits
liebre (f)	hare
lima	lime
zumo de lima	lime juice
limón (m)	lemon
zumo de limón	lemon juice
lionesas	choux pastry with icing filled with custard
lomo	loin
lomo de cerdo	lion of pork
lomo de cordero	loin of lamb
longaniza	pork sausage

lubina — sea bass
  lubina al horno — baked sea bass
  lubina cocida — boiled sea bass

macarrones (mpl) — macaroni
  macarrones con queso — macaroni cheese
macedonia de frutas — fruit salad
madalenas — small, round sponge cakes
malta — malt
mandarina — tangerine
manos (fpl) de cerdo — hand of pork
mantequilla — butter
manzana — apple
  pastel de manzana — apple pie
  tarta de manzana — apple tart
mariscos (pl) — seafood, shellfish
martini (vermút) (m) — martini (vermouth)
mayonesa — mayonnaise
mazorca — corn on the cob
mejillones (mpl) — mussels
  mejillones a la marinera — mussels à la marinière
  mejillones al vapor — steamed mussels
melocotón (m) — peach
melón (m) — melon
menestra de verduras — mixed vegetable soup
menta — mint
menú del día (m) — set menu
merengue (m) — meringue
merluza — hake
  filete (m) de merluza empanado — filleted hake fried in egg and breadcrumbs
  filete (m) de merluza rebozado — filleted hake fried in egg and flour
  merluza a la bilbaína — filleted hake fried in egg and flour

merluza cocida	boiled hake
merluza en rodajas	sliced hake
mermelada	jam
mermelada de albaricoque	apricot jam
mermelada de ciruela	plum jam
mermelada de fresa	strawberry jam
mermelada de grosella	gooseberry jam
mermelada de melocotón	peach jam
mermelada de naranja amarga	orange marmalade
mero	sea perch
mero al horno	baked sea perch
mero asado	roasted sea perch
miel (f)	honey
miel sobre hojuelas	puff pastry with honey
minestrone (f)	minestrone soup
morcilla	black pudding
morcilla de arroz	black pudding with rice
morcilla de cebolla	black pudding with onion
mortadela	salami
morteruelo	kind of pie made with minced hare (Cuenca)
mostaza	mustard
mousse (f)	mousse
muslo de pollo	chicken leg
nabo	turnip
nabo sueco	swede
naranja	orange
zumo de naranja embotellado	orange squash
zumo de naranja natural	fresh orange juice
nata	cream
nata espesa	double cream
nata fresca	fresh cream
nata líquida	single cream
nata montada	whipped cream

natillas (fpl)	custard
nécora	baby crab
nuez (f) nueces (pl)	nut, walnut
ostra	oyster
paella	rice with seafood, vegetables and chicken (Valencia)
paella de pollo	chicken paella
paella mixta	mixed paella (chicken and shellfish)
palmera	flat, light pastry
palomitas	popcorn
pan (m)	bread
pan de leche	milk loaf
pan de molde	sliced white bread
pan de pasas	raisin bread
pan integral	brown bread
panquemado	kind of bun (Valencia)
pan rayado	breadcrumbs
una barra	a loaf of bread
panecillo	roll
parrillada de carne	mixed grill
pasas	raisins
pasta	pasta
pastas de té	biscuits
pastel (m)	cake, pie
pastel be bizcocho	sponge cake
pastel de fruta	fruit cake
pastel de ternera	veal pie
pasteles (mpl)	small cakes, pastries
lionesas	choux pastries with icing filled with custard
miel sobre hojuelas	puff pastry with honey
tocinos de cielo	cakes with candied egg yolk

yemas	small cakes made with egg yolk
patatas	potatoes
croquetas de patata	croquette potatoes
patatas al montón	fried potatoes
patatas asadas	roast potatoes
patatas bravas	potatoes in red spicy sauce
patatas en puré	mashed potato
patata en salsa verde	potatoes in parsley sauce
patatas estofadas	stewed potatoes
patatas fritas	chips
patatas hervidas con verduras	potatoes boiled with onion and vegetables
patatas nuevas	new potatoes
patatas paja	potatoes cut very thin and fried
patatas salteadas	sauté potatoes
pato	duck
pato a la naranja	duck in orange sauce
pavo	turkey
pavo trufado	turkey stuffed with truffles
pechuga de gallina/pollo	breast of chicken
pepinillo	gherkin
pepino	cucumber
pera	pear
percebe (m)	type of edible barnacle found only in Spain
perejil (m)	parsley
perro caliente	hot dog
pescadilla	type of small hake
pescado	fish
pez (m) espada	swordfish
pierna de cordero	leg of lamb
pimiento	pepper
pimiento rojo	red pepper
pimiento verde	green pepper

pimientos rellenos de arroz y carne picada — peppers stuffed with rice and minced meat

pinchos — snacks served on bar counters

piña — pineapple

pisto manchego — ratatouille

  revuelto de pisto — ratatouille with scrambled egg

plátano — banana

platija — plaice

plato — course

  comida de /tres/ platos — /three-/ course meal

  plato combinado — mixed dish of different kinds of food

pollo — chicken

  muslo de pollo — chicken leg

  pechuga de pollo — chicken breast

  pollo al vino — coq au vin

  pollo empanado — chicken fried in breadcrumbs

  pollo trufado — chicken meat loaf

  sopa de pollo — chicken soup

pomelo — grapefruit

  gajos de pomelo — grapefruit segments

  zumo de pomelo — grapefruit juice

porrusalda — dish of cod, potatoes and leeks (Basque)

postre (m) — dessert

potaje (m) — type of thick vegetable soup

  potaje de garbanzos — chick pea soup

primer plato — starters

puerro — leek

pulpo — octopus

puré (m) de fruta con nata — fruit purée with cream

  puré de guisantes — pea purée

  puré de patatas — mashed potato

queso — cheese

queso azul	blue cheese
queso curado	rather dry and tasty cheese
queso cremoso	cream cheese
queso de bola	large round cheese (red outside)
queso gallego	creamy cheese
queso manchego	hard white cheese
queso roquefort	Roquefort cheese
requesón	cottage cheese
quisquilla	shrimp
rábano	radish
rabo de buey	oxtail
sopa de rabo de buey	oxtail soup
rape (m)	large white fish
rape en salsa verde	white fish in parsley sauce
ravioli (mpl)	ravioli
relleno	stuffing, stuffed
remolacha	beetroot
reo	sea trout
repollo	cabbage
requesón	cottage cheese
revuelto de pisto	ratatouille with scrambled egg
riñón (m)	kidney
riñones al jerez	kidneys in sherry sauce
rodaballo	turbot
ron (m)	rum
ruibardo	rhubarb
sal (f)	salt
salchicha	sausage
salchicha de Frankfurt	Frankfurter
salchichón (m)	salami
salmón (m)	salmon
salmonete (m)	red mullet
salsa	sauce

salsa bechamel	béchamel sauce
salsa blanca	white sauce
salsa de manzana	apple sauce
salsa de menta	mint sauce
salsa de pan	bread sauce
salsa Tabasco	Tabasco sauce
salsa tártara	tartare sauce
salsa vinagreta	vinaigrette sauce
salsa worcester	Worcester sauce
salvia	sage
relleno de salvia y cebolla	sage and onion stuffing
sandía	water melon
sandwich (m)	sandwich
sangría	mixture of wine, fruit and lemonade, sometimes with liqueur added
sardina	sardine
sardinas en escabeche	pickled sardines
sardinas fritas	fried sardines
sardinas rebozadas	sardines rolled in batter and fried
sepia	cuttlefish
sepia a la plancha	griddled cuttlefish
sesos	brains
setas	edible toadstool
sidra	cider
solomillo	sirloin
solomillo de cerdo	pork fillet
sopa	soup
sopa de ajo	soup with bread and garlic
sopa de cebolla	onion soup
sopa de pescado	fish soup
sopa del día	soup of the day
sorbete (m)	sorbet
suizos	danish pastry

suquet (m)	a dish of mixed fish (Catalonia)
surtido	assortment
tapas	appetizers found in bars. They usually consist of olives, anchovies, prawns, eels, squid, or any regional speciality and are almost a meal in themselves.
té (m)	tea
té chino	China tea
té indio	Indian tea
té manzanilla	camomile tea
té menta	mint tea
té tila	linden blossom tea
una taza de té	a cup of tea
una tetera de té	a pot of tea
ternera	veal
lengua de ternera	calves' tongue
ternera mechada	veal stuffed and rolled
ternera rehogada	veal sautéed in oil and garlic
timbal (m) de salchichas	sausage pie/pastry
timbal de hígado	liver pie/pastry
tocino	bacon
tocinos de cielo	cakes with candied egg yolk
tomate (m)	tomato
ensalada de tomate	tomato salad
tomate relleno	stuffed tomato
zumo de tomate	tomato juice
tordo	thrush
torrijas	sliced fried bread, previously dipped in milk and sprinkled with sugar
torta	pancake
tortilla	omelette

tortilla con queso	cheese omelette
tortilla española	Spanish omelette
tortuga	turtle
sopa de tortuga	turtle soup
tostada	toast
trucha	trout
trucha a la navarra	trout stuffed with ham, and fried in an almond and parsley sauce
turrón (m)	kind of nougat, made of almond, honey etc
uva	grape
vaca	beef
vainilla	vanilla
valenciana	sponge cake
venado	venison
verdura	vegetable
vichyssoise (f)	vichyssoise
vieira	scallop
vinagre (m)	vinegar
vino de la casa	house wine (usually good and more economical)
vodka	vodka
yema	small cake made with egg yolk
yogur (m)	yoghurt
zanahoria	carrot
zarzuela	a dish of mixed fish
zumo	juice
zumo de naranja	orange juice
zumo de pomelo	grapefruit juice
zumo de tomate	tomato juice

Señalizaciones españolas

Spanish signs

ABIERTO	Open
ABROCHENSE LOS CINTURONES DE SEGURIDAD	Fasten safety belts
ACCESORIOS	Accessories/parts (garage)
ACCESORIOS DE AUTOMÓVIL	Car accessories
ACEITE	Oil
ADUANA	Customs
AGENCIA	Agency
AGENCIA DE VIAJES	Travel agency
AGUA POTABLE	Drinking water
AIRE	Air
ALIMENTACIÓN	Food
ALOJAMIENTO	Accommodation
ALQUILER DE COCHES	Car hire

ALQUILER DE HABITACIONES	Rooms to let
ALQUILERES	Rentals
ALTURA MÁXIMA	Maximum headroom
AMBULANCIA	Ambulance
ANDÉN	Platform
ANFITEATRO	Amphitheatre
ANTIGÜEDADES	Antiques
ANULADO	Cancelled
APARCAMIENTO (COMPLETO)	Parking/car park (full)
APARCAMIENTO DE GARAJE	Garage parking
APELLIDO	Surname
ARRIBA	Up
ARTESANÍA	Craft shop
ARTÍCULOS QUE DECLARAR	Goods to declare
ASCENSOR	Lift
ASIENTO	Seat
AUTOBÚS DEL AEROPUERTO	Airport bus
AUTOCAR	Coach
AUTOMÁTICO	Automatic
AUTOPISTA	Motorway
AUTORIZADO MAYORES 14 AÑOS Y MENORES ACOMPAÑADOS	'A' film (for children over 14 or those accompanied by an adult)
AUTORIZADO MAYORES DE 18 AÑOS	'X' film
AUTOSERVICIO	Self-service
AVERIADO	Out of order
AVISO	Warning/notice
BANCO	Bank
BANDEJAS	Trays
BARCAS PARA ALQUILAR	Boats for hire
BASURA	Litter
BIBLIOTECA	Library
BIENVENIDO A	Welcome to

BILLETES	Tickets
BOCADILLOS	Snacks/sandwiches
BODEGA	Wine bar
BONOBÚS	Cheap rate bus ticket (available from some kiosks and some major banks)
BUZÓN	Letterbox
CABALLEROS	Gentlemen
CAFETERÍA	Café
CAJA	Cash desk
CAJA CERRADA	Till closed
CAJERO	Cashier
CALIENTE (C)	Hot (water)
CAMARERA	Chambermaid/waitress
CAMBIO	Exchange/rate of exchange
CAMPO DE GOLF	Golf course
CANTINA	Buffet/Bar
CARGA MÁXIMA 4 PERSONAS O 300 KG	Maximum load 4 people or 300 kg (lift)
CARNICERÍA	Butcher's
CARTA	Menu
CARTAS	Letters (letterbox)
CEDA EL PASO	Give way
CENTRO CIUDAD	Town centre
CERRADO (DURANTE HORA DE ALMUERZO)	Closed (for lunch)
CIRCO	Circus
CIUDAD	Town (letterbox)
CLÍNICA	Surgery/clinic
CLÍNICA DENTAL	Dental surgery
COBRADOR	Bus conductor
COCTELERÍA	Cocktail bar
COCHE RESTAURANTE	Restaurant car
COMIDAS PARA LLEVAR	Take-away meals

COMPLETO	Full
CONFERENCIAS INTERNACIONALES	Overseas telephone calls
CONSERJE	Porter
CONSIGNA	Left luggage office
CONSULTA MÉDICA	Surgery
CONSULTAS EXTERNAS	Outpatients
CONTROL DE PASAPORTES	Passport control/immigration
CORREO	Mail
CORREO AÉREO	Airmail
CORREOS	Post Office
CRUZ ROJA	Red Cross
CUENTAS CORRIENTES	Accounts
¡CUIDADO!	Watch out!
¡CUIDADO CON EL PERRO!	Beware of the dog!
CURVA PELIGROSA	Dangerous bend
CHALECOS SALVAVIDAS	Life jackets
DENTISTA	Dentist
DEPARTAMENTO DE JUGUETES	Toy department
DEPARTAMENTO DE MUEBLES	Furniture department
DEPARTAMENTO DE NIÑOS	Children's department
DESTINO	Destination
DESVÍO	Diversion
DE VENTA AQUÍ	On sale here
DIRECCIÓN DE HOTEL	Hotel management
DISCOS	Records
DISCOTECA	Disco
ELECTRODOMÉSTICOS	Electrical goods
EMBARQUE	Embarcation/boarding
EMERGENCIAS	Emergencies
EMPUJAR/EMPUJAD	Push
EN BENEFICIO DE TODOS ENTREN Y SALGAN RÁPIDAMENTE	To avoid delay, enter and leave as quickly as possible (underground)

ENTRADA	Way in/entrance
ENTRADA (LIBRE)	Admission (free)
EQUIPAJE	Luggage
EQUIPAJE DE MANO	Hand luggage
ESCALERAS	Stairs
ESCUELA	School
ESPEREN	Wait (pedestrians)
ESTACIÓN DE AUTOCARES	Coach station
ESTACIÓN DE FERROCARRIL	Railway station
ESTACIÓN DE SERVICIO	Petrol station
ESTANCO	Tobacconist
EXCURSIONES DE MEDIO DÍA	Half-day tours
EXCURSIONES DIURNAS	Day trips
EXCURSIONES EN AUTOCAR CON GUÍA	Conducted coach tours
EXTRANJERO	Abroad (letterbox)
FABRICADO EN	Made in
FACTURACIÓN	Check-in (desk)
FARMACIA	Dispensing chemist
FILA	Row (in theatre)
FIN	The end
FLORISTA	Florist
FRÁGIL	Fragile (parcels)
FRÍO (F)	Cold (water)
FUEGO	Fire exit
FUERA DE SERVICIO	Out of order
GARAJE	Garage
GASOLINA	Petrol
GIROS	Money orders
GRATIS	Free
GUARDARROPA	Cloakroom
GUARDERÍA INFANTIL	Nursery/crèche
GUÍA	Guide

HABITACIONES	Rooms
HABLE (AQUÍ)	Speak (here)
HELADOS	Ice creams
HOMBRES	Men
HORARIO	Timetable
HORARIO DE SALIDAS	Departure times
HORAS DE CONSULTA	Surgery hours
IGLESIA	Church
INFLAMABLE	Inflammable
INFORMACIÓN	Information/Enquiries
INFORMACIÓN DE VUELOS	Flight information
INGRESOS	Admissions (hospital)
INTERMEDIO	Intermission
INTRANSFERIBLE	Not transferable (ticket)
INTRODUZCA (MONEDA)	Insert (coin)
JABÓN LÍQUIDO	Liquid soap
JOYAS	Jewellery
JOYERÍA	Jeweller's
JUGUETES	Toys
LAVABOS	Toilets
LAVANDERÍA	Laundry
LIBRE	Vacant
LIBRERÍA	Bookshop
LIBROS DE BOLSILLO	Paperbacks
LÍMITE DE ALTURA	Height limit
LÍMITE DE PESO	Weight limit
LIMPIEZA EN SECO	Dry cleaning
LIQUIDACIÓN TOTAL	Closing down sale
LISTA DE CORREOS	Poste restante
LUNES–SÁBADO	Monday–Saturday
LLAME	Call (on bell)
LLEGADAS	Arrivals

MÁXIMO 2 HORAS	Maximum 2 hours (parking meters)
MERCADO	Market
MERCERÍA	Haberdasher's
MERIENDAS	Light refreshments/afternoon teas
METRO	Underground (trains)
MODAS	Fashions
MUEBLES	Furniture
MUELLES	Docks
MULTA	Fine (payment)
NADA QUE DECLARAR	Nothing to declare
NIÑOS	Children
NO APARCAR, LLAMAMOS GRÚA	No parking – or your car will be towed away
NO ENTREN NI SALGAN DESPUÉS DE OÍR EL SILBATO	Do not enter or leave train after whistle has sounded (underground)
NO MOLESTAR	Do not disturb
NO PISAR EL CÉSPED	Keep off the grass
NO SE ADMITEN PERROS	No dogs allowed
NO SE FÍA	No credit
OBRAS	Roadworks
OCTANO	Octane
OCUPADO	Engaged (toilet)
OFERTA ESPECIAL	Special offer
OFICINA DE OBJETOS PERDIDOS	Lost property office
OFICINA DE VIAJES	Travel agency/office
ÓPTICO (OFTALMÓLOGO)	Optician (ophthalmic optician)
PABELLÓN	Ward (Hospital)
PANADERÍA	Baker's
PARA ALQUILAR	To let

PARADA (DE AUTOBÚS)	(Bus) stop
PARTICULAR	Private
PASAJEROS EN TRÁNSITO	Transit/transfer passengers
PASAPORTES	Passports
PASEN	Cross now (pedestrians)
PASO A NIVEL	Level crossing
PASO A NIVEL CON GUARDA	Manned level crossing
PASO A NIVEL SIN GUARDA	Unmanned level crossing
PEAJE	Toll (motorway)
PEATONES	Pedestrian
PELIGRO	Danger
PELIGROS: OBRAS	Roadworks
PELUQUERÍA	Hairdressing salon
PELUQUERÍA DE SEÑORAS	Ladies hairdressing salon
PERFUMERÍA	Perfumery
PIEZAS DE RECAMBIO	Spare parts
PISCINA	Swimming pool
PLANTA BAJA (B)	Ground floor (lift)
POLICÍA	Police
POR FAVOR...	Please...
POR LA OTRA PUERTA	Use other door
PORTERO	Porter
PRECAUCIÓN	Watch out!
PRIMERA CLASE	First class
PROHIBIDA LA ENTRADA	No entry
PROHIBIDO	Prohibited
PROHIBIDO ACAMPAR	No camping
PROHIBIDO APARCAR	No parking
PROHIBIDO BAÑARSE	No swimming
PROHIBIDO EL PASO	No access
PROHIBIDO ESTACIONARSE	No waiting
PROHIBIDO USAR A LOS MENORES NO ACOMPAÑADOS	Children must be accompanied (lift)

PROPIEDAD PRIVADA PROHIBIDA LA ENTRADA	Private property: no trespassing
PUENTE AÉREO	Madrid–Barcelona flights
PUERTA	Gate (airport)
PUERTO	Port
PUESTO DE SOCORRO	First aid
PULSE BOTÓN PARA CRUZAR	Press button to cross
R.A.C. (REAL AUTOMÓVIL CLUB)	Spanish equivalent of the Automobile Association
RAZÓN: AQUÍ	Enquiries here
RAZÓN COMERCIAL	Business address
REBAJAS	Sales
RECIÉN PINTADO	Wet paint
REFRESCOS	Cold drinks
REGALOS	Gifts
REPARACIÓN DE CALZADO	Shoe repairs
REPARACIONES	Repairs
RESERVADO	Reserved
RESERVADO SOCIOS	Members only
RESERVADO SUBIDA Y BAJADA DE VIAJEROS CARGA Y DESCARGA	Parking reserved for passengers entering and leaving vehicles, and for loading and unloading
RESERVAS	Reservations/Advance booking
RESTAURANTE	Restaurant
RETRASO	Delay
REVISTAS	Magazines
ROPA DE SPORT	Casual wear
ROPA INTERIOR	Underwear
RUTA ALTERNATIVA	Alternative route
S.A. (SOCIEDAD ANÓNIMA)	Co. Ltd.
SALA DE ESPERA	Waiting room
SALDOS	Sales
SALIDA	Out/exit

SALIDA DE EMERGENCIA	Emergency exit
SALIDA DE INCENDIOS	Fire exit
SALIDAS	Departures
SALIDAS DE AUTOCAR	Coach departures
SALIDAS INTERNACIONALES	International departures
SALIDAS NACIONALES	Domestic departures
SALÓN	Lounge
SANCIÓN	Fine
SE ALQUILA	For hire/to let
SEGUNDA CLASE	Second class
SE HACEN FOTOCOPIAS AL MOMENTO	Photocopies done on the spot
SE HACEN LLAVES	Keys cut here
SELLOS	Stamps
SEÑORAS	Women
SE PROHIBE FUMAR	No smoking
SE PROHIBE HABLAR CON EL CONDUCTOR	Do not speak to the driver
SE PROHIBE LA ENTRADA	Do not enter
SE RUEGA...	Please...
SE RUEGA A LOS CLIENTES QUE COJAN UNA CESTA	Customers must take a basket (supermarket)
SERVICIO A DOMICILIO	Delivery service
SERVICIO DE CAMARERA	Ring for service
SERVICIO DE HABITACIÓN	Room service
SERVICIO GRATUITO	Free service
SERVICIO (NO) INCLUIDO	Service (not) included
SERVICIOS	Toilets/Services (motorway)
SESIÓN(ES) DE HOY	Today's performance(s)
SE VENDE	For sale
SILENCIO	Silence
SÍRVASE COGER UNA CESTA	Please take a basket (supermarket)
SOBRECARGA	Additional charge
SÓLO...	...only

SÓLO BUS	Buses only
SÓLO CARGA Y DESCARGA	Loading and unloading only
SÓLO EMPLEADOS	Staff only
SÓLO MAQUINAS DE AFEITAR	Shavers only
SÓLO MOTOS	Motorcycles only(parking)
SÓLO TAXIS	Taxis only
SÓTANO (S)	Basement (lift)
SUPER	Super (petrol)
SUPLEMENTO POR EXCESO DE EQUIPAJE	Excess baggage charge
TAQUILLA	Box office
TARIFA	Fare/price
TEATRO	Theatre
TEJIDOS	Fabrics
TEJIDOS PARA MOBILIARIO Y DECORACIÓN	Furnishing fabrics
TELÉFONO	Telephone
TELEGRAMAS	Telegrams
TERMINAL (AÉREA)	(Air) terminal
TERMINAL INTERNACIONAL	International terminal
TERMINAL NACIONAL	National terminal
TIMBRE	Bell
TIRAR	Pull
TRANSFERENCIAS BANCARIAS	Money orders
TÚNEL	Tunnel
ULTRAMARINOS	Grocer's
VADO PERMANENTE	Do not obstruct entrance: No parking at any time
VENENO	Poison
VESTUARIO	Changing room
VINOS Y LICORES	Wines and spirits
VOLTAJE	Voltage
VUELO	Flight

| ZAPATERÍA | Shoe shop |
| ZONA AZUL | Parking limited to 1 ½ hours (town centre) |

Clave para el automovilista

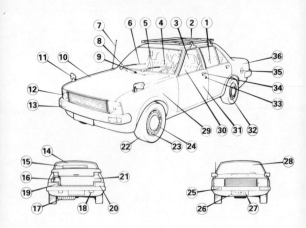

1 asiento trasero	back seat
2 baca	roof rack
3 apoyacabezas	head restraint
4 asiento delantero	passenger seat
5 cinturón de seguridad	seat belt
6 canto de goma del limpiaparabrisas	windscreen wiper blade
7 antena	aerial
8 brazo de limpiaparabrisas	windscreen wiper arm
9 lavacristales	windscreen washer
10 capó	bonnet
11 retrovisor exterior	exterior mirror
12 faro	headlight
13 parachoques	bumper
14 luneta trasera	rear window
15 luneta térmica trasera	rear window heater
16 rueda de recambio	spare wheel
17 depósito de gasolina	fuel tank
18 intermitente de emergencia	hazard warning light
19 luz de frenos	brake light
20 luz trasera	rear light
21 maletero	boot
22 neumático	tyre
23 rueda delantera	front wheel
24 tapacubos	hubcap
25 luz de posición	sidelight
26 placa de matrícula	number plate
27 matrícula	registration number
28 parabrisas	windscreen
29 guardabarros delantero	front wing
30 asiento del conductor	driver's seat
31 puerta	door
32 rueda trasera	rear wheel
33 cerradura	lock
34 manecilla de la puerta	door handle
35 tapón de depósito	petrol filler cap
36 guardabarros trasero	rear wing

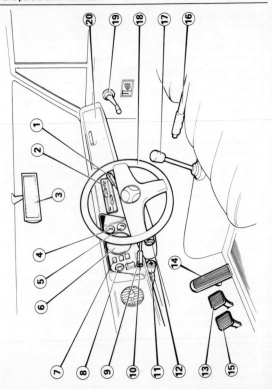

1 conmutador para luces	dipswitch
2 calefacción	heater
3 retrovisor	interior mirror
4 termómetro del agua	water temperature gauge
5 amperímetro	ammeter
6 indicador de velocidad	speedometer
7 testigo de la presión del aceite	oil pressure warning light
8 indicador del nivel de la gasolina	fuel gauge
9 bocina	horn
10 intermitente	direction indicator
11 stárter/dispositivo de arranque en frío	choke
12 encendido	ignition switch
13 pedal de freno	brake pedal
14 acelerador	accelerator
15 pedal de embrague	clutch pedal
16 freno de mano	handbrake
17 palanca de velocidades	gear lever
18 volante	steering wheel
19 manivela para abrir la ventanilla	window winder
20 guantera	glove compartment

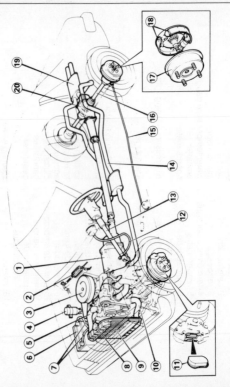

1	caja de cambios	gearbox
2	caja de fusibles	fuse box
3	filtro de aire	air filter
4	bobina de encendido	ignition coil
5	tubo flexible superior	radiator hose (top)
6	batería	battery
7	hilos conductores	leads (battery)
8	tapón del radiador	filler cap (radiator)
9	radiador	radiator
10	tubo flexible inferior	radiator hose (bottom)
11	forro de freno de disco	disc brake pad
12	cable de velocímetro	speedometer cable
13	columna de dirección	steering column
14	tubo de escape	exhaust pipe
15	cable de freno de mano	handbrake cable
16	eje trasero	rear axle
17	tambor de freno	brake drum
18	zapata de freno	brake shoe
19	silencioso	silencer
20	diferencial	differential

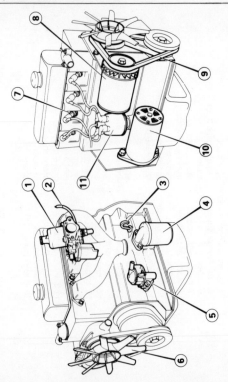

1	carburador	carburettor
2	cable	cable
3	varilla del nivel de aceite	oil dip stick
4	filtro de aceite	oil filter
5	bomba de gasolina	fuel pump
6	ventilador	fan
7	bujía	sparking plug
8	dínamo	alternator
9	correa del ventilador	fan belt
10	motor de arranque	starter motor
11	distribuidor	distributor

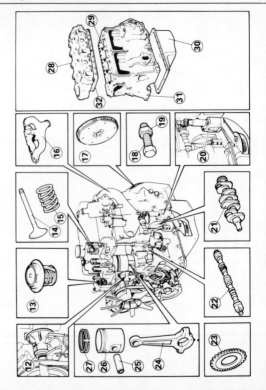

12	bomba de agua	water pump
13	termostato	thermostat
14	válvula	valve
15	resorte	spring
16	colector de admisión y escape	manifold, inlet and exhaust
17	volante	flywheel
18	tornillo	bolt
19	tuerca	nut
20	bomba de aceite	oil pump
21	eje cigüeñal	crankshaft
22	eje de levas	camshaft
23	ruedas de cadena	sprocket
24	biela	connecting rod
25	bulón de pistón	gudgeon pin
26	pistón	piston
27	aros de pistón	piston rings
28	culata de cilindros	cylinder head
29	cilindro	cylinder
30	colector de aceite	oil sump
31	bloque de cilindros	cylinder block
32	junta	gasket

Números, días de la semana y meses del año

Números

0 oh	43 forty-three
1 one	54 fifty-four
2 two	65 sixty-five
3 three	76 seventy-six
4 four	87 eighty-seven
5 five	98 ninety-eight
6 six	100 a hundred
7 seven	101 a hundred and one
8 eight	211 two hundred and eleven
9 nine	322 three hundred and twenty-two
10 ten	433 four hundred and thirty-three
11 eleven	544 five hundred and forty-four
12 twelve	655 six hundred and fifty-five
13 thirteen	766 seven hundred and sixty-six
14 fourteen	877 eight hundred and seventy-seven
15 fifteen	988 nine hundred and eighty-eight
16 sixteen	1000 a thousand
17 seventeen	1001 a thousand and one
18 eighteen	2112 two thousand one hundred and twelve
19 nineteen	3223 three thousand two hundred and twenty-three
20 twenty	4334 four thousand three hundred and thirty-four
21 twenty-one	10,000 ten thousand
32 thirty-two	

Días de la semana

Lunes	Monday
Martes	Tuesday
Miércoles	Wednesday
Jueves	Thursday
Viernes	Friday
Sábado	Saturday
Domingo	Sunday

Meses del año

Enero	January
Febrero	February
Marzo	March
Abril	April
Mayo	May
Junio	June
Julio	July
Agosto	August
Septiembre	September
Octubre	October
Noviembre	November
Diciembre	December

Equivalencias

Moneda británica

GB: Pound = £   Pence = p   £1 = 100p

Monedas (*Coins*)
½p a half penny (a half p.)
1p a penny (one p.)
2p two pence (two p.)
5p five pence (five p.)
20p twenty pence (twenty p.)
50p fifty pence (fifty p.)
£1 a pound, one pound

Billetes (*Notes*)
£1 a pound, one pound
£5 five pounds
£10 ten pounds
£20 twenty pounds
£50 fifty pounds

En el banco le preguntarán cómo quiere el dinero:

¿Cómo lo quiere?   How would you like the money?
en billetes de /una libra/   in /ones/
en billetes de /cinco libras/   in /fives/
en billetes de /diez libras/   in /tens/
en billetes de /veinte libras/   in /twenties/

(Números vea 1.26)

Distancias

1,6 kilómetros = 1 milla   1 mile = 1.6 kilometres

Millas	10	20	30	40	50	60	70	80	90	100	Miles
Kilómetros	16	32	48	64	80	97	113	128	145	160	Kilometres

Longitud y talla

Algunas equivalencias:

Británicas			Métricas
1 inch	(pulgada)		= 2.5 centímetros
6 inches			= 15 centímetros
1 foot	(pie)	= 12 inches	= 30 centímetros
2 feet	(pies)	= 24 inches	= 60 centímetros
1 yard	(yarda)	= 3 feet = 36 inches	= 91 centímetros
1 yard 3 inches			= 1 metro

Tallas de ropa (incluye medidas de busto/caderas)

GB	EE.UU	Europa	pulgadas	cm.
8	6	36	30/32	76/81
10	8	38	32/34	81/86
12	10	40	34/36	86/91
14	12	42	36/38	91/97
16	14	44	38/40	97/102
18	16	46	40/42	102/107
20	18	48	42/44	107/112
22	20	50	44/46	112/117
24	22	52	46/48	117/122
26	24	54	48/50	122/127

Medidas de cintura

GB/EE.UU (pulgadas)	22	24	26	28	30	32	34	36	38	40	42	44	46	48	50
Europa (cm)	56	61	66	71	76	81	86	91	97	102	107	112	117	122	127

Medidas de cuello

GB/EE.UU (pulgadas)	14	$14\frac{1}{2}$	15	$15\frac{1}{2}$	16	$16\frac{1}{2}$	17	$17\frac{1}{2}$
Europa (cm)	36	37	38	39	40	41	42	43

Zapatos

GB	3	$3\frac{1}{2}$	4	$4\frac{1}{2}$	5	$5\frac{1}{2}$	6	$6\frac{1}{2}$	7	$7\frac{1}{2}$	8	$8\frac{1}{2}$	9	10	11	12
EE.UU.	$4\frac{1}{2}$	5	$5\frac{1}{2}$	6	$6\frac{1}{2}$	7	$7\frac{1}{2}$	8	$8\frac{1}{2}$	9	$9\frac{1}{2}$	10	$10\frac{1}{2}$	$11\frac{1}{2}$	$12\frac{1}{2}$	$13\frac{1}{2}$
Europa	36		37		38		39		40		41		42	43	44	45

Sombreros

GB	$6\frac{5}{8}$	$6\frac{3}{4}$	$6\frac{7}{8}$	7	$7\frac{1}{8}$	$7\frac{1}{4}$	$7\frac{3}{8}$	$7\frac{1}{2}$	$7\frac{5}{8}$
EE.UU.	$6\frac{3}{4}$	$6\frac{7}{8}$	7	$7\frac{1}{8}$	$7\frac{1}{4}$	$7\frac{3}{8}$	$7\frac{1}{2}$	$7\frac{5}{8}$	$7\frac{3}{4}$
Europa	54	55	56	57	58	59	60	61	62

Las tallas de guantes son las mismas en todos los países

Pesos

Algunas equivalencias:

ounces (oz.) (onzas) y *pounds* (lbs.) (libras)
         16 *ounces* (16 ozs.) = 1 *pound* (1 lb.)
grams (gms.) (gramos) y *kilograms* (kgs.) (kilogramos):
         1000 *grams* (1000 gms.) = 1 kilogram (1 kilo/kg.)

1 ounce (oz)	=	25 grams (gms.)
4 ounces (ozs) ($\frac{1}{4}$ of a pound)	=	100/125 grams
8 ounces ($\frac{1}{2}$ a pound)	=	225 grams
1 pound (16 ozs)	=	450 grams
1 pound 2 ounces	=	500 grams ($\frac{1}{2}$ kilogram)
2 pounds 4 ounces	=	1 kilogram (1 kilo)
1 stone	=	6 kilograms

Peso Corporal

El peso corporal en Gran Bretaña se suele medir en 'stones' (1 *stone* = 14 *pounds*)

Algunas equivalencias:

Libras	Stones	Kilogramos
28	2	12½
42	3	19
56	4	25
70	5	32
84	6	38
98	7	45
112	8	51
126	9	57½
140	10	63
154	11	70
168	12	76
182	13	83
196	14	90

Medida de líquidos

En Gran Bretaña los líquidos suelen medirse en 'pints', 'quarts' y 'gallons'.
'Pints' se emplean para cantidades mas reducidas, a menudo embotelladas: por ej; *a pint of milk* (leche). 'Gallons' se emplean para cantidades mayores: por ej; *a gallon of petrol* (gasolina).

Algunas equivalencias:

1 pint = 0.57 litres (litros)
2 pints = 1 quart
8 pints = 1 gallon
1 gallon = 4.55 litres

Litros		**Medidas británicas**
0.5	=	1 pint (20 fluid ounces) (20 fl. ozs.)
1	=	1.7 pints
5	=	1.1 gallons
10	=	2.2 ..
15	=	3.3 ..
20	=	4.4 ..
25	=	5.5 ..
30	=	6.6 ..
35	=	7.7 ..
40	=	8.8 ..
45	=	9.9 ..

Temperaturas

	Fahrenheit (°F)	**Centigrade** (°C)	
Punto de ebullición	212	100	Boiling point
	104	40	
Temperatura corporal	98.4	36.9	Body temperature
	86	30	
	68	20	
	59	15	
	50	10	
Punto de congelación	32	0	Freezing point
	23	−5	
	0	−18	

Para convertir Fahrenheit en Centígrados se restan 32 y se multiplica por 5/9. Para convertir Centígrados en Fahrenheit se multiplica por 9/5 y se añaden 32.

Temperaturas: Podemas decir '75 degrees' (75 grados) o '75 degrees Fahrenheit/Centigrade; (75 grados Fahrenheit/Centígrados). El término 'Centigrade' se usa más a menudo que 'Celsius' (Celsio).

Presión de los neumáticos

kg/cm^2		lb/sq. in.	kg/cm^2		lb/sq. in.	kg/cm^2		lb/sq. in.
1.40	=	20	1.68	=	24	2.10	=	30
1.47	=	21	1.82	=	26	2.39	=	34
1.54	=	22	1.96	=	28	2.81	=	40

NB El sistema métrico decimal se está extendiendo
progresivamente en Inglaterra.

Paises, monedas, nacionalidades y lenguas

Pais, area o continente	Moneda principal	Descripción y nacionalidad	Idioma(s) principal(es)
Africa	Africa	African	—
Africa del Sur	South Africa	South African	Afrikaans/English
Albania	Albania	Albanian	Albanian
Alemania	Germany	German	German
A. Occidental	West G.	Deutschmark	German
A. Oriental	East G.	Ostmark	German
Arabia Saudita	Saudi Arabia	Riyal	Saudi Arabian	Arabic
Argelia	Algeria	Dinar	Algerian	Arabic/French
Argentina	Argentina	Peso	Argentinian	Spanish
Asia	Asia	—	Asian	—
Australia	Australia	Dollar	Australian	English
Austria	Austria	Schilling	Austrian	German
Bahrain	Bahrain	Dinar	Bahraini	Arabic
Bélgica	Belgium	Franc	Belgian	Flemish/French
Birmania	Burma	Kyat	Burmese	Burmese
Bolivia	Bolivia	Peso	Bolivian	Spanish
Brasil	Brazil	Cruziero	Brazilian	Portuguese
Bulgaria	Bulgaria	Lev	Bulgarian	Bulgarian
Canadá	Canada	Dollar	Canadian	English/French
Colombia	Colombia	Peso	Colombian	Spanish
Costa Rica	Costa Rica	Colon	Costa Rican	Spanish

Cuba	Cuba	Peso	Cuban	Spanish
Checoslovaquia	Czechoslovakia	Koruna	Czech	Czech/Slovak
Chile	Chile	Escudo	Chilean	Spanish
China	China	Yuan	Chinese	Chinese
Chipre	Cyprus	Pound	Cypriot	Greek/Turkish
Dinamarca	Denmark	Krone	Danish	Danish
Ecuador	Ecuador	Sucre	Ecuadorian	Spanish
Egipto	Egypt	Pound	Egyptian	Arabic
Eire	Eire	Punt	Irish	English/Irish
El Líbano	Lebanon	Pound	Lebanese	Arabic
El Perú	Peru	Sol	Peruvian	Spanish
El Sudán	Sudan	Pound	Sudanese	Arabic
Escocia	Scotland	Pound	Scottish/British	English/Gaelic
España	Spain	Peseta	Spanish	Spanish
Estados Unidos de América (EE. UU)	United States of America (USA)	Dollar	American	English
Etiopía	Ethiopia	Dollar	Ethiopian	Amharic
Europa	Europe	—	European	—
Finlandia	Finland	Markka	Finnish	Finnish/Swedish
Francia	France	Franc	French	French
Gales	Wales	Pound	Welsh/British	English/Welsh
Ghana	Ghana	New Cedi	Ghanaian	English/Akan
Grecia	Greece	Drachma	Greek	Greek
Guatemala	Guatemala	Quetzal	Guatemalan	Spanish
Guyana	Guyana	Dollar	Guyanese	English
Holanda (Países Bajos)	Holland (The Netherlands)	Guilder	Dutch	Dutch

Pais, area o continente		Moneda principal	Descripción y nacionalidad	Idioma(s) principal(es)
Hong Kong	Hong Kong	Dollar	from Hong Kong	Chinese/English
Hungría	Hungary	Forint	Hungarian	Hungarian
India	India	Rupee	Indian	Hindi/English
Indonesia	Indonesia	Rupiah	Indonesian	Bahasa Indonesian
Inglaterra	England	Pound	English	English
Irak	Iraq	Dinar	Iraqi	Arabic
Irán	Iran	Rial	Iranian	Farsi
Irlanda del Norte	Northern Ireland	Pound	Irish/British	English
Islandia	Iceland	Krona	Icelandic	Icelandic
Israel	Israel	Pound	Israeli	Hebrew/Arabic
Italia	Italy	Lira	Italian	Italian
Jamaica	Jamaica	Dollar	Jamaican	English
Japón	Japan	Yen	Japanese	Japanese
Jordania	Jordan	Dinar	Jordanian	Arabic
Kenia	Kenya	Shilling	Kenyan	Swahili/English
Kuwait	Kuwait	Dinar	Kuwaiti	Arabic
Libia	Libya	Dinar	Libyan	Arabic
Luxemburgo	Luxemburg	Franc	a Luxemburger	French/German
Malasia	Malaysia	Dollar	Malaysian	Malay/Chinese
Malta	Malta	Pound	Maltese	Maltese/English
Marruecos	Morocco	Dirham	Moroccan	Arabic/French
Méjico	Mexico	Peso	Mexican	Spanish
Nicaragua	Nicaragua	Cordoba	Nicaraguan	Spanish
Nigeria	Nigeria	Naira	Nigerian	Hausa/Ibo/Yoruba English

Noruega	Norway	Krone	Norwegian	Norwegian
Nueva Zelanda	New Zealand	Dollar	a New Zealander	English
Pakistán	Pakistan	Rupee	Pakistani	Urdu
Paraguay	Paraguay	Guarani	Paraguayan	Spanish
Polonia	Poland	Zloty	Polish	Polish
Portugal	Portugal	Escudo	Portuguese	Portuguese
Reino Unido (= Inglaterra, Irlanda del Norte, Escocia, Gales, Las Islas Normandas)	United Kingdom (UK) (= England, Northern Ireland, Scotland, Wales, Channel Islands)	Pound Sterling	British	English
Rumania	Romania	Leu	Romanian	Romanian
Singapur	Singapore	Dollar	Singaporean	Malay/Chinese/Tamil/English
Siria	Syria	Pound	Syrian	Arabic
Suecia	Sweden	Krona	Swedish	Swedish
Suiza	Switzerland	Franc	Swiss	French/German/Italian
Tailandia	Thailand	Baht	Thai	Thai
Tanzania	Tanzania	Shilling	Tanzanian	Swahili/English
Túnez	Tunisia	Dinar	Tunisian	Arabic/French
Turquía	Turkey	Lira	Turkish	Turkish
Unión de Repúblicas Socialistas Soviéticas (URSS)/Rusia	Union of Soviet Socialist Republics (USSR)/Russia	Rouble	Russian/Soviet	Russian

Pais, area o continente		Moneda principal	Descripción y nacionalidad	Idiomas(s) principal(es)
Uruguay	Uruguay	Peso	Uruguayan	Spanish
Venezuela	Venezuela	Bolivar	Venezuelan	Spanish
Vietnam	Vietnam	Dong	Vietnamese	Vietnamese
Yugoslavia	Yugoslavia	Dinar	Yugoslavian	Serbo-Croat
Zaire	Zaire	Zaire	Zairean	French/Lingala
Zimbabwe	Zimbabwe	Dollar	Zimbabwean	English/Shona/ Ndebele

Algunas ideas para el viajero

Direcciones

Oficina de Turismo de Londres (London Tourist board), frente a Platform 15 (andén nº 15), Victoria Station. (Tfno. 730–0791 – se hablan idiomas). Diariamente de 9 a 6.

British Tourist Authority (Delegación Británica de Turismo), St James's Street, nº 64. SW1, (Tfno 499–9325). Lunes a Viernes de 9 a 6; Sábados de 10 a 1

London Transport, Estación de metro de St James's Park y otras estaciones de metros importantes. (Tfno 222–1234, servicio de 24 horas). Diariamente de 8 a 6. Planos gratis de autobús y metro.

Conducta social

La gente a veces se da la mano al encontrarse y al despedirse. El beso y el abrazo se reserva para la gente que se conoce muy bien, pero nunca entre hombres.

Mr/Mrs/Miss. se usan con el nombre y apellido o sólo con el apellido. por ej. en presentaciones o por teléfono.

Para llamar la atención de alguien, por ej. un camarero, hágaselo ver. Como último recurso diga 'Excuse me'. Nunca dé palmas o chasquee los dedos. etc.

En las colas: respete siempre el turno en las colas de autobuses, billetes etc.

El regateo es muy poco corriente, igual que los descuentos.

Preguntas de caracter personal. A no ser que haya mucha confianza, se considera de poca educación preguntarle a alguien cuanto gana.

Echar papeles o desperdicios está mal visto además de severamente multado.

Regalos – a menudo se envian flores o se regálan bombones a cambio de la hospitalidad recibida.

Alojamiento

Póngase en contacto con el London Tourist Board o British Tourist Authority. El alojamiento va desde:

Grandes Hoteles internacionales.

Hoteles más pequeños, más económicos.

Habitaciones (Rooms)/Cama y desayuno (Bed and Breakfast). Busque el anuncio de Vacancy/B & B, en casas particulares. Son más baratos que los hoteles y el precio incluye desayuno cocinado, a la inglesa.

Hostal/alojamiento tipo estudiantes. Póngase en contacto con Budget Accommodation (London Tourist Board, Victoria Station), consulte la publicación Time Out. Youth Hostel Association es sólo para socios.

Para desplazarse

Si viaja en tren, autobús o metro, pida un billete económico de ida y vuelta en el día ('cheap day return'), billete de excursión, de fin de semana, semanal etc.

Las horas punta (rush hour) en Londres son aproximadamente de 8 a 9.30 de la mañana y de 4.30 a 6.30 por la tarde. Evítelas.

Planos (maps) se pueden comprar en la mayoría de papelerías y librerías. El callejero de Londres más completo es el A–Z.

En taxi En Londres y otras grandes ciudades se puede parar un taxi en la calle, si tiene la luz amarilla encendida. Fuera de Londres los taxis se encuentran en las estaciones. El precio lo marca el taximetro. Añada un 10% de propina. También se puede conseguir un taxi por teléfono.

En autobús urbano se paga al cobrador, a no ser que sea automático. Diga a dónde va y le dirán el precio. Se paga por trayecto. Guarde el billete por si el revisor se lo pide. Haga señal con la mano al autobús para que se detenga en la parada. Compruebe a qué hora sale el último autobús. La mayoría de servicios terminan sobre las 11.30 de la noche.

Hay unos pocos autobuses rápidos, rojos, de un solo piso, en Londres, para los cuales tiene que llevar cambio exacto.

En metro compre el billete para su destino en la taquilla o máquina automática. No pierda el billete pues lo tiene que entregar al final del trayecto. Los vagones son de clase única y en la mayoría no se permite fumar.

NB Compruebe la dirección y el destino en las señales e indicaciones del andén, y manténgase a la derecha en las escaleras mecánicas.

En tren (British Rail) hay 1ª y 2ª clase. La mayoría de la gente viaja en 2ª. que es muy cómoda. Generalmente no se necesita reservar billete.

En autocar de larga distancia existe una red de servicio de autocares, económica, por todas las Islas Britanicas. Detalles en Victoria Coach Station, Eccleston Bridge, Victoria, London SW1. Oficina de Información abierta de 8 a 6.

Para cambiar moneda

Los bancos abren de 9.30 a 3.30 de lunes a viernes, excepto festivos. Sin embargo, puede cambiar moneda en los bancos de:
　　Harrods, Knightsbridge
　　John Barker & Co., Kensington High Street
　　Selfridges, Oxford Street
de 9 a 5 lunes a sábado.

Oficinas de cambio (Bureau de Change). cobran una mayor comisión. Algunas abren día y noche.

De compras

Las tiendas abren generalmente de 9.30 a 5.30, y cierran los domingos y festivos. Algunas tiendas del centro de Londres cierran los sábados por la tarde y los diferentes barrios cierran tarde un día a la semana, a las 8. Fuera de Londres cada población tiene un día en que cierran temprano, a la una de la tarde.

Oficinas de Correos tienen el mismo horario que el comercio, excepto que los sábados cierran a la una. Hay una oficina de correos abierta día y noche en Trafalgar Square. Los sellos sólo se venden en las oficinas de correos o en máquinas fuera de ellas.

Comida y bebida

Para comer fuera de casa puede elegir entre Snack bars, cafés, autoservicios y restaurantes. En los restaurantes se sirve el lunch desde las 12 del mediodía y puede ser difícil comer después de las 2 de la tarde. Es difícil conseguir cena en cualquier parte después de las 11–11.30. En hoteles de las zonas rurales es difícil incluso cenar después de las 8.30.

Tomar una copa: recuerde los horarios de los pubs. Abren generalmente de las 11 de la mañana a las 3 de la tarde y de las 5.30 a las 11 los días laborables y de 12 a 2 de la tarde y 7.00 a 10.30 de la noche los domingos.

NB Sólo se permite la entrada e los pubs a los niños mayores de 13 años. que pueden tomar bebidas no alcohólicas. Sólo los mayores de 18 años pueden consumir bebidas alcohólicas en lugares públicos.

Propinas

Restaurantes si el servicio no está incluido, 10/15%.

Hoteles conserjes sobre 20p, servicio de habitación, 20p y encargos también sobre 20p.

Taxis 10%.

Peluquerías 10/15%.

Mozos de estación sobre 50p por bulto.
No se da propina en cines, teatros, pubs y bares.

Espectáculos

Para saber lo que ponen puede mirar la cartelera de espectáculos de los periódicos de la mañana o de la tarde. En Londres la revista Time Out da información detallada.

Para hacer reservas reserve en taquilla o en una agencia (la agencia cobra comisión). Las entradas sobrantes se venden a veces como una hora antes de la representación. Vea la ilustración del plano general de un teatro, aunque cada teatro tiene un diseño especial.

NOTA: Matinales comienzan de 2 a 3 de la tarde.
         Sesiones de noche, de 7 a 8 de la tarde.

Museos y Galerías de Arte la mayoría cierran los festivos y domingos por la mañana.